To The
Arctic Circle

My Nomadic Experiment

Book I

Morgan Stafford

First printing: 2019

This book is based on daily journaling from the occurrences, experiences, and research on people and places. Names were changed in order to maintain the anonymity of the individuals I encountered and friends I visited along the way.

Book Design: Morgan Stafford

Cover Design: Morgan Stafford & Kevin Gilbert

Visit the author website at **www.nomadicexperiment.org**

ISBN: 9781795421133

Table of Contents

Maps

THE THIRTY-FOUR (34) maps provided in this book were created by the author. Some are original, some were recreated, and some were created to illustrate my path and direction during parts of my travels where a map was not used or required. All were drawn on 9in X 6in ruled paper in a stenographer notebook which fit well in the map pouch on top of the tank bag. The research and creation to draw the maps was an entertaining and relaxing pleasure. I hope you find them helpful.

1

Taos, New Mexico

*"It takes a lot of courage to show your
dreams to someone else."*

—*Erma Bombeck*

IT WAS NOT a random decision to find myself in Taos, New Mexico. After seven months and just short of 25,000 miles of motorcycle travel in North America, I was ready to stop. No, Taos was not random at all. It satisfied a promise I made to myself many years ago—spend time in New Mexico. Like so many, I had been bitten by the Southwest bug and favored Northern New Mexico. In my early forties, the area captured my heart and transformed my spirit. Now, in my early sixties, I was here.

It was autumn, the perfect season to be in Taos with the yellows of the cottonwood and aspens patching color in thick conifer growth on surrounding mountains. For three weeks I would live a fantasy, having rented an adobe house built in the twenties; tin roof, blue door, natural setting with a hammock strung between two apple trees. Low ceilings had exposed wood beams, and the floors sagged from age. I had agreed to care for three cats living at the house, two feral and one a lethargic homebody. The house was a home with a restful atmosphere. It possessed the spirit of the two artists I rented it from, now convalescing in a nearby condo.

I had been so many places during my seven-month tour of the Lower Forty-Eight, Canada and Alaska. Things now, somewhat a blur. So I needed to refresh and recharge before I became jaded by continual travel. Once having a dream to cross the country on a motorcycle, I had far surpassed that, and the freedom of the road had opened my eyes to what I could do with my newly created life, my love of motorcycling, and my deep love for travel. Stopping in Taos, I put a space holder at a temporary end of what I had named, "My Nomadic Experiment." An experiment that had only begun.

During my time on the road, I realized that the recipe for my own happiness was to ride until I became road weary, then stop until I felt the urge to go again. It was my comfortable balance. Typically, it was not long before I became antsy and, once again, was ready for movement.

I had wondered if I possessed "The Travel Gene," or the DRD4-7R gene, as it was called scientifically. Research stated that a small percent of the population had the gene embedded in their DNA, which caused a person to embrace movement, change, and adventure. Supposedly, a holdover from a prehistoric time when humans roamed nomadically in search of food. I already identified with all those blues songs about wandering and rambling: "Going down that long lonesome road Babe, where I'm bound, it's hard to tell." I always felt the pull of a life to travel over the idea of nesting into a cozy home life. The quaint adobe house would provide a respite from the road and a taste of domesticity while researching to choose my next direction.

In the mornings, I kept the kitchen door open to the outside, hoping the two feral cats would come in and eat. Only one ever did while meowing up at me, agitated at my presence. The other sat outside staring in with no intention of entering. During the night, the two would come through an open window while I slept. The third stayed on my bed—the most peaceful creature I had ever encountered.

The house tucked in the wooded corner lot felt like it was deep in the country. However, it was just a short walk to the Taos Plaza at the center of town. The road to get there was along a ridge with magnificent views open grazing land spread before the Sangre de Cristo mountains displaying seasonal colors and spectacular sunsets, particular to the Southwest.

So much of who I was at the age of sixty-two was a result of the thirty-five years I traded to make retirement possible. I retired on the twenty-eighth of February, 2015 after twenty-five years of service with the Department of Defense. I had worked since the age of fourteen, having to obtain a worker's permit to get my first job. I recall my father's words before signing the authorization: "Son if I sign this, you'll be working the rest of your life." He was reluctant to approve, thinking I was too young to work. But I was adamant. A job meant money, and money meant freedom. For the most part, my father was right. Except for short periods in my twenties when I would work to save enough for periods of lengthy travel. Other than that, I have been working ever since he signed the permit. Then I chose a career where there was no escaping a life of work. I made it through and now had entered the stage I worked my entire life, thus far, to get to.

I always kept my retirement at the forefront of my life plans—my carrot on the horizon. I was fortunate, but not lucky. My retirement did not fall into my lap. It required work, maintenance, discipline, and the hope that I would live to obtain my carrot and reap the benefits.

It was a culmination of choices that directed me to create this thing I was calling, "My Nomadic Experiment." My conundrum had been to create a plan for my life in retirement that would give me a domestic life with a home base and, at the same time, give me the freedom for lengthy travel. My evaluation made me aware that having both was for the affluent. Knowing the strain and burden of home ownership and the size of my retirement portfolio I had to make some creative choices. So, like an animal with his foot in a trap, I chose to let my house go to free myself. I put a plan in motion, with a serious dedication to selling my house. My house was my albatross and had owned me too long. Possession of the house meant nothing to me, and my relationship was defined best in the lyrics of a Beck song, "I'll just hold onto nothing and see how long nothing lasts."

I was embracing a mental transformation, along with the reinvention of my life. I was familiar with the phrase "you can't take it with you" and thought it clever and true. Now the expression was especially true—and poignant. It caused me to ask: If I can't take it with me, why am I keeping it? From that question, my emotional and mental state to rid myself of possessions entered a place of ease. So I chose to let everything go instead of storing belongings for some nebulous future when I might settle. This was My Nomadic Experiment, and it would be but so nomadic if I kept a home to nag me. I even felt a storage unit contradicted my philosophy of total freedom. So I sold, gave away, and donated, only retaining those few things I found to be most precious, knowing I would regret their loss. The effort to divest brought me closer to peace, causing me to dig deeper into my psyche and trust the loss of belongings, knowing less had indeed become more.

So, on a heavily packed adventure touring motorcycle, I left Virginia Beach, Virginia a week after the date of my retirement. I had a reservation for a three-day ferry ride to Haines, Alaska, from Bellingham, Washington, scheduled three months out. This gave me a gracious period to explore the Lower Forty-Eight, having spent months hovering over maps in preparation.

In a nutshell, I spent the previous eighteen months divesting my earthly belongings; house, clothes, furniture, guitars, surfboards, SUV, etc. I retained two trunks in my late father's bedroom, filled with treasured items. During the period of my divestment, I maintained a positive attitude, never wavering from my objective to be free from things that owned and restricted me. My divestment was with patience and discretion, in a staggered manner taking me from a three-thousand-square-foot house to a twelve-hundred-square-foot condo, to a five-hundred-square-foot cottage and, finally, a 1200cc adventure touring motorcycle.

I did not read a book to learn how to construct this new lifestyle. It was my creation and constructed methodically, checking boxes from a list: selling my house, my belongings, choosing a motorcycle, buying parts, luggage, clothing and planning routes. An approach that allowed me to successfully turn a concept into a life—a creative process to transform my life into art. Now, in Taos, New Mexico, I was reviewing and evaluating my experimental life thus far and wanted to record the tale for myself and for others.

2

The Motorcycle

*"Love is the feeling you get when you love
someone as much as your motorcycle."*

—*Hunter S. Thompson*

I WAS FIFTY-FIVE years of age when I got my first motorcycle. Like most men, I had always wanted a motorcycle, but it had been drilled into my head that riding a motorcycle meant certain death. Motorcycle accidents were usually detailed in horrific stories, causing me to deny my desire to buy a bike.

I don't recall what occurred to cause me such stress. Maybe work, maybe family, a girlfriend—I only remember being unusually stressed. I was pacing the garage, listening to Lightning Hopkins on my workshop stereo and drinking beer. Suddenly, my stress was relieved with an epiphany, a confident clarity with the immediate awareness that I could drop dead and whatever issue caused me stress would be resolved with my absence—a reminder of the brevity of life. Then, somehow I drew an equation between my mental health and buying a motorcycle. The following day I was at a Triumph shop choosing my first motorcycle.

It seemed that all my fellow Baby Boomers either had or wanted a Harley Davidson. I had nothing against the Harley, other than loud pipes and the idea of joining the Harley culture of the weekend outlaw biker. Like Marlon Brando, Bob Dylan, and Steve McQueen, I preferred the Triumph, liking the British bike and the company responsible for inventing the motorcycle. So, I bought a Triumph America, a cruiser style bike with a Bonneville 850cc engine; a fantastic choice for my first motorcycle.

Nothing will teach you to ride a motorcycle like riding a motorcycle. Motorcycles are dangerous and should be thought of as so. It's an agreed risk every time you throw your leg over the seat. It's also addictive, and now I cannot imagine my life without a bike. Motorcycling an open road is sensory overload, therapeutic, and a hunger that had to be fed. I wanted to turn my dream of long travel into long-term motorcycle travel. So, I created a plan to get there.

A few years before buying my first motorcycle, the sport of adventure motorcycling began to take shape. The growth has much to do with the Scottish actor Ewan McGregor and friend Charley Boorman who rode around the world on their BMW GS1190 adventure bikes. A PBS series was made, and a book was written to document their adventure, both entitled, *The Long Way Around*. The book flooded me with inspiration. So I read other books on motorcycle travel, including to the classic, *Jupiter's Travels* by Ted Simon, who inspire McGregor and Boorman and others who considered motorcycle travel on a global scale. Then there was Glen Heggstad, "The Striking Viking," who wrote, *One More Day Everywhere: Crossing 50 Borders on the Road to Global Understanding*. Heggstad was inspiring, with his unique approach to people, cultures and his expression of global peace. Traveling on the motorcycle was about the experience of people, geography, landscape—more than merely moving fast on two wheels.

In 2012, Triumph debuted the Tiger Explorer 1200, a blatant attempt to compete with the BMW 1200GS. The adventure touring market was experiencing severe growth to produce motorcycles capable of handling rugged roads of world travel while heavily packed. Design of the Explorer began in 2006, six years before its launch. Once on the showroom floor, several friends told me that it was the bike I should ride for the type of traveling I pursued. So, in 2013, I bought the Explorer and have had no regrets. I have established a trusted relationship with my motorcycle, even referring to it as "Brother." It takes me down amazing roads and through severe backcountry and I continue to appreciate the engineering, the craftsmanship, and the durability of the bike.

In hindsight, choosing the motorcycle was the easy part. To prepare for the type of adventure travel I had in mind, there were needs I had to address. First was aftermarket parts to outfit the bike and make it mine; mine and ready the way I deemed necessary. All those "add-ons" were called "farkles"—an adventure motorcycle term. Walking up to another adventure bike you check out their farkles—an act that made me feel like a dog sniffing another dog's butt. Aftermarket items included bash plates, exhaust guards, a radiator guard, crash bars, on and on. I was going to live off the bike, so there was nothing weekendish about my plans.

Pannier is a French word meaning "handbag," and traditionally meant baskets slug over a beast of burden. The term conveyed to motorcycle luggage. A friend recommended a particular brand, so I made the order. Later, I regretted not having evaluated the product more before procurement. They looked good, but during the first month, I crushed one of the corners causing it to leak. The fabrication was flimsy with little attention to structural integrity to protect against impact. The crushed corner was there to remind me of my poor decision and to research and choose carefully.

Choosing clothing took time due to my personal vanity. I would be living in a protective jacket and pants, and neither would be cheap. They had to suit four seasons and functional in a range of temperatures, achieved through layers and venting. Safety features necessary for protection were integrated hard spots, under durable material with multilayered stitching. And, to be transparent, the suit had to be visually appealing.

Boots were equally difficult to evaluate with so many to choose from. Like the jacket and pants, I would be living in them. I was looking for style and comfort but rugged and protective. I found a hybrid, that was a crossover for a rough day on the bike and all-day comfort.

My condo and beach cottage became a parts department with boxes stacked with newly received items. Weekends were spent installing new parts and learning the bike. It became a labor of love and forced me to begin a specific collection of maintenance tools to include in my cargo. There was a point when I had to stop buying and installing to conclude the endless effort.

The first item to arrive was crash bars to protect the upper fairing of the bike. A set for the lower area to protect the engine already existed. Overkill, but not for my extreme plan. The aluminum bash plate arrived for the underbelly of the engine protecting against rough unpaved roads I would encounter. I bought a guard for the exhaust pipes which attached between the bash plate and a radiator guard. The installation of each required a rubber mallet, a little muscle, beer, and profanity.

Parts kept coming—a protective guard for the headlight, secondary engine covers, larger baseplate for luggage, a GPS mounting carriage, and a windshield extension. I swapped my side mirrors for a type that folded back, instead of breaking off if the bike was dropped. I found foot pegs with a broader base to take the pressure off my arches.

My forty-six-liter panniers arrived increasing the breadth of the bike. Like the bash plate, exhaust, and radiator guard, the installation was not what you would call, "plug and play." It required tenacious perseverance, pride, and stubbornness with me twisting and bending the frame structure to match black and white instruction pictures. Once again—a mallet, muscle, beer, and profanity.

The bike was outfitted, ruggedize, and ready. I bought a forty-liter square canvas pack for the back, which mounted to the larger baseplate. And two, twenty-two-liter waterproof, end-to-end bags to strap on my panniers, both for camping gear. And, on the seat behind me, a forty-liter waterproof duffle bag.

A big choice in the luggage category was the tank bag, which I initially thought did not look cool. Ironically, the tank bag was my most used luggage item. It contained those readily accessible items like maps, books, glasses, snacks, and such. Function took over with looking cool taking a back seat.

I was lucky to have been born in a time with this new type of motorcycle travel and an industry that catered to those requiring such sophisticated equipment, luggage, and clothing. As a fellow biker told me, "Adventure motorcycling is the fastest growing sport nobody knows about." I was glad I discovered the sport and was now prepared to take to the open road.

3

Departing a Life

"Get busy living or get busy dying."

—*Andy Dufresne*

BEFORE MY DEPARTURE, there were several things I had to address knowing the road would be my home. I had researched the advantage of taking up residency in a state that did not impose an income tax on their residents. Living in Virginia, I was paying six percent annually. For that reason, I found a domicile in Texas with an operation that would provide me an address and offered mail forwarding, for an inexpensive yearly fee. The effort would give me convenience and increased income. Most of all, it made me free to focus on My Nomadic Experiment.

In my beach cottage, I spent my nights devouring an atlas of the United States to prepare for three months in the Lower Forty-Eight before boarding a ferry to Alaska. I left with a detailed route, marked in yellow highlighter on Rand McNally state maps. I had tailored my itinerary to visit family, friends, and places I had dreamed of seeing. On the ferry, I would have time to develop my route for Alaska and the Yukon Territory. My route in the US was dictated by it still being winter, and the risk of inclement weather as spring fought for its place in the Midwest. This could result in vicious thunderstorms and tornadoes. For that reason, I designed my route south until I felt spring had fully planted its feet. Once I finished Texas at the Mexican border, I would wiggle north through New Mexico and into Utah, still too early to see the north rim of the Grand Canyon. I could plan as much as possible and map my route to finite detail, but ultimately I would have to remain flexible, respond to what may occur, and what I might encounter.

In a nutshell, what I had done was divest ninety-nine percent of my earthly belongings, sold my sizeable beautiful house during a two year staggered downsize. I rented a small condo, then a tiny beach cottage while retiring from a thirty-five-year career. I had to control my engrained domestic mentality to not question what I was doing and trust my instincts while I moved in the direction of another life. I had changed my values in regards to what I considered important. The reinvention of my SELF was more in-depth than I originally planned. Soon, I would transcend plan and purpose to live the outcome of my own creation. I would be NOMADIC and begin my EXPERIMENT and was interested to see how it would affect me as time passed. What would life on the road do to me? Who would I become after removing so much that defined who I was?

On the morning of March ninth, 2015, I left Virginia Beach, Virginia, on my fully loaded Triumph Explorer with no thoughts of returning. My plan— both finite and nebulous, precisely as I wanted it. It afforded me time to explore the unknown and anticipate the planned. With all my preparation for leaving, it felt unnatural, frantic, and scrambled—the mood bothered me. Everything was on the bike, but I had little recollection of where. I dealt with the bewilderment by just leaving, knowing the arrangement of items would be in flux with ample time to learn their location.

Once on the road, I was pleased the bike handled the heavy load. It raised the vertical center of gravity, which made Brother roll sweetly into curves. As loaded as I was, I eventually encountered other bikers with more cargo—some with a passenger. As with everything I was doing, it was an adjustment.

The morning I left was cloudy with fog and the air chilly and wet from ocean wind. Temperatures were in the upper thirties with an expected high of fifty. It was not spring yet.

Starting the bike, I found my departure challenging to comprehend, bombarded with emotions, both sour and sweet. Having worked so hard and waited so long and now, with the simple act of loading the bike I was riding away and into a new life. I force myself to be conscious that it was actually taking place—my dream, now a reality. At sixty-two years of age, I realized, the last time I was this free was when I was twenty-two—forty years ago. What I was doing felt authentic, adventurous, and personally satisfying and nothing I ever saw in an AARP magazine. Now, all that had delivered me to my day of departure would disappear behind me. I was feeling more alive than I had ever felt. I could not help but remember the words of the character Red at the end of *Shawshank Redemption:* "I find I'm so excited I can barely sit still or hold a thought in my head. It's an excitement only a free man can feel. A free man at the start of a long journey, whose conclusion is uncertain." For me, all NOW was NEW and in front of me. So I eagerly pointed Brother into the prospects of my unknown future.

4

STAGE I: Mile 0 - 996

The Road, My Home - Wernher von Braun
Baggie of Ashes

"In the end, we'll all become stories."

—*Margaret Atwood*

LEAVING VIRGINIA BEACH, my route was marked by a yellow highlighter on a state map, folded to fit in a map pouch attached to my tank bag. My view was of the road before me and, looking down, the route of my destination. This was to be my world, for thousands of miles and through so many landscapes.

The previous evening my sister and mother came to say goodbye with my mind too busy to feel sentimental about leaving what remaining family I had. My mother was eighty-eight and in the care of my sister. I knew, at that age, there was a chance I would not see her again. I received their blessings to go live my life. Considering gifts from the universe, this would be my first.

My first stop would be Morehead City, North Carolina, four hours south. I had been married for twenty years, into a family from that small coastal town. My ex-wife's mother, now in her late eighties, still lived in the family home. I made arrangements to spend the night and enjoy the familiarity of my past. She was a real Southern lady, who keep fit and read to remain mentally sharp. We shared good conversation and she, as always, was curious about my travels and my plans. Although confident in what I was doing, she offered comments that bolstered me with affirmation. I was grateful that I made my first stop a place that had once been a second home.

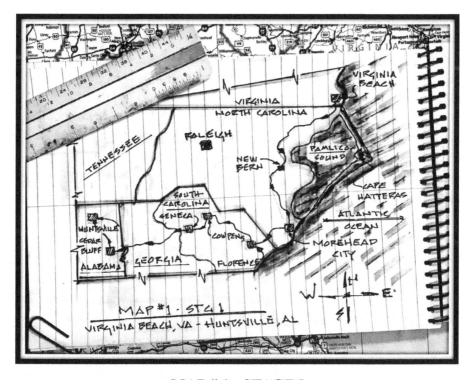

MAP # 1 - STAGE I
Virginia Beach, VA - Huntsville, AL

The next morning we enjoyed breakfast while sharing goodbyes. It would be as it would be many times in my travels—I would drive away full in spirit and grateful. I rode west and crossed into South Carolina.

In Florence, I got a room in a motel that catered to eighteen wheelers and my first motel stop. I learned there would be a methodology to unloading and loading the bike. First removing my tank bag taking it into the room with my helmet and gloves. Then I would remove all that was strapped on the back. I was lucky to have panniers that were easy to remove to bring inside, both holding items I needed for my evening. If I chose to keep them attached, I would cover the bike to deflect curiosity of the wrong type.

A buffet breakfast came with the price of my room. My MO became that if breakfast was offered—be there. It saved time and money. I stood in line with big truck driving men, wearing ball caps, and oversized T-shirts that hung over bay frontage. They breathed laboriously while spooning parcels of food on plates, well exceeding the necessary caloric count for their day. I left too full myself and vowed to never eat all I could eat again.

Across northern South Carolina, I chose a direction to avoid the busy grid of Spartanburg, a route that would cross Georgia on my way to visit friends in Huntsville, Alabama. The terrain was taking a subtle change as I entered the foothills of the Piedmont with a slight roll to the land and forests of sugar pine, paper pine, and bright green grass sprouting in seasonal change.

I passed through the small town of Cowpens, the site of the Revolutionary War Battle of Cowpens. A large monument commemorated the battle and Brigadier General Daniel Morgan who served under Washington. His bravery and command changed the war and was considered one of the most gifted battlefield tacticians of the Revolution. The Battle of Cowpens was his tactical masterpiece and part of the Southern Campaign. South Carolina had more Revolutionary War battles than any other state. I gazed out on the battlefield to imagine the short skirmish. Imagining myself a farmer with a musket at war with the mother country for his freedom. My stop at Cowpens was the type of interest I would look for, wanting to comb the country for history, geography, and geology.

I spent the night in Seneca, the following morning crossing into Georgia with rolling hills turning into steep mountains in bare woodlands of the Chattahoochee National Forest. The sky was overcast with temperatures in the low forties and felt like it could snow. I was out of the Piedmont and into the Southern Highlands of the Blue Ridge, a part of the Appalachians—my first taste of mountains. The road cleared my mind of everything but rolling into the next banked turn. I enjoyed the gyro effect as acceleration pushed the bike around tight bends while I twisted the throttle, trying to make the back wheel pass the front—a feeling only a biker knows.

Monte Santo was high on a mountain and overlooked the city of Huntsville. The road to the top was steep and winding with boulders to both sides. My friends lived on top of the mountain. Elliot, like me, was a retired Federal employee, following a career with the Bureau of Land Management.

Huntsville is located at the southern tip of the Appalachian Mountains, on the Cumberland Plateau, tucked in a knuckle of the Tennessee River. It was a beautiful city that had expanded to satisfy the needs of the space industry. At the end of WWII, the US captured and moved Wernher von Braun and over 1,500 scientists, engineers, and technicians to the United States. Braun, was a space engineer and architect, credited for inventing the V-2 rocket and the Saturn V for the US. Braun was also a member of the Nazi party and the SS. He and fellow workers were brought to the US as part of Operation Paperclip, established to design the rockets that launched America's first space satellite and series of moon missions, all taking place at the Redstone Arsenal Ordinance Guided Missile Center in Huntsville. The operation set the stage for the American space program and gave birth to NASA.

Two packages waiting for me in Huntsville from people I had provided a forwarding address to. One, a Bob Dylan T-shirt; a retirement gift from a friend. The other package, the ashes of a high school friend which came with a note from his wife, expressing gratitude for me agreeing to spread her husband's ashes on my travels. Hearing about my plans, she contacted me and asked the favor of scattering Jack's ashes through National Parks. Now, having the ashes of my old friend in front of me, I felt overwhelmed. My agreement to her request had been casual. Now holding the baggie of ashes, I felt what I had agreed to do to be somewhat daunting. It was difficult to connect my current life at sixty-two, with my life when I knew my friend, forty or more years ago—especially while holding his remains in a sandwich baggie.

Jack was a big Irish guy who loved life and loved to laugh. If I had approached the spreading of his ashes with some level of spirituality, I would have felt corny, pretentious, and I would not be able to keep a straight face. And, for sure, wherever Jack was, he too would have rolled his eyes.

I sealed the bag while reflecting on my friend from a lifetime ago. Surreal is a trendy word but seemed the only word to best describe the feeling I had while holding his ashes. So, I stowed them in a pannier for now. I was at the beginning of my reinvention and an epic journey—a life-changing odyssey. And now, riding along with me—the ashes of a man who left the world too early. It affirmed the truth that there is no guarantee of a tomorrow. Spreading Jack's ashes along my travels would add another layer, another dimension, and more texture to my journey.

5

STAGE II: Mile 966 - 1893

The Trace - Jackson - The Flood - Hair Loss

*"Ashes to ashes, salt to salt, you go down
in this flood, it'll be your own fault."*

—*Bob Dylan*

I LEFT MY friends in Huntsville after a five-day visit. Elliot and I shared stories about our time in federal employment, concluding that whatever issues we had during our long career, it now afforded us the luxury of retirement and for that we were grateful.

I headed west through Athens, Florence, Muscle Shoals, and Tuscumbia—the birthplace of Helen Keller. My direction was to Mississippi, in search of the Natchez Trace Parkway and surprised I knew nothing about, "The Trace" as it was called; a four-hundred- and forty-mile route, beginning south of Nashville, Tennessee and ending in Natchez, Mississippi. The path, originally created by animals in pursuit of salt lick and later used by Choctaw and Chickasaw in tribal migration, eventually became a trail in the early Mississippian culture for trade. Thomas Jefferson wanted to connect Daniel Boone's Wilderness Trail to the Trace to gain access to south-central Mississippi. The Wilderness Trail was an east to west route opened by Daniel Boone in 1775 from what is now Kingsport, Tennessee and through the Cumberland Gap of Virginia into Kentucky. The Trace was the only reliable land link between Mississippi and Louisiana, originally called the "Columbia Highway," its origin at the foothills of the Columbia Gap. People who traveled the route dubbed it, "the devil's backbone" due to rough conditions and encounters with highwaymen (robbers and thieves).

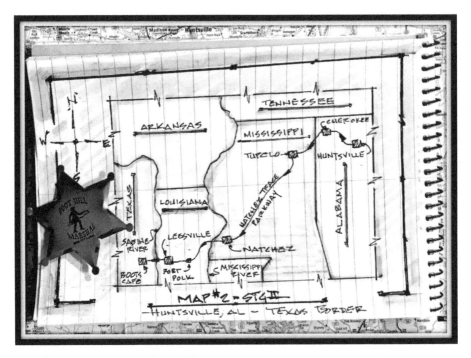

MAP # 2 - STAGE II

Huntsville, AL - Texas Border

The Trace was used in the Revolutionary War by Andrew Jackson. Its where Meriwether Lewis either committed suicide or was murdered at a roadhouse, in route to Washington, D.C. In the early nineteen-hundreds, the Daughters of the American Revolution chose to resurrect the Trace for its historical significance creating a parkway along the routed Trace.

Riding the Trace was comfortable with slight hills, mild turns, and thickly wooded landscapes. The ride was peaceful, meditative, with the easy handling of Brother giving me time to reflect on all I had done to get where I was. I stopped in Tupelo, finding a seedy but tolerable motel. Pulling up, people stared while smoking at the open doors of their rooms with some shouting compliments about my bike. A microbrewery was directly in front at a strip mall, with a Thai restaurant across the street. The next morning I woke to steady rain and chose to stay another night, spending my day arranging luggage to acquaint myself of their locations. The next day I headed back to the Trace, a bit fuzzy from one too many craft beers at the microbrewery. On the way, I hunted down the birthplace of Elvis to have my picture taken on the King's front porch. From there I continued west to the town of Oxford to see the home of William Faulkner, making a lunch stop at a country cafe for coffee and a BLT. Then I was back on the Trace, hoping to be in Vicksburg by nightfall.

The town of Vicksburg held a particular fascination for me, having read Shelby Foote's, *The Beleaguered City: The Vicksburg Campaign, December 1862 - July 1863.* During the Civil War, Union naval bombardment from the Mississippi River lasted two weeks—a torturous takedown of a city filled with stubborn and tenacious Southerners who eventually surrendered. The Union victory made a decisive change in the Civil War, cutting off trade along the Mississippi River.

Back on the Trace, the sky was gray and becoming increasingly overcast. The road offered few options for exit, so I knew when the rain came I would have to endure a wet ride. The rain started as an aggravating mist. I stopped for coffee at a gift shop in an old gristmill then was back on the Trace. The misting rain was thick, covering the shield of my helmet, forcing me to peer over wet glasses to see. I had my Gore-Tex liner in, but the damp exterior caused a chill, so I stopped and pulled on another layer. Five miles down the road the mist became light rain. I set the bike to cruise at fifty with conditions uncomfortable and dangerous due to my impaired visibility. Light rain became a spring deluge, the visibility causing me to wonder if I could be seen. Seeing an exit for Jackson, I took the ramp. Road conditions were rough and in need of repair, the asphalt ruggedly cracked and buckled. During my coming months, I would develop a masterful eye for road conditions and encounter every type imaginable.

The part of Jackson I entered was depressed, impoverished, and unappealing. Cement building structures showed a beginning but unfinished with rusted reinforcement bars protruding in bent arrangements from pilings that looked like modern art. Nasty crabgrass grew high at unmaintained medians where billboard signs were ubiquitous, advertising everything from hair products to the Gospel of Jesus. I was a curiosity at stop lights and must have looked out of place, judging by the stares I was getting. The roughly paved road led to a city skyline with buildings looking dank in the wet air. It reminded me of pictures I saw of Moscow winters. I wished I was back on the Trace in the pouring rain. Then I remembered that Jackson was where Johnny Cash got married in a fever.

I checked in the first motel I saw, next to I-10 with the sound of passing eighteen-wheelers. While unloading Brother a young man not much more than twenty stood at the door of his room wearing a ball cap twisted to the side, holding a beer and a cigarette. He shouted over, "kinda wet out there, isn't it?" An uninviting comment filtered through a beer buzz stating the obvious. Even with my high dollar motorcycle outfit, I was soaked to the bone. I looked at him long enough to know I would not look at him again—or respond. He flicked his cigarette to the parking lot and slammed the door—responding to my nonresponse.

Scoping out the area, it was comprised of fast food and filling stations. I changed into dry clothes and surrendered to a hamburger. I sat to watch an older man with what I thought to be his grandson. They were enjoying a hamburger meal with an expression of happiness that was captivating and seemed to pardon all that had not been good about Jackson.

Around three in the morning, I sprang out of bed as my body convulsed to rid my stomach of the hamburger. At daylight, it was raining, and I felt numb from the restless night of intermittent vomiting forcing me to spend another day in "Moscow."

The next day I escaped from Jackson, Mississippi and made it to Vicksburg for a short stop before back on the Trace, until terminating in Natchez. I found a restaurant that specialized in tamales in a barn. Seeing it as unique, I stopped for lunch and was reminded of how unexciting tamales are. I ordered six, regretting my order after chewing through three, then found the road for Louisiana.

Cross the Mississippi from Natchez, and you're in Louisiana. Over the bridge, a detour directed me south along the levee; an unexpected blessing. It was another rough, bleached out, asphalt road. The river levee was to my left, covered in brown weeds, ignored and as unkempt as the road. To my right, acres of lifeless brown dirt covered flat land that disappeared on the horizon. The sky was blue with an afternoon sun glaringly bright. A mile away a tractor strained in a cloud of dust with the faint chug of an old engine. A solitary tree stood in miles of empty wasteland. A few years back, I read *Rising Tides*, by John Goldman, an account of the 1927 flood of the Mississippi; the most destructive flood in US history. The flood covered 27,000 square miles stretching across much of Arkansas, Mississippi, and Louisiana. It reached depths of thirty feet. The flood, the result of political corruption and a government that chose to divert overflowing waters from the city of New Orleans by relieving levees with dynamite to open farmland. It displaced over 630,000 people with promises by the Government to reimburse their losses—promises that were never kept. The detour, serendipitously, put me in a place where I was shocked to realize I was seeing the landscape I had visualized while reading Goldman's book.

I had fears of running out of gas, having seen nothing since the bridge except ghostly shacks, a few abandoned cars, and miles of plowed dirt, everything appearing forgotten and ignored. My gas light came on at the same time I saw a gas station. The station seemed to be an after-work meeting place for farmers covered in brown dirt. It was an odd underworld, less than two thousand miles from Virginia Beach, in the same country—America in its rawest form. Inside the station was food fried in thick batter, mostly unrecognizable except for the chicken. Men stood in line to direct a robust woman with heavy arms to fill Styrofoam containers with their dinner. Twelve-packs of Budweiser were bought to wash down the heavy food and to sink them in tranquility before repeating their day, the following day. I filled my gas tank while answering questions about my mysterious looking bike. They were kind, open, and hard working for their place in poverty. I felt a chill when I considered their inescapable place in a life of labor—a moment that made me aware of how opportunity had given me fortune.

I got clarity for my direction to continue west, my ride having been random and relaxing for miles in an area that sparked my imagination to relive descriptions from a fabulous book. The road west took me through a thick forest of paper pine with amber floors of pine needle pelt, collecting light from a descending sun—a descending sun that became an annoyance as it bored holes in my eyes. Sunsets would be a daily issue on my circuitous route west. A buzzard dropped so low I thought it was targeting my helmet. Months later I heard stories about bikers colliding with raptors that took them down. Something eventually is gonna getcha…

I was hot, so I stopped at a country store to hydrate. I found a Zero bar, a throwback from my to childhood. Standing in the parking lot, two teenage girls appeared curious about me and my bike, expected the way I was loaded and the way I was dressed. One girl asked, "Are you a bounty hunter?" "Why?" I asked. "You look mean," she said. I guess it was my hair, which was near my shoulders. I admit that I grew it as a comment on my pending freedom, but all that hair was getting on my nerves and hot under my helmet. Her comment inspired me to make a change.

I passed Fort Polk where my father went to Army boot camp before being deployed to Germany at the end of WWII. It was difficult to get my father to talk about his time at war, always tight-lipped about his experience. When I was a child, he and I would watch the TV series *Combat* with Vic Morrow. During each episode, soldiers would walk the streets of bombed European towns, and I would picture my father a member of the platoon—making my father bigger than life.

In Leesville, I found a room in a town an hour from the Texas border. Following breakfast, I inquired about where I could get a haircut and was directed to Billy's Barbershop.

Walking in the door, Billy eyed me while turning a swivel chair in my direction. He was an easy going, clean cut, Southern gentleman in his early seventies with silver hair and an honest face. I told Billy how I wanted my hair cut and he restated in terms a barber would use: "Layered back, just above the ears, tight at the neck." I didn't fully understand but agreed to anything that would put a lot of hair on the floor. Hair that was no longer a comment about my freedom——now my life was the comment.

Small talk with Billy led to what I was doing. His voice changed tone while detailing a period in his youth when he owned a Triumph. He twisted the chair toward the mirror so I could approve his work, then brushed me off, then asked to walk me out to see my bike. Seeing Brother, his half grim told me he missed his bike as his eyes shifted between me and the bike. Beneath his quiet, modest nature, there remained a wild undercurrent. Saying goodbye I felt sure he stood in the parking lot to watch me ride away, wishing he was riding with me.

My destination of Livingston, Texas had me cross the border of Texas and Louisiana separated by the Sabine River. I crossed a rusted steel truss bridge where the speed limit was fifty-five in Louisiana, changing to seventy-five as soon as I entered Texas. An eighteen-wheeler on my tail let me know about the twenty-mile-an-hour increase while I escaped his aggressive push by pulling off into the gravel lot of the Boots Cafe.

The cafe looked creepy from the outside with the interior paneled with rough cut cedar. Cowboy curios and knickknacks decorated cabinets and the counter near the register: spurs, hand-carved covered wagons, cowboy hats, and belt buckles sat about in an attempt to give the restaurant Texas ambiance. A pretty young girl rolled up in a wheelchair with a sweet smile and a soft voice. I ordered breakfast and called it lunch while wondering what happened to put the young girl in a wheelchair. Then I remembered that Texas was where my mother was born and raised.

6

STAGE III: Mile 1893 - 2194

Livingston Domicile - Texas Cousin
Lone Star Family Graves

"Mama, don't let your babies grow up to be cowboys."

—*Waylon Jennings*

I GOT A motel room in Livingston and reviewed my plan to change my residence from Virginia to Texas. I chose Texas because it was one of eleven states in the US that did not impose a state income tax. The town of Livingston was the home of a business operation for those who lived in recreational vehicles. For a yearly fee, I could get a Texas address and mail forwarding. Going completely "off the grid" and not receive mail was too extreme. I needed to be connected for reasons of taxes, investments and credit cards.

On my first morning in Livingston, I jumped into action, somewhat apprehensive that things would not go smoothly due to some unexpected glitch. Arriving at the office of the business, I was greeted by a cordial staff who walked me through the process to register, providing an itemized list I needed to accomplish. Then they set me up with mail forwarding, provided me with an ID card with my new address and informed me that I was their first customer to live off a motorcycle.

The list consisted of changing the address on my motorcycle insurance, a state motorcycle inspection, state registration and tags, and to obtain a Texas drivers license, and registered to vote. I was surprised at how smooth I accomplished the list with no surprising glitch.

There was a particular irony of me becoming a Texas resident, my mother having been raised in the state until relocating to Portsmouth, Virginia, as a teen. At seventeen she got a job behind a drug store soda counter and met my father before he went off to war. Through my mother, there had always been the reflection of her past in detailed stories about her Texas background, and her

impoverished youth. As a child, she was forced to pick cotton with her mother and sisters, while her father was in some phase of vagrancy.

Growing up, family vacations were to Texas. Myths and stories would fill our time while I tried to put faces to the characters she described. Now a resident, my interest in my Texas history was reignited. I was on my way to meet family and learn more, happy to include some genealogy to my travels.

Heading back to the motel I passed a small cinderblock Mexican restaurant, so I stopped in for a celebratory lunch. I ordered a beer to find Livingston was a dry county. A waitress brought me chips, salsa, and slipped me a cold Corona long neck. She spoke little English, and from what I understood, the beer was a gift. I ate one of the best Mexican meals I've ever eaten, and the gracious lady brought another cold beer with another bright smile as if she knew how pleased I was about my day.

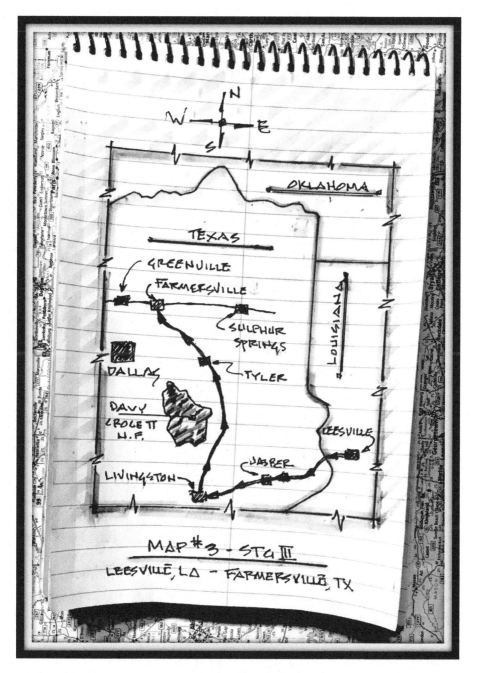

MAP # 3 - STAGE III
Leesville, LA - Farmersville, TX

The next morning I left Livingston for Farmersville to find a Texas cousin I had never met. She was the daughter of my mother's sisters, and family members had encouraged me to meet her because of our similarities. Like me, she had been a college English Major and knew how to tell a story with flair. Her stories were mostly about her wild and lawless cowboy family. The Texas side of my family was filled with crazy lore and unbelievable tales about outlaws and tragedy.

Maria was the youngest of four children and the only one alive. A beautiful woman with big blond hair, a mind loaded with common sense, and a sassy Texas mouth—you didn't know her long before knowing it was best to stay on her good side. During my short visit, I was quick to realize that it should be she, not me, writing.

On the weekend we drove north to Clarksville where our mothers were born. It was also the town that my second cousin, William Humphrey, set the location of his novel, *Home from the Hill;* an epic tale based on our great-great-grandfather, Earl Albert Napoleon Bonaparte Humphrey. The story detailed his life as a philanderer and the struggles of his wife and son in the small Texas town. The book was made into a major motion picture, starring Robert Mitchum as Humphrey.

On the way to Clarksville, Maria felt it mandatory that we stop at a favorite restaurant once hearing that I had never experienced a chicken fried steak—an idea she considered unacceptable. The restaurant was a wooded A-framed, open barn with tables full of people that made a sea of cowboy hats. Eating a chicken fried steak was a Texas right of passage, and my confession of not having the experience was similar a confession that I was a virgin. The waitress came for our order, and my cousin pointed at me and in her best Texas twang said: "He's never had a chicken fried steak." The waitress threw her head back with a hearty laugh. So I ordered it with mashed potatoes, pinto beans, and sweet tea, initially requesting unsweetened tea which raised another question about my manhood. The fried steak came, covered with gravy and hanging off both sides of the plate. To prove myself I ate it all and mopped the gravy from my plate with manly torn pieces of biscuit. It was delicious and glad for the experience, but it turned into a rock in my gut and stayed too, too long.

Clarksville, Texas, about a hundred mile: ville was just east of the town of Paris, close tc child were in a 1965 Ford Galaxie station wagc down with inflatable mattresses covered in blan] We were separated from our parents in the front of food, a Coleman stove, and a cooler. The lor grandmother but considered a family adventure. Along the way, we stopped at parks in mountain areas, camping and eating meals cooked at picnic tables. We were the typical middle-class family.

Downtown Clarksville had changed. As I remembered, the movie, *Home from the Hill* began with a group of older men sitting on the edge of a fountain, centered in the town square. Now, the fountain was gone and the square a tacky attempt to create a park-like setting with benches and cement paths circling a granite Civil War statue of a Confederate soldier. What was once open with intermingling traffic circling the monument and fountain, was now an open field surrounded by depressed businesses. I turned a full circle to see every store closed on a lifeless Saturday.

We made our way to graveyards, which is what people did in the country on weekends. I regretted not having a tape recorder for the family stories my cousins told while pulling weeds around headstones and brushing their tops clean of dirt. For each name she pointed to, he had a story, again convincing me that she should be writing stories about our family history.

We made a visit to both the Lone Star Cemetery and Clarksville Cemetery, and I had to wonder how many Lone Star cemeteries there were in the Lone Star State. At the Clarksville cemetery, we visited the plots of Maria's mother, father next to her sister and brother. She never met her older sister who, at nineteen months, was tragically stepped on by a galloping horse. Her death was just after I was born and she would have been the cousin closest to my age. While staring at her headstone, with a black and white photo covered in oval glass, I wondered what she would have been like if she had lived. The picture of the dark haired, dark eyed, pretty girl dressed in white, gave me an emotional

idea of a mother losing three children was difficult to com-
..

The marker for my younger male cousin, Maria's youngest broth-
r, was flat to the ground and engraved with a cowboy riding a bull. He
had been a paraplegic since his teens, the result of a diving accident.
He died in his fifties from heart failure, following much in his life in a
wheelchair.

My oldest male cousin committed suicide at thirty-two after living a wild cowboy life. He had a short career on the National Rodeo
Circuit, once performing in Madison Square Gardens. He was cremated, and his ashes were spread at his favorite hunting spot in east Texas.

Growing up in Virginia and hearing about my family far away
in Texas was like hearing about mythological gods. My mother was
quick to let us know how different she had been raised in comparison
to her life after meeting my father. To her, she had bettered herself by
marrying into an old Virginia family who knew how to set a table in a
sophisticated manner. I, on the other hand, always held a fascination
for the wild Texas bunch, our lesser known kin. Our visits were short,
lasting long enough to identify the differences in the manner we were
raised, which always had a way to point out that I was a bit of a dandy
in comparison to the feral manner of how my cousins were reared.

Onto the Lone Star Cemetery, where my grandfather and grandmother were buried along with my great-grandfather and great-grandmother. I remembered Granny, as we called my great-grandmother, as
being tall, strong, and quietly and in charge. She lived to the age of
ninety-four, rare for the Texas side of the family. Her first husband
was Earl Albert Napoleon Bonaparte Humphrey, who had a business
selling his particular breed of hog called Pole-China. I owned a small
leather journal of his sermons hand-written in illegible cursive with
a blue fountain pen. Pole, as they called him, was a "Hell, Fire, and
Brimstone" preacher, as my mother would say. Pole was shot in the
back while running from an angry husband. He lived a contradictory
life, preaching a sermon from one side of his mouth, while living dif-
ferently, and always in pursuit of any woman he could bed.

I stayed with my cousin for a week, spending several evenings with her husband driving country roads, feeding cows, and drinking beer. In saying goodbye, my cousin said: "Why don't you come here, buy a house, and let's grow old together." It was a heartfelt compliment and made me feel happy for bringing her into my life.

7

STAGE IV: Mile 2194 - 3260

**Jailhouse - Wildflowers - Luckenbach
Divvying Ashes**

"The problem is, you think you have time."

—*Buddha*

EVERYONE WAS AT work the morning I left Farmersville, good-byes taking place the night before. My cousin was exactly as everyone had described her and I was amazed at how she turned out to be such a stand-up gal having been raised around such wild ass cowboys who skirted the law. I took out for the Hill Country after hearing so much about wildflower season.

Fredericksburg was the epicenter of an annual wildflower event, and my timing was accidentally fortuitous. Creating a long route to avoid Dallas, I made my evening stop the small town of Hamilton, west of Waco. Like so many Texas towns, it had a grand courthouse on Main Street. I got a room, a shower, a Mexican dinner, then walked the town peering through empty store windows, the town as depressed as Clarksville. I felt like I was staring at the world in a fishbowl, an omniscient alien observer—and I was dig'n it.

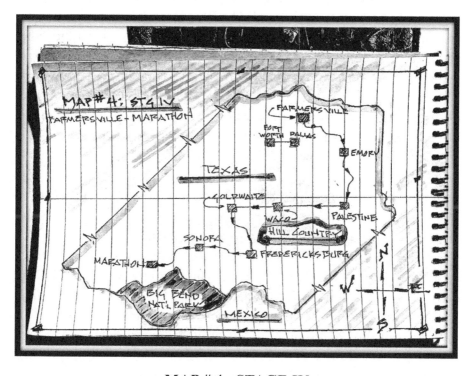

MAP # 4 - STAGE IV

Farmersville, TX - Marathon, TX

The following morning I had breakfast in the town of Goldthwaite, once I recognized a two-story brownstone jailhouse from the mini-series *Lonesome Dove*, written by Texas author William McMurtry. The jailhouse was where they tried to contain an Indian renegade named Blue Duck. While escorting him to a second-floor cell, Blue Duck grabbed the sheriff by his lapels and ran through a large window, sending both to their death. Now the building was offices for city business.

Across the street, I walked in the Wagon Wheel, to find a breakfast buffet with a line of folks, tall and wide, all filling plates with country cook'n. The waitress confirmed the building across the street was the jailhouse from *Lonesome Dove* and then I asked if I could order off the menu. She looked at me suspiciously for not choosing the buffet with the same look for never experiencing a chicken fried steak.

Closer to Fredericksburg, I began to see bluebonnets in thick fields along both sides of the road. The Blue Bonnet looked like a flower cultivated for the floral industry, looking like a small indigo tulip about six to nine inches tall. Stiff leaves grew from the stem, colored in a transition from light burgundy to brown to green. They grew prolifically along the roadsides and in fields covering acres. And not just bluebonnets but California poppies of brilliant orange, purple lupine, black-eyed Susans, and bright red Indian paintbrush. Fields looked like a French Impression painting by Monet or Mary Cassatt.

In the early afternoon, I rode into the town of Fredericksburg, finding a room at a quaint collection of white-washed cottages close to Main Street. I was given a ten percent discount for being a motorcyclist, then offered directions for wildflower viewing.

Fredericksburg, the heart of the Hill Country, was a surprise with its distinct German heritage. There were bars and restaurants, some located down brick staircases to cellars that felt European. That evening I dined on schnitzel, bratwurst, and drank German beer.

I spent three days riding roads around Fredericksburg. My first ride to Enchanted Rock near the town of Llano. Then to Kerrville and Bandera—considered the Texas Cowboy Capital. Last, I drove to the famous town of Luckenbach, once the home of Willie Nelson. Throughout, the landscape was amazing and not just because of the magnificent wildflowers, but the roll of the land, and the unique taupe colored rock, characteristic of the Hill Country.

I knew of Luckenbach from the 1977 song by Willie Nelson and recall the spoken introduction: "The only two things in life that make it worth living is guitars tuned good and firm feelin' women." Willie changed up Country Music with his songs and joined greats, like Hank Williams, George Jones, and Johnny Cash. To find the tiny German town, all you had to do was follow the traffic. It was comprised of a post office, a souvenir shop, and a bar near a low wooden stage. All types milled around with plenty of parked Harleys and most was holding a longneck. Near the stage were picnic tables under large oaks with chickens roosting on limbs. A band was playing with an elderly lady singing a slow country moan, two old men played acoustic guitar, one man played banjo, while an old lady pumped a concertina accordion. There was a carnival atmosphere, so I got my own longneck, sat on the edge of the stage, and took it all in.

Once in Texas, I realized how big the state was. Leaving the Hill Country, I headed south to Big Bend National Park at the border of Mexico. It was Sunday morning, drizzling rain and chilly with winter poking a finger at the incoming spring. It dawned on me that it was Easter Sunday. Then realized how out of touch I had become with the calendar—other than my commitment to board a ferry. Having been in contact with no one and ignoring the news gave me no reference to upcoming holidays. Through the gray day and the annoying drizzle, I remembered Easter during my childhood when I would get a basket of candy and an unwanted new suit and bowtie for church. Now, living a nomadic lifestyle, I wondered if I would ever give holidays attention again. Would there be a reason?

In the town of Sonora, I stopped for breakfast, checking my map to create my route to the town of Marathon, thirty miles north of Big Bend. Drinking coffee to escape the weather, I glared out at the gloom of steady drizzle and chose to get a room. I made my dinner a tuna sandwich from a gas station while chilling beer in a trash can. The gray day made me lethargic, so I surrendered to a nap.

The next morning sun was piercing through closed curtains. I loaded Brother for a long and leisurely ride through more Texas towns with grand county courthouses. Thirty miles east of Marathon the high indigo-colored mountains of Big Bend came into view, undulating in the desert heat. I experienced an excitement that I had not felt since leaving Virginia. This is how my life would be—making plans and then arriving.

Marathon is an old Texas town located in the middle of the Chihuahua Desert. A destination for those who seek the obscure and the wide-open landscape. I found a one-room cabin a short walk to the small town. My other lodging option was the Cage Hotel built in the twenties to host wealthy cattle barons. I cleaned up and walked down to the bar of the old hotel for a dinner of buffalo while watching basketball.

Back in my room I open my pannier and pulled out the baggie of Jack's ashes and placed it on the table in front of me. Pawing through my duffel bag, I found a small plastic aspirin container; the type you would buy at a gas station. Laying the container next to the baggie of ashes I evaluated how many spreadings I could perform. To conserve, I decided to begin with a half container to see how little was subtracted from the bag. The allotment was good for many spreadings in North America.

It was my first time touching the cremated remains of a human. I was surprised at how finely ground the ashes were——like baby powder. It was difficult for me to process that the powdery substance was what remained of a person I once threw a football with, paddled a canoe with, and roughhoused with. I placed the small tubular, half filled container in my coat pocket while thinking about the act I had agreed to. The next day I would visit Big Bend, my first National Park since leaving. I made the decision to share the experience with my old friend.

8

STAGE V: Mile 3,260 - 3,552

Big Bend Spreading - Terlingua
Marfa Posse

"Live in seclusion, so you can live for yourself."

—*Fredrick Nietzsche*

BIG BEND NATIONAL Park is the nation's largest National Park yet one of the least visited. Because of that, I knew I had to go. Located in southwest Texas on the US-Mexico border in a remote location, the park occupies one hundred and eighteen miles of the border, defined by the Rio Grande and the Rio Bravo rivers. The park is named after a large bend in the Rio Grande. From Marathon, the park is directly south. At the visitor's center, I purchased my Senior's Pass to all US National Parks, a benefit for getting old.

On my ride to Marathon, whenever I was asked where I was headed, and I replied, "Big Bend," the response was "Make sure you go to Terlingua." I knew nothing about the town or its history, but it seemed to be a hideout for those on the lam, and I was told not to ask anyone's name.

The day was hot, park ranger telling me that temperatures would reach a hundred. All the vents of my black pants and jacket were open. In the park, I planned to meander the roads and enjoy the rugged desert landscape, then find a location to spread my friend's ashes. I wanted to finish the day in Terlingua.

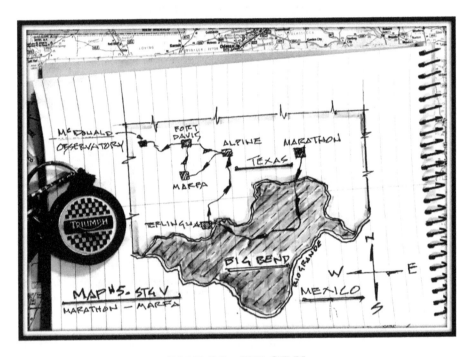

MAP # 5 - STAGE V
Marathon, TX - Marfa, TX

The road through the park was an empty, two-lane asphalt with a mountain range on both sides. There were cactus poppy with shoots of yellow and salmon color and a scattering of yucca and Indian Paint Brush accenting the desert floor.

At a pull off, I spotted a man photographing a line of mountains, so I pulled over in a rush to get his attention before he got away. I explained that I had a friend's ashes to spread

while holding up the container then asked if he would take my picture. He agreed, so I handed him my iPhone.

He asked questions about the person who was now ashes. The man looked to be in his fifties, slight in build, wearing a baseball hat. He said he was from LA and had jumped in his car choosing a random direction. I directed him on how to take the photo, telling him to take the shot on my count of three as I tossed the ashes. The instructions would be my continued method.

The man told me about losing his wife, explaining how he and his son took her ashes to Northern California to a group of redwoods she enjoyed. His voice was void of emotion while sharing the story, making me think that time had smoothed the rough edges of his loss. Our short exchange made me aware of how difficult it is to use words to describe a life. In my perception, once the ashes of my friend hit the desert floor, they were of no more or no less value than the sand where they landed. Ashes to ashes, dust to dust, and no matter what station you may have held on earth, you would be no better than the next person once mixed in the soil of a West Texas desert.

I reached a sign directing me to Terlingua, feeling zapped from the long hot day. Terlingua has been referred to as "The Bottom of the World." A living ghost town having once been a mining community in the late 1880s with a population near 2,000, all in pursuit of minerals in the mercury-based quicksilver family. Terlingualite was one of the minerals that gave the town its name. I liked the name and how it rolled off the tongue. Because of the remote location and issues with hostile Indians, the mining industry diminished, and eventually, the town was abandoned. Now it's a place where people lived off the grid...way off the grid.

The sign for the El Dorado Motel was plywood nailed to upright post, painted white with black letters from a homemade stencil. Below the name was a black painted scorpion. The motel was macabre, but luring in an underworld manner; a hangout for the egregious and the nefarious. Below an awning to the side of the cinderblock motel sat car seats circling a cooler that served as a table. Four men and a Hispanic lady sat drinking beer and smoking. A hubcap used as an ashtray was centered on the plastic cooler, filled with crushed butts. They greeted me like we were old compadres which made me suspicious.

Inside was a foyer with an open window to an office where a woman stood, appearing confused as she stared down at the disarray of strewn paper on a desk. Looking up, she asked if she could help me, but directed her eyes back to the mishmash of documents. I asked if a room was available and she unconsciously nodded. From their dark bar, I heard a *Carpenter's* song, seeming very out of place. I asked the price, and she looked me square in the eyes in a voice like we were making a drug deal, "It's ninety dollars, but if you pay cash it's sixty." I opted for the cash deal.

The rooms were cinderblock boxes with views of the endless desert. I showered and changed into jeans and a T-shirt and went to the bar and had a dinner of buffalo meat and pinto beans. Following, I took out through the odd town of Terlingua during that magical time between night and day with the dimming of a colored sky and a thick line of darkness on the horizon that could be confused as mountains or clouds. The time of the day made the town feel harmless, innocent, even sad. The road was brown gravel following the natural flow of the landscape. I walked in the direction to what looked to be an old hotel. Structures along the path seemed to be placed to satisfy available space with no concept of order—a first come, first serve, unspoken approach. There were trailers, odd enclosures adapted from parts of old trucks, a few Quonset huts, and one dwelling in what looked to be a rusted water tank. I passed an old graveyard on a slope, littered with oddly arranged markers and crosses hammered in the hard caliche and tilted in all directions, the site enclosed by a sloppily built stone wall. I had the passing thought of ending up on the lam in the 1800s and coming down this far to meet my end and be buried on the slope. There were two stone pillars to each side of the entrance with welded metal crosses centered to the top, one bent at an angle. The sight of the deformity and the colors of the evening sky were a fitting statement for a place ugly—yet beautiful.

What I thought was a hotel on the top of a hill was the Starlight Theatre and Saloon. Inside, a man was playing guitar, and a young woman accompanied him with a pan flute. He had a long white beard, wore a cowboy hat, with a stomach so big he had to keep his legs open to provide it space. The music was dirge-like, fitting my mood from the old graveyard. After two beers and the melodic lullaby of their "you too, are gonna die one-day" performance, I began my walk back through the random network of gravel roads to the El Dorado.

Now very dark, I regretted not having a flashlight as I barely saw the road. Back at the motel, the same group lingered in their timeless exchange of banality under the awning, the hubcap filled higher with ashes and butts. I stopped to say hello, and a guy spoke out "I passed you on the road?" I shrugged in question. He screamed out "You gotta be careful Mannnnnn, the rattlesnakes come out at night for the heat of the road."

From Terlingua, I was about a hundred and fifty miles from Marfa. I had watched a *60 Minutes* expose that dubbed the town "The Capital of Quirkiness." Once no more than a railroad water stop, the town had become a mixture of the culturally vibrant, cutting-edge artists of the minimalist movement and a place where the Anglo and Hispanic mixed in what seemed to be a social utopia. Most were transplants from LA, New York, and Chicago but the local cowboy culture did not look down on them as "comehereins." In fact, they embraced them. Marfa was the filming location for the movie, *Giant,* James Dean's last movie.

I found a motel just out of town and unloaded Brother while a wicked storm drove through with hail, high winds, and racing tumbleweeds, ending quickly with a show of rainbows. Another blast followed to repeat the same show.

The storm pushed the heat out to clear the sky as I watched from my doorway while sipping a cold Lone Star. Into town, I randomly chose a restaurant on Main Street. Inside, with the doors shut, it felt like I was in the West Village of Manhattan. There were no cowboys, just city people with pointed cat glasses, fashion tattoos, and haircut in odd ways to look like they just got out of bed. The atmosphere was cold, cliquish, and the bartender a jerk. I ate my Nova Scotian Wild Caught Salmon and drank my lightly oaked chardonnay with a hint of citrus and felt secure with who I was. I complimented myself on not being a pack animal and having a distaste for what I saw as "Funky for Funky's Sake." I went back to the motel for another Lone Star in the open doorway to enjoy the clear night, and a sky filled with Texas stars.

The next morning I was greeted with my rear tire going flat—my first incident. I had preconditioned myself, knowing there would be incidents and I would choose to block emotions and not judge them good or bad, but just approach them to find a solution.

As I dragged an air hose to Brother at a filling station, a large van pulled up. The man driving called out "Do you know how to patch that?" I answered back "I'm getting ready to learn." He and his wife hopped out and, at the time, I did not know I was about to take Motorcycle Tire Patching 101.

Both had pleasant smiles, looked cool, and fit like acrobats. They said they were going to the motorcycle races in Austin, having spent the night in a yurt—totally a Marfa thing to do. Looking over my bike, he said, "Loaded!" I scrambled through my luggage in pursuit of my patch kit, finding my harmonica, my Bible, a half-roll of toilet paper, all to eliminate all that was not a patch kit. We inflated the tire to capacity and rolled the bike forward until we found the nail causing the leak. His wife walked from the van with cups of espresso from their espresso machine. The plugs I had were called mushroom plugs, and my new friend had a history with the type. Finding the nail, he took my needle-nose pliers and pulled the embedded perpetrator out, saying "Now we have a hole." Then we went through the process of installing the plug, while I read the instructions and he refreshed his memory. It was evident that he liked doing what he was doing and I had to think he viewed my flat tire as an opportunity to practice his tire patching technique.

The plug was a success, and I was invited to the side of the van for another cup of espresso. It made me buzzed with energy and a bit chatty. We shared a few stories, and I asked him about his occupation.

He casually said "I'm a Neurosurgeon" and his wife followed with "I'm a nurse." It explained his surgical manner in plugging my tire. The entire event was, as they say, "Golden." I thought about a quote from Glenn Heggstad's book, which he repeated each time he encountered problems: "Just wait for the posse."

9

STAGE VI: Miles 3,552 - 4,388

Less Hair - Buddha Friend
Extraterrestrials - Billy the Kid
Yuppies and Ashes

"We are things that have the illusion of having a self."

—Rustin Cohle

LEAVING MARFA, I spent my morning riding a triangle between Alpine, Fort Davis, back to Marfa. At Fort Davis, while sitting outside eating a tuna sandwich, I decided to get another haircut. Seeing a salon within view, I walked in to see a tall, lanky blond who exuded a "Been There, Done That, "bored-with-life" attitude. I told her to cut my hair too short to comb having reached a new level of personal honesty, car-ing less and less about my appearance. My life was the road, true stories, photographs, and the purging of my past. The motion of Brother was creating gems that would shine brightly in my recollection.

Freshly shorn, I gassed up and sped north to the McDonald Observatory on one of the highest mountains in Texas: Mount Locke in the Davis Mountains. Bikers in Fredericksburg advised me to do the climb, but the hairdresser warned me, saying the road was rife with accidents, some deadly. It is seldom the road, rather those riding reckless, with abandon to give a road a lousy reputation. The observatory road was not threatening, supporting my theory of how a road can get a bad rap. Steep, hairpin curves were fantastic with views to open range and high peaks—the highest since Virginia.

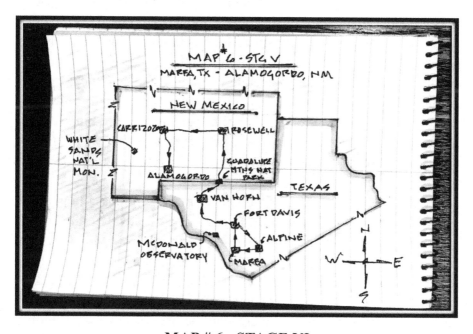

MAP # 6 - STAGE VI
Marfa, TX - Alamogordo, NM

I head northwest seventy miles to Van Horn. A town established as a mail stop on the Butterfield Overland Stagecoach Trail and named after Lieutenant Van Horn, a Union officer in the Civil War who was in command of a garrison in the area. Its main street parallels I-10, between Fredericksburg and El Paso.

The El Capitan Hotel, a grand building, constructed of red brick, stands on the corner in town. Like the Cage Hotel in Marathon, the hotel catered to cattle barons of the day. Miles before entering the town I could see colossal neon letters on the rooftop supported by a grid of steel beams: EL CAPITAN. Passing the magnificent hotel, I turned to see a long row of motels advertising competitive rates as low as twenty-six dollars a night. I chose one, checked in, showered, and to satisfy my curiosity made my way to the old hotel for dinner.

After an unexciting salad with bad service, I took my beer out to the wood-paneled lobby for a big leather chair. The atmosphere lit my imagination of a time when it was busy with men who came for business and pleasure, happy to spend their money, coming from the open range where they could only spend time. I had a spontaneous urge to call a college roommate. After a month on the road, I was in search of an energetic exchange with someone familiar. If I called Zack, I would get that and be entertained and inspired—always a new joke, always a sage word. Only a few months older, I had always viewed him as much wiser, seeming to possess an old soul in a Buddha kind of way. I did not doubt myself or question my choices but the period of dusk and the antiquity of the motel put me in a sullen mood, so I made the call, and as always, I was revitalized as he validated my adventurous solo journey.

US Route 90, which I had followed since Del Rio, terminated at I-10. To the other side, Route 54 led to Carlsbad, New Mexico, and a road to Roswell. I passed through Guadalupe Mountains National Park along the border of Texas and New Mexico, with El Capitan Peak at 8,749 feet, the highest point in Texas. The abrupt rise of the mountain peak is magnificent in its singularity on the open landscape, making a dramatic announcement while standing guard over the Chihuahua Desert like a protective mother. It was a natural landmark and a milestone used by travelers on the Butterfield Stagecoach route. The country was stark, yet beautiful, and I wondered why I felt at home in a landscape so unfamiliar to what I had known in my life.

The name Roswell is attached to the 1947 UFO incident that never came to truth or, for that matter, to rest. Questions continue about the original event, the result of a US Air Force weather balloon crashing on a ranch outside of Roswell. Suspicion was that the US government was performing a coverup and prohibiting the public from the crash site resulting in a highly publicized rumor that the government was hiding aliens and the wreckage. Somehow, from that came the image of aliens that we know today. The Roswell Incident is an example of what can be created from nothing to provide something to satisfy the imagination of the masses. Personally—I keep the door cracked in question.

Interest in the 1947 incident waned shortly after it began. Then a resurrection in interest in 1970 due to revived publicity involving claims of alien abductions—conveyed mostly by grocery store checkout journalism. It was indeed something you can dismiss with a condescending grin or the wave of the hand, but since 1970, accounts of alien abduction have been on the rise. Numerous people have come forward to claimed abduction, all seeming normal and respectful. Or was it one unstable person following the actions of another? Or...? For me, it's a pragmatic trap to not question that which has no concrete proof. I have to confess—I find it intriguing to consider space aliens have visited earth.

The pungent smell of curry greeted me as I walked in the motel office, a scent I knew from so many motels managed by people from the Indian subcontinent. With temperatures in the nineties, I was ready to ice down some beer. Settled in my room, I engaged in my standard procedure of rearrangement, moving the table where I could see the TV, grabbing my laptop and iPhone for picture downloads and my journal to chronicle my day's observations. The next morning, I bought a T-shirt with an alien on the front but left it in the next room for the maid—campy not being my thing.

The road to Alamogordo was lonesome and passed through the town of Carrizozo. Like Terlingua, Carrizozo rolled off the tongue, and I could hear the dark voice of James Coburn speaking the town's name in the movie *Young Guns*. Traveling through Picacho, Lincoln, Capitan, New Mexico, I was in Billy the Kid and Pat Garrett country. I held a fascination for outlaws, an attraction that began with black and white TV shows depicting good guys in white and bad guys in black.

Billy the Kidd was a punk with a lot of balls and his fame came when he hooked up with the English cattleman John Tunstall. Billy was hired on with other young men, referred to as regulators; armed guards for Tunstall during the Lincoln County War; conflicts over Tunstall raising cattle in areas occupied by a consortium nurturing a monopoly. Tunstall was murdered by Lincoln County officers causing "The Kid" to roam New Mexico seeking revenge —supposedly killing one man for every year of his twenty-one-year life.

I encountered thick black clouds and driving wind with tumbleweed sweeping across the road like fast-moving prairie animals, one becoming entangled in the crash guard. Pulling off to read a historical marker and remove the wiry brush from Brother, I stood to watch a passing freight train a mile in length. The open landscape, the wicked black sky, and the screech of steel on steel mixing with the husky thrust of locomotives painted a Woody Guthrie moment. A picture of America and a reward for my nomadic life on the road.

The historic sign spoke of Carrizozo's establishment in 1899 from the ghost town of Twin Oaks, once a thriving mining town known for its relationship with Billy the Kid, Pat Garrett, and the governor of New Mexico, Lew Wallace; Wallace was also the author of, *Ben Hur.*

I found the town uninviting but wanted coffee. At a convenience store, I poured a Styrofoam cup of black fluid that had been stewing all day. Trying to pay I was not charged but looked at strangely for wanting to drink the sludge. Standing in the parking lot, I stared at the threatening sky wondering when the rain would come.

A sheriff pulled up in an SUV with the County Sheriff official emblem on the door. He was in uniform, wore a cowboy hat, and stepped out to enter the store. I called over: "Excuse me, you're a Lincoln County Sheriff right, like Pat Garrett?" With a broad smile he walked over and turned while pulling his sleeve at his upper arm to display a patch of Pat Garrett's image and the Lincoln County courthouse.

Nearing Alamogordo, the black sky met the desert heat over land looking like a snake pit. Wavy thermal views of the Sacramento Mountains stood in the distance, barren and scorched. White Sands National Monument was a half hour south, so I checked into a motel for a two-day stay. I researched the difference between a National Park and a National Monument finding the first was created by Congress and the later created by the President.

Alamogordo is located in the Tularosa Basin of the Chihuahuan Desert. Like Carrizozo, it was established on the El Paso and North-eastern Railway. The town is known for the Trinity Test Site and the explosion of the first atomic bomb. The first bomb was a mock-up named "The Gadget" and constructed similarly to "Little Boy," the first of two bombs used to end WWII. The experimental bombing took place southwest of Socorro in the Jornada del Muerto Desert; the Alamogordo Bombing and Gunnery Range under the direction of Robert Oppenheimer.

Robert Oppenheimer had a challenging job that required a unique moral compass. To design and engineer the most destructive device ever known was more daunting than words can explain. Considering scientists behind sandbags, waiting for an explosion with no guarantee that molecular diffusion would end was hard to comprehend. It seemed to me to be such an irresponsible risk and made me think about their bravery while being resentful and confused about the gamble our military forced them to take—the possibility that the chain-reaction would continue to never end—atoms splitting atoms and splitting more atoms, continually. It was Russian Roulette on a global scale.

White Sands is what it is…for miles, a beach without an ocean. Sand, white and beautiful. Following a half-hour of riding sand dunes, I found an overlook at the end of an extended deck. A clean-cut couple of the yuppy breed exited from their fussy sports car. Leaning on a rail, I stood to wait as they walked to where I stood. It was apparent they saw me as suspicious, given I was dressed in a black motorcycle outfit in such heat. The closer they got, the more I felt I was piercing their protective orb. My impression was they spoke little to each other and preferred not to talk to anyone else and appeared to be a culmination of choices inspired by commercials, advertisements, and fads. Once they approached, I asked the favor of taking my picture and received a faint mumble of acceptance from the gentrified gentleman. He took the camera from me between index finger and thumb like he was afraid of bacteria. I climbed over the railing, jumping down to the white sand while giving my systematic instruction for how to take the picture. As soon as the picture was taken he extended his arm hastily, returning my iPhone with no offer to ensure the photo was good. His girlfriend, or wife, or pixie stood in the background with hanging arms and laced fingers. They were quick to turn, stepping in unison back to the safety of the sports car. It was then I became aware that asking people to photograph spreadings was a social experiment that I would enjoy along the long road.

10

STAGE VII: Miles 4,388 - 4,666

Techno Whining
Cathedrals, Basilicas, Chapels
Riding the Rails

"Perhaps the best I can do is to document my experiences of being me, of having been, of becoming."

—*Bjorn Halvorsen*

I BOUGHT A techno gadget before leaving Virginia called an Air-Card; a device to give me internet connection when WiFi was not available. Somehow, it had become necessary to always have an internet connection. I received the item just before leaving and did not ensure it worked before departing. So I was heading to Albuquerque, following numerous calls to a helpline I was directed to a maintenance office for assistance. Like securing my domicile in Texas, internet access on the road was another effort to maintain my nomadic life.

So, from Alamogordo, I rode north through mountains surrounding Ruidoso…more Billy the Kid country. I rode from desert heat to chilly air in high elevations. I passed a drive-in from the fifties and pulled in to enjoy a hamburger wrapped in wax paper while sitting at a cement table near a screen door to the kitchen. I basked in the warm sun smelling ground beef grilling while voyeuristically overhearing conversations in Spanish that were "no comprende." The sky was cloudless blue, and I was chilled from brisk winds. The morning news warned of dangers from high winds. The wind was an element I had not considered when I considered the weather.

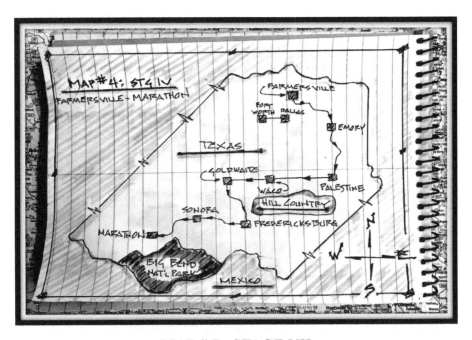

MAP # 7 - STAGE VII
Alamogordo, NM - Santa Fe, NM

Leaving Ruidoso, I did the climb over Pajarito Mountain at 7,987 feet near the small town of Hondo. Vistas were breathtaking as the road dropped to flat open prairie heading through Lincoln, Capitan, and back through Carrizozo as I created a zig-zag pattern to enjoy the New Mexico landscape—in no rush to get anywhere.

In Albuquerque, I found the store I was searching for at a shopping mall. Walking in, I was greeted by the quintessential computer whiz-kid who understood technology from birth. Where my generation continued to struggle, the millennials were born with a computer chip in their brain which gave them an innate technological understanding. The young man downloaded the necessary software onto my laptop to connect with the AirCard and Shazam—it worked, and I was out the door. Ironically, I learned that if there were no WiFi there would most likely be no satellite connection with the device. But WiFi had become ubiquitous with connections almost everywhere.

I set out to cruise the streets of Albuquerque in hopes to find a motel but saw nothing but convenience stores, tire shops, electronic stores, and car dealers—nothing inviting. I spot a sign for I-25 north. The spontaneity of my lifestyle allowed me to head for Santa Fe, less than an hour away. Off the ramp and on the interstate, heavy wind gets under my helmet almost pulling my head off. I found the trailer of an eighteen-wheeler to block stiff gusts coming out of the northwest.

Closer to Santa Fe, the twin adobe towers of the Basilica of Sant Francis of Assisi came into view. The sun was setting to create a colorful sky—blues, purples, and yellow. Along the way, rutted tracks of the Santa Fe trail remain in open prairie, the interstate following this historic route.

Centered in Santa Fe, the Cathedral Basilica of Saint Francis of Assisi was completed in 1717. An account of its origin is detailed in Willa Cather's *Death Comes for the Archbishop*. It was painted by Edward Hopper, an artist I admired because of his precise drafting skills. Northern New Mexico is peppered with beautiful adobe chapels and cathedrals, in locations ranging from the state capital of Santa Fe to villages with a few haciendas in open farmland. Their history dates back to 1590's to 1670's, a period of dominance during the Spanish Expedition. The landscape is beautiful with rolling mountains, foliage, and brush in soft earth tones, and small villages of tin-roofed barns with grazing cattle and sheep. The land seemed to possess both the spirit and atmosphere of Spain and Mexico, both simple and picturesque.

Francisco Vasque de Coronado led a Spanish Expedition comprised of four hundred Spaniards in arms, about 1,500 Indians, and four monks. Their pursuit—the rumored Seven Cities of Cibola or Seven Cities of Gold. The quest took him as far as present-day Kansas before turning back empty-handed. Some believe early explorers witnessed sun hitting pueblo walls in Taos where straw in the Adobe appeared to be gold. From New Spain, they traveled the Colorado River, the Grand Canyon, and the Rio Grande near Taos to establish New Mexico in 1598. They maintained a presence for over one hundred and fifty years until Apache revolts caused their departure in 1676.

The Spaniards murdered for wealth with the monks displayed more interest in spreading Christianity through the new-found country, leading to many churches and Indians converted to Christianity. So, after a few hundred years, what remains are beautiful churches and unique culture of Spanish heritage, the remnants an invasion by another country, proceeding the colonization of Jamestown, Virginia in 1607.

Taking an off-ramp, I weaved through Santa Fe until I found a motel close to the old Plaza in the center of town. I planned a three-night stay and replace the tire I had patched 1,200 miles ago in Marfa, Texas. Searching the internet, I found a motorcycle shop, the following day I calling the shop to hear an articulate German accent answer the phone. Explained that I was on the road and in need of a rear tire he investigated his stock then told me I was in luck. The sophisticated German owner had served an apprenticeship with Mercedes Benz in Germany, which led to a position as a shop foreman in a large facility in Dresden. From there he was sent to the US to manage a Mercedes Benz maintenance shop. It was there he decided to pursue his dreams involving motorcycles, working as a BMW tech until establishing his shop in Santa Fe specializing in vintage motorcycle restoration.

He had a functional motorcycle shop with cycle parts, clothes, and partially completed antique BMWs on the floor. Bike pictures covered the wall; Fonda and Hopper from *Easy Rider*, McQueen from *The Great Escape*, and Brando from *The Wild Bunch*. The floor was open, allowing me to watch him work. His movements were exact, intentional, and performed with careful precision. I coveted his abilities. Attempts to engage in small talk resulted in a one-word response. His wife, a thin blonde, sat at a desk peering through thick glasses at paperwork, answering the phone, and feeling no obligation to keep me company—so I toured the shop like a museum.

He backed the bike off the ramp, grabbed a helmet, and tore off standing on the pegs. He was back in a few telling me it was all good. I paid, bought a shop T-shirt, and gave my thanks.

I spent the next two days in Santa Fe being a tourist. My first visit, the Loretta Chapel located at the far end of the Plaza. The chapel was built for nuns called the Sisters of Loretta. Once a Catholic church, it was now a museum, occasionally used for weddings. A unique feature of the chapel was the helix-shaped spiral staircase spanning between the sanctuary and the choir loft. The chapel was commissioned in 1872 by the Diocese of the Cathedral of Saint Francis as a convent for the Sisters of Loretta, named Our Lady of Light Chapel. The architect and overseer of the construction, Antoine Mouly, died before the completion, leaving the chapel without a staircase to the choir loft. To remedy their need for this necessary feature, the nuns undertook a novena: a nine-day period of prayer to Saint Joseph, the Father of Christ. On the eighth day, a very unkempt man with tools arrived at the chapel door on a donkey looking for work. Under the direction of the nuns, he would build the staircase. He informed the sisters he require total privacy, locking himself in the chapel for three months, then mysteriously disappeared.

Entering the chapel, the nuns were amazed. A spiral staircase was created of non-native wood, the type…still in question. The construction was mysterious with no supports or buttresses in a vertical span of a three hundred and sixty-degree spiral design supported only at the floor and loft attachment. A search for the mysterious man went as far as to put a notice in the local Santa Fe newspaper. The man was never found. The nuns could only conclude that their novena was answered and it was Saint Joseph who built the staircase.

I left the chapel questioning how much was true and how much was a fable. And like my thoughts about space aliens, I wanted to believe.

For dinner, I found a trendy restaurant in one of the original adobe buildings and dined on brook trout, rutabagas, and organic string bean the waitress bragged about. Following my meal, I wandered the plaza finding a cellar bar having Johnny Cash night. It was a bar that had history: "If these walls could talk;"—small, dark, and a throwback to the sixties with black lights and day-glow posters. Hipsters, hippies, and homeless sat at a row of bar stools. I spotted a bottle of Spaten beer through their glass-front fridge—an old favorite of mine. I order one, and a guy to my right says, "That's an expensive beer, isn't it?" I saw he was drinking a sixteen-ounce PBR. "Yes, it is," I respond.

The man looked rough and called me "Brother," insisting on shaking my hand—a drunken archetype I had encountered many times. His face was sad, yet trusting, and I sensed a great deal of pain. Robust with strong hands, dressed in faded jeans, he had a thick, full beard that grew over high cheekbones below intense, piercing blue eyes too intense to blink.

On the floor, against his stool, leaned a framed backpack with a bed-roll. It was then I realized he was homeless. He mentioned "riding the rails." Then he spoke about plans of "jumping a train" to Florida, saying he had a son. Although a bit drunk his disposition was pleasant mentioning time in the army and Iraq. I began to weave some assumptions about the path of his life that got to this stage, this place, this point, right here. He repeatedly spoke about his son, the rails, and his time in the desert. Unfortunately, all I saw, on the other side of those clear unblinking eyes, was a pain. A pain he smothered with false optimism and alcohol. We finished our beers, and I ordered us both one of the expensive ones. The act made me feel philanthropic, then shallow for being proud of the small act.

Walking back to the motel I thought, "riding the rails" in 2015. I had just met a John Steinbeck character. I love hearing stories from people who have a real story. Talking to the man I shared beers with it made me realize how my life has not strayed that far outside the lines. Even now, as I lived off a high-priced motorcycle, staying in motels in my Gucci life on the road.

11

STAGE VIII: Miles 4,666 - 5,335

Chimayo Spreading - A Veteran's Father
Four Corner Spreading
Monument Valley on Steroids

*"Absorb what is useful, discard what is useless,
and add what is specifically your own."*

—*Bruce Lee*

I LEFT SANTA Fe and rode to Taos. Thoughts of the road excited me, knowing I would pass through beautiful New Mexico country, the towns of Chimayo and Espanola, then cross the Rio Grande Gorge. Taos was only fifty miles northeast from Santa Fe, but I wanted to make a day of it and ride to the small town of Abiquiu, the home of Georgia

O'Keefe, the painter who captured the essence and soul of Northern New Mexico.

The two-lane road rolled and weaved through the countryside on the way to the Hispanic town of Espanola. When I mentioned Chimayo and Espanola during my travels in New Mexico, I received warnings of gang violence and motorcyclists being harassed. There would always be such warnings of places, people, and dangerous roads. Snakes, bears, gangs, the police, high winds; there were always people who had something to warn you about. But I knew most of those people were afraid to leave the security of their home.

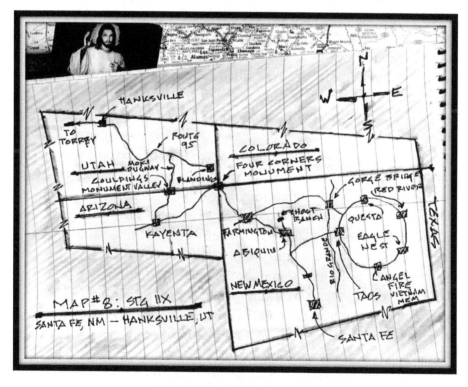

MAP # 8 - STAGE IIX
Santa Fe, NM - Hanksville, UT

The ride from Santa Fe to Chimayo was euphoric. I dreamt of riding a motorcycle through the area with the sand-brown mountains, the cottonwood trees, and the feeling of being in another country—even another era. I felt the warm sunshine under the perfect blue skies which, for some reason, were always bluer in northern New Mexico. It was bliss.

In Chimayo I stopped at the El Santuario de Chimayo, a church I considered the holiest of holy places, even after spending time in Jerusalem. It had much to do with the simplicity of the structure and how it so perfectly represented the surrounding farming community; its people exuding a sincere and honest belief. The Santuario was built in the mid-1800s over a small pit of dirt, said to possess healing powers. The church became a pilgrimage for the sick, many arriving on crutches and somehow transformed to walk away. It was the power of faith that changed the lives of people who came; a pilgrimage site with more Catholics coming to the small Catholic church than any other in America. The atmosphere was filled with a gathered spirituality for those open to the energy. I felt it and left enriched.

The chapel is small, enclosed by an adobe wall. You entered through two large wooden Spanish gates. Two chapel towers in the style of Gothic architecture stood to each side of carved doors for the entrance of the church; simple, beautiful, and pure. Centered at the entrance was a wooden cross on a brick foundation, the base wrapped with plastic flowers and rosary beads. A woman near my age walked in so I asked if she would photograph me spreading Jack's ashes. I felt it necessary to leave some of my Irish Catholic friend at this very holy place. I placed ashes onto the foundation of the cross as she took the photo, conscious to be aware of the act I was performing and not wanting the act to become habitual or void of connection. But even in the richly spiritual place, I found it difficult to comprehend that the ash dust on my hand was the remains of a person I once knew. His early death caused me to consider the fragility of my own mortality. Bringing Jack on my travels was adding a cathartic dimension.

Out of Chimayo through Espanola and north to Taos, I stopped in Abiquiu for lunch at a Lebanese restaurant, filling myself with fresh river trout. I was enjoying the pace of my new life and deflected innate demands to always expect and apprehend what would be next. My intent was to reconstruct my psyche and slow down—appreciate the now.

At Abiquiu, I passed O'Keefe's home before entering an open area that fronted the large Saint Thomas Church; another adobe marvel. The town was empty and felt abandoned. Once a Spanish settlement, there was little difference compared to photographs taken a hundred years earlier when the area was filled with encampments for Native Americans. Up the hill, on a gnarly dirt path stood the Masada, a tiny adobe church with a single bell tower. Three wooden crosses stood at a cliff edge with dark blue mountains in the distance. It felt like a foreign country with the Masada being the most quintessential picture of New Mexico—the adobe structure appearing to be rooted in the landscape.

Ghost Ranch, twenty miles north, was originally part of a 1766 Spanish Land Grant by Charles III of Spain and now, a retreat and educational center operated by Presbyterians. Located in red rock cliffs, its part of what is called the Piedra Lumbre; The Shining Rock. After the property passed through numerous hands, it was bought by Authur Pack, the publisher of a nature magazine in the early thirties. One of his articles stated that the northern New Mexico area was "the best in the world." Georgia O'Keefe, a young painter Manhattan painter, read the article and was inspired to visit the location—she never left. She lived at Ghost Ranch for ten years before buying a home in Abiquiu. The landscape became her artistic playground.

From Ghost Ranch I headed back to Espanola, riding along the Chama River and through a tight canyon of vertical red rock. High winds funneled through causing a ferocious twist to create an eddy of circular entrapment. Spinning wind was ladened with debris—plastic bags, desert grass, and tumbleweed.

From Espanola, I turned west for Taos, crossing the Rio Grande Gorge bridge; the seventh highest in America; a steel deck arched bridge built in 1963, spanning a 1,300-foot deep crack in the earth.

The skies had darkened, and the temperatures dropped with winds blowing hard for most of my ride with open prairie along the backdrop of the Sangre de Christo mountains. An eerie line of thunderclouds followed while heavy crosswinds buffeted me as I rode across the exposed two-lane bridge. I took my eyes off the road to stare down at the narrow sliver of a river more than five hundred feet below. At the center of the bridge were railed platforms to both sides of the walkway to providing a bump out to stand and view the gorge. In the movie, *Natural Born Killers*, the characters played by Woody Harrelson and Juliette Lewis stood to on one of the platforms to proclaim their love in a macabre manner.

The "Gorge Bridge" as it's called has a history of suicides, with authorities investigating means to prevent such horrible deaths. I heard the bridge was proclaimed as a "suicide destination" with people traveling to make the jump. It was hard to wrap my brain around the concept of a "suicide destination."

Taos is different than Santa Fe; more rustic, less polished, with a population of Indians appearing to be of Spanish heritage. The town was built around the Taos Pueblo near the home of Kit Carson; American frontiersman, mountain man, fur trapper, wilderness guide, Indian agent and American army officer. Carson left Kentucky at sixteen to pursue a frontier life to became a legend from biographies and dime store novels. He was a Union Brigadier General in the Civil War and, with a group of mostly Hispanics successfully halted the forward aggression of the Confederacy into New Mexico. Following the war Carson continued to fight Indians in the west; the Navajo, Apache, Kiowa, and the Comanche.

I got a room a few blocks from the Plaza. The town was casual and full of modern-day Hipsters—skinny jeans, little hats, tattoos, piercings, and attitude. I graduated high school in 1971, following the peak of the Hippie movement. By the mid-seventies, it was no big deal to dress any way you wanted. People adjusted to dirty jeans and long hair—it was fashionable and no longer a statement. Now, in 2015, there was another counterculture making a social statement—a statement about what, I wondered. The Hipster movement, if it was a movement, expressed a certain freedom with fashion and void of ideology. I found it to be a counterculture of style without purpose.

The next morning I looped the Enchanted Circle which began with a ride to the town of Questa, passing Wheeler Peak, the highest in the state at 13,761 feet. The ski town of Red River was at the top and then Eagle Nest, and Angel Fire. I stopped at a Vietnam Memorial, established in 1968 by the parents of a son lost in Vietnam. There was a chapel within a modern structure honoring those from New Mexico who lost their lives in wars on foreign soil.

There was a blustery cold wind at the memorial, exposed on a high mound in open range. The grounds of the chapel had cement walkways with red bricks, four abreast to each side. Names of men and women fallen in war were inscribed on the tops of the bricks. Below their names, their date of birth, and then their date of death. Being the only person at the site, I walked a slow pace to the sound of thrashing windblown flags.

Back to Brother, I saw an RV in the empty parking lot. A man stepped out wearing a camouflage Army cap and walked over with a stiff hobble. He asked me questions about my bike and where I had traveled and then spoke about his days riding a motorcycle saying his back was too bad to ride now because of remaining shrapnel. Then he told me how he and his wife drove up from Albuquerque to meet the caretaker of the memorial to move their son's brick next to their son's best friend's brick on the walkway. I asked for clarification while processing his statement. He described a firefight in Afghanistan where his son and his son's best friend lost their lives together. He and his wife felt it fitting that because the two had always been so close—raised together, joined the Army together, and died together—only fitted that their bricks be together on the walkway—side by side. I was speechless, with nothing to say that would not sound trite. I could only give earnest praise for what he, his son, and his son's friend had given. I was as chilled from his story as I was from the blustery wind. I rode down the hill heading back to Taos feeling guilty for being so fortunate. How was I alive while such courageous men were plucked from the earth so early? Why was my friend, now ashes in a baggie? I felt guilty for my fortune—my life, and for being alive.

After three days in Taos, I crossed the Gorge Bridge heading north to Tres Piedras, Tierra Amarillo, Chama, and the southern foothills of the Rockies. Approaching Colorado, I drove an east-west road paralleling the border heading to Farmington.

Known for motorcycle gangs and meth labs, Farmington, New Mexico is a rough town. I slept, got up quickly and pulled off the road to take a picture of a billboard that read, "ADULT VIDEOS." Below, a smaller billboard with a picture of Jesus that read, "JESUS IS WATCHING YOU." I believe it defined the town's struggle.

It was my first visit to the Four Corners, where four states intersect: Arizona, Utah, Colorado, and New Mexico. The Four Corners Monument is managed by the Navajo Nation with an admission price of five dollars and located in a dry, desolate area with a few trailers selling fry bread and Navajo tacos.

The "Quadripoint" as it is called, is an attractively designed multi-brown paved surface. In the center a bronze plate with a grooved cross-shaped recess marking the intersection of the four states with passages segregated at each "FOUR STATES - MEET HERE - IN FREEDOM - UNDER GOD."

Scanning the area, I spotted a young man and asked that he photograph me rubbing my friend's ashes in the recessed cross. I knelt on one knee, poured the ashes from the container into the recess then rubbed portions equally in four directions. He took the picture, and we began a comfortable conversation. The young Air Force officer was interested in the loss of my friend, a rare interest as compared to others who photographed spreadings with little interest.

Heading west I rode through more Navajo country, dropping down to Kayenta, Arizona, then north to Monument Valley at the border of Utah—perhaps the most photographed landscape in America. It's immortalized by way of magazines, commercials, and cowboy movies, the area an iconic image of the America West. It's where Forrest Gump stopped running. The five square mile area is located on the Colorado Plateau in Navajo Territory; a cluster of sandstone buttes rising from the desert floor to heights of a thousand feet. Few know where the vertical rock structures are located.

All rooms at the Goulding's Lodge face the iconic rock formations. I checked in, unpacked, then poured two fingers of Jack Daniels and sat on my balcony to enjoy the vertical marvels with a sunset painting a backdrop of blue and pink. I heard loud pipes from Harley Davidsons arrive with their throaty rumble—my view too mesmerizing to investigate.

I woke early, excited to begin my tour of Utah. Packing Brother, I stood in a row of five Harleys with five guys moving about, spewing locker room talk while loading for their day. I joined in the bravado also excited about a great day on the motorcycle. All five had shipped their bikes from Seattle to Las Vegas to ride the Four Corners area. One seemed to be the spokesman, a tall cowboy figure with a bottom lip packed with dip. He circled Brother while sliding questions from the side of his mouth curious about my bike. Without asking he threw a leg over the seat and rocked the bike off the kickstand. He grabbed the grips and peered forward as if he was riding, then stepped off saying he liked the way it felt. He asked questions about my travels, and after I detail my plans, he gathered his buddies. All were envious, and like many guys on group rides, they were just taking a week away from the wife and family for a trip they had planned for all year.

Before taking off, the spokesman sat on the curb near my bike appearing contemplative. He looked over Brother with fascination while packing dip deeper into his bottom lip. In an authoritative tone, he asked "Which direction are you heading?" I began to detail my route, but he cut me off: "Go to Mexican Hat and pick up 261. It takes you above The Valley of the Gods. It's a gravel road that T-bones Highway 95 and heads west to Hanksville. It's spiritual." He sounded like some Greek god with his commanding tone.

With all of his compadres on their Harleys, the man of all men was the last to mount. Throwing a finger high in the air he made a circular pattern that meant "Let's roll boys." I had to grin at the bravado but felt a chill in appreciating their moment. It was men, going out to be meat eaters in a pack and it was a glorious thing. For a moment I wished that I was included. Taking his direction, I rode north to Mexican Hat for a quick breakfast. Then I found Route 261, a uranium mining road built in the fifties with unbelievable views overlooking the Valley of the Gods. It was a switchback of loose gravel—a ride that required attention for thirty-eight miles before reaching US 95. Traffic was sparse, mostly big haul trucks, everyone moving slowly and carefully. It was difficult not to get lost in the expansive views to a horizon of hazy transition between earth and sky.

The road was steep forcing me to stay steady on the throttle. In places, the gravel was deep causing the front tire to get squirrelly as it searched for a solid surface. At the road's end, I took a left for Hanksville, ninety miles away. With one look I knew that Harley guy was right—it was spiritual——it was "Monument Valley on steroids." The road rolled in soft curves while passing imposing red rock cliff faces casting huge shadows on desert plains littered with millions of years of scattered rock. Passing one cliff wall, another would enter in view, each formation more individual and unique than the previous.

My gas gage had haunted me. In Mexican Hat, I checked the level and felt confident. Sixty miles into the ride I began to do the math. My gas light came on the moment I spotted a filling station as I entered Hanksville. The station was a cave in the side of a rock cliff.

Harley Zeus did me right. I had an unusual and innate trust in the man, beguiled by the relaxed manner he mounted Brother—uninvited. He caused me to think about the word spiritual, which he used to describe the road I just finished. For some, it had to do with religion. For Harley guy, I believe it was about renewal through experience and motorcycling a perfect open road gave him that. Something unexplainable that made him feel richer and revitalized. I know it's what it meant to me.

12

STAGE IX: Miles 5,335 - 5,998

Red Rock Spreading - Fish Taco Pontificator
Utah 95 Again

"Hell is other people."

—*Jean-Paul Sartre*

FROM TORREY, UTAH, it's eight miles east of Capitol Reef National Park, yet another Utah park filled with colorful variegated canyons, ridges, cliffs, and buttes. Utah is a treasure trove of parks with roads to the parks equaling the scenery in the parks.

I found a pull-off to get a closer view of one of the more unique monolithic red-cliff walls. I saw an elderly couple stepping out of a camper in the same euphoric state as me. We nodded, share cordialities, and I ask the lady if she would photograph me while spreading ashes.

She seemed touched and agreed. We exchange small talk, and I learned they were from Florence, Oregon, a town I was familiar with so we lingered quietly for a bit between the cliff walls.

During lunch, I gave thought to my next direction. I had been so impressed with the "Spiritual" US 95 that I wanted to ride it again, so I detailed a plan.

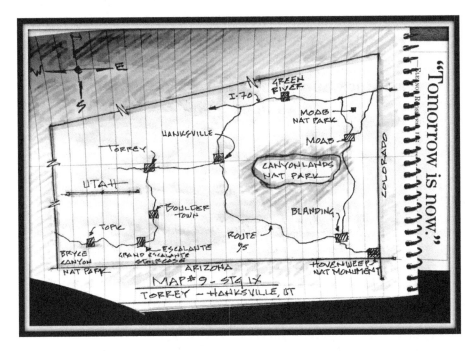

MAP # 9 - STAGE XII
Kingman, AZ - Lone Pine, CA

Capital Reef is located mid-state, so I rode back to Hanksville, then north to Moab and Arches National Park. I was circling my way back for my second ride of the magnificent highway from the start in Blandings, Utah. At the southeast corner of the state, I could visit Hovenweep National Monument, high on my list as an intriguing Anasazi dwelling. My plan was flexible enough to do the 'spiritual' ride to Hanksville again.

The town of Hanksville was settled by Mormons; The Church of Latter Day Saints. The Mormons dominated much of Utah, with many sites beginning as missions to settle intermountain areas. Hanksville is at the confluence of the Freemont River, Muddy Creek, and the Dirty Devil River, the town once a hideout for Butch Cassidy and The Wild Bunch.

Just before nightfall, I rode into Green River, a small town off I-70. The town consisted of the main drag with a few restaurants and a big truck stop which I made my dinner option once I found a room. I sat at their counter for soup, ham on white bread and wine that tasted like party punch. Looking around the place with its fifties decor and the sound of diesel engines running in the parking lot it was depressing.

The next morning I rode I-70 as a shortcut to get to my objective to visit Arches National Park in Moab, another Utah park known with monolithic arches shaped by time into odd curiosities, appearing to be made by a god with a sense of humor. Following a forty-minute loop through the park, my first stop was to the famed Delicate Arch, one of the more photographed formations in the West. It stands alone, now protected and enclosed and not allowed to be touched by human hands. I stopped a young hiker and asked if she would photograph me spreading Jack's ashes. She agreed, took the picture, handed the iPhone back, and stepped away quickly. Sensing a discomfort, I chose not to engage.

A light rain began with warm temperatures. Back to Moab clouds cleared, followed by a muggy heat, making the Gore-Tex under my jacket and pants feel like a sauna.

At Moab, there was a long main road with plenty of motels and restaurants. Following one ride through town, I circled back to a clutter of cabins in a pocket of high cliffs. Moab was commercialized for continual crowds of mountain bikers, dirt bikers, backpackers, and rock climbers—an epicenter for the granola mentality. I just wanted a room so I could get out of the damp and sticky Gore-Tex.

After a shower and a nap, I inquired about a place for dinner and was directed to a microbrewery across the street. Walking inside it was large, open, and noisy with a big horseshoe-shaped bar and few empty seats. I sat next to a man who appeared to be in his seventies; wiry, rough, and academic. He was eating fish tacos, so I ask how they were. In a peculiar manner, he motioned with his hands that he could not talk while ambitiously forcing the end of a soft taco into his mouth. I saw they had an extensive beer selection, so I asked the bartender if it was real beer or the 3.2 percent I had been putting up with since entering Utah. " Nope," he said, "it's the real stuff." The fish taco guy wiped his mouth, telling me to order the tacos, now ready to talk.

We begin a conversation about Moab, and he let me know that he had been coming to the town for a million years. A quick read told me that this would be a man you listened to and there would be little room for exchange—a "Knower of All Things." It was not going to be a conversation, but a lecture. The man was intelligent, yet domineering, and I chose to weather his pontification hoping he would offer me information of value or maybe entertainment. Now it was my turn to stuff fish tacos in my mouth.

He asked what I was doing in Moab, so I explained how I was traveling and then shared my plans for Alaska. He stepped to another level of all-knowingness and, like others I had met, began to instill fear about heading into the wild of that rugged state. I encountered a man in Texas who worked hard to scare me about Alaska saying "Once you get up there man, you're a part of the food chain and you might just get off your bike to take a leak and before you know it there'll be a bear running out of the woods to tear you apart." I was fine with his comment, but when he started saying "You'd have to be a dumb ass to go up there by yourself, then repeated " a dumb ass" twice it rubbed me wrong, so I told him I was not a "dumb ass" but he may very well be a "candy ass." Going to Alaska, like riding a motorcycle was a chosen risk.

The knowledgeable man in Moab was more about making me aware of what to expect, and I appreciated what he shared. It turned out that he had a long history of wilderness life, having traveled the country as a botanist. He filled my ear with tales of people being trampled by stampeding moose or caribou while sleeping in tents. He shared stories of bear attacks with warnings that made me fearful and excited. He told me that he never knew what wilderness was until he went to Alaska, saying it was truly the last untamed land in the US. I had been reading about Alaska but mostly about road conditions. Abruptly, the wiry professor type jumped from his bar stool saying he had to go while shooting a rigid hand in my direction for a handshake. "Good Luck," he said. His pontifications left me exhausted but gave me things to think about regarding my time in Alaska.

One thing the man said that stuck: "You need to find out about local bear etiquette, where ever you go. Then said that the way a person would behave around a brown bear, a black bear, and a grizzly would be completely different and it would be up to me to know the difference—if I wanted to save my own life. I put bear spray on my shopping list.

I left Moab, heading north to Canyonlands National Park, which I found to be an impressive combination of the Grand Canyon and Arches National Park. I had become a connoisseur of buttes, mesas, monoliths, and cliff walls with an increased understanding of how formations originated from the erosion of wind, ice, deluges, more wind and a lot of time. As the character Red said in *Shawshank Redemption*, "Geology is the study of pressure and time" and it was pressure and time that made all the rock formations I was fortunate to see.

There was no speed limit through the twist and turns of Canyonlands, so I made the most of the ride. I found a place to stop and hike up to a massive arch and high cliff overlook. Along the steep trail, I met a guy who asked if I was riding the Triumph in the parking lot, telling me he had a BMW 1200 at home. Then confessed that he rarely got on the bike anymore, saying he just got tired of riding. With how I felt about Brother, I found his attitude hard to understand.

Once up to the arch there were people set up with tripods, video cameras, and one German fellow walking on the top of the massive stone arch with his phone attached to a selfie extension. He was a daredevil, and made everyone nervous.

I asked the guy I just met to photograph me spreading Jack's ashes in front of the massive arch. Jack's daughter had mentioned that her father "Loved Utah," so I planned to scatter his ashes in each park I visited. He took the picture then we shared polite conversation before I pointed Brother to Blanding, hoping to make it by nightfall.

73

Blanding was an ideal stop for two reasons: a short ride to Hovenweep and the beginning of US 95—my redo of that "spiritual" ride to Hanksville. I got a good nights sleep, followed by breakfast, and then headed south to the Anasazi dwelling of Hovenweep.

You get to Hovenweep National Monument by way of winding roads in open grasslands populated by wild horses that run free. In 1854 a missionary under Brigham Young was led to the dwellings by Ute and Navajo guides, trepidatious about any visit to the area—the Indians believed the ruins to be haunted. The settlement was occupied from 8,000 years BC to 200 years AD; habitants said to be ancestral Puebloan and Anasazi Indians. They were located along shallow tributaries that ran through vast, deep canyons to the San Juan River consisting of caves in cliff sides and stone buildings with mud mortar enclosures. A square stone masonry tower rises out of the canyon floor appearing to me to be too sophisticated for the time it was built. Along the edge of the canyon were structures referred to as castles with equally sophisticated stonework. Following the mysterious disappearance of the Anasazi, the dwellings were later occupied by Paiute and Navajo tribes.

It was a two-mile hike out and around the canyon tributaries. Wildflowers were in bloom and views down into the stone cavity caused my imagination to picture what it must have been like when occupied with a thriving civilization. The canyon would have been teaming with activity and voices in a language of the earliest people, the smell of cooking game with smoke rising from the canyon floor.

Twisting my way back through the open roads to Blanding, I stopped several times for wild horses that crossed and hovered near the roadside. I watched white stallions running before open fields of lavender to create a lasting image in my mind.

I completed my second ride on US 95 to Hanksville, and it was as amazing as my first—well worth a redo. At the same filling station, I stopped at a week earlier, I got gas and coffee, weary from my long day on the bike. Three guys on BMWs pulled up beside me, none too friendly or maybe I was too talkative, which I believe occurs when you travel alone—occasionally, I could bend someone's ear. In talking about the road, I asked: "was that not amazing?" I got slight nods from each. Thinking we were of the same ilk, I thought we shared the same enthusiasm about the road we just finished—but I was wrong. I love the motorcycle for how it allows me to experience travel but realize all motorcyclist do not feel the same. For some, it's about the bike and the road. The ride on US 95 could have been a spiritual experience in a car but seemed much more so, on Brother while threading my way through such a glorious and natural environment.

On my way to Torrey I encounter what I encountered the week before—a blazing sunset. Passing Capital Reef, I stopped to view petroglyphs on a cliff wall. I felt good about surrendering to my impulse to ride 95 again. It was a gift.

13

STAGE X: Miles 5,998 - 6,787

The Staircase - Bryce
Kanab & Montezuma's Gold

"Never look back, the past is a wilderness of horrors."

—*The Wolfman*

I WOKE UP in Torrey, Utah—same motel, same room, one week later. The temperature on my iPhone said thirty-four degrees, my coldest morning yet. I would get the chance to try my heated gear.

Getting my fill of coffee and cereal in the lobby, the manager told me that if I were heading to Bryce, I would have to cross the mountain. Earlier she had talked to a friend who said the road was clear, then added: "It's gonna be cold."

By the time I was fully packed the sky had accumulated winter clouds of gray lines stacked like corn rows—a cold front ushered in by high winds. Gust was forecasted to be between thirty and forty miles an hour. I plugged in my heated jacket and gloves, turned on my heated seat, and installed a chin cover to the bottom of my helmet to enclose the void. There was an order in preparing for a cold day on the bike. My gloves had to be pulled on last; otherwise, I'd never fasten my helmet or button my jacket. A few times I put on my helmet, glasses, and gloves on to remember the key was in my pocket and not in the ignition.

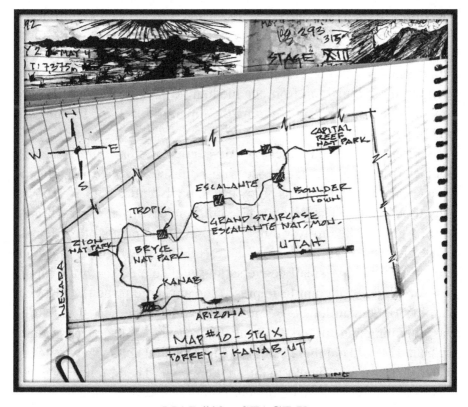

MAP #10 – STAGE X
Torrey, UT – Kanab, UT

I was both excited and apprehensive to find out how well my heated gear worked. I left Torrey on US 12, a Scenic Byway. Utah was so beautiful I had to wonder how one road could be designated scenic over another. I began my climb up Boulder Mountain at 9,600 feet. Knowing how cold it was in Torrey, I knew it would be much colder in those snowy clouds. With every mile, the snow got closer to the road until I passed through thick conifers covered in snow—a winter wonderland. A sheen on the road caused me concern thinking it may be black ice. I let the accelerator out easy keeping my hand off the brake, conscious not to downshift. I sat straight in the seat and held my knees tight to the gas tank, aware that the bike could slide uncontrollably, knowing there was a proper way to hit the tarmac. Through multiple turns, I precariously made my way over the shiny surface with quiet prayers echoing in my helmet. I crossed the summit of Boulder Mountain, passing a sign that read "9,600 FEET." I was now surrounded by open terrain, a transition from the meditative silence of quiet forest to howling wind in open land, trading the threat of black ice for the dangers of powerful winds.

From the summit, the road descended a slope until reaching Boulder Town to a stop in the road with a bookstore/coffee shop. Inside I was welcomed by a braless hippy girl in her twenties with dreadlocks behind a counter. The place was comfortable with a wood burning stove. I got a coffee to warm my innards and the palms of my hands. Three guys sat at the wooden counter of the snowboarding dropout variety, one making small conversation intellectually with the hippie girl—an obvious attempt to impress. She appeared to be the real deal with her Bohemian looks. But my impression of the guy was that he was slumming and still on dad's meal ticket. One of his friends said to me "Kind of cold out there, isn't it?" I nodded and held up a wire to my heated coat saying "Thanks to this, not too bad." Then I felt a tug at my coat as a man pulled a dangling cord on my jacket. Turning he said "I knew you must've had something to keep you warm. I was behind you from the summit, and I saw it was twenty-six degrees at the top. I told my wife, he must be freezing." We laughed, and he walked to the door turning to say "Living the Dream" while giving me a thumbs up.

Continuing south I passed through Dixie National Forrest, planning to end my day in the town of Tropic near Bryce Canyon National Park. I entered the Grand Staircase Escalante National Monument or "The Staircase" as it is called—an expanse of sizable adobe-colored rock sparsely populated with small pines peppering rock cliffs that grew in cracks and crevices of oddly shaped formations. My view from the steep downhill was across open land to a distant horizon. To use words like amazing, awesome, or magnificent to describe what I was seeing would be trite. My slow descent was a euphoric sensation similar to surfing—sensory overload and dreamlike—an out-of-body experience that made me feel incredibly alive.

The Grand Staircase Escalante National Monument was designated by Bill Clinton in 1996 and not without controversy. The designation of national monuments falls under the Antiquities Act of 1906, with the purpose of protecting significant natural, cultural, and scientific features of the country. Clinton's designation was the most significant National Monument in US history at nine million acres. Miners and construction workers found his designation controversial, as it froze a large portion of southern Utah from business and growth. I had no opinion on his act, but I did appreciate the unspoiled beauty unobstructed by industry.

In Tropic, I found a motel attached to a restaurant with a grocery store. There was a country atmosphere with taxidermy animal heads mounted on walls of aged wood. Trout was on the menu, so I asked the waitress "Is the trout fishy?" I was half joking but searching for an honest answer and glad she understood. With a slow delivery she replied, "No, it's a very mild fish." I was careful having ordered fish that tasted like the bottom of a bait bucket. I relaxed with my dinner, proud for making such a day unfold, wanting to imprint the experience in my mind like the pages of a book that I could revisit.

My morning ride to Bryce Canyon National Park was short. It was another Utah park sharing the commonalities of rock, rock color, rock type, vegetation, similar, but unique in their own way. I considered the shock for the Mormons when first seeing the unusual formations so different from the topography of the east from where they came.

Bryce Canyon National Park is really not a canyon but a series of amphitheaters along the eastern side of the Paunsaugunt Plateau. The park is distinctive for the many geological formations known as Hoodoos, named so because they looked similar to the human form and appeared ghostly; a term used in the south by early African-Americans to describe ghosts. The formations were plentiful, the result of stream erosions of an ancient river. Vertical wall cliffs and arches enclosed the park, situated to allow viewing of a landscape filled with strange human-like formations of eroded rock.

At a cliff edge overlook, I was enjoying the vistas in the crisp, clear April air. Hoodoos and Ponderosa pines remained spattered with winter snowfall. I had Jack's ashes in my coat pocket so when I encountered a couple near my age, I asked the man if he would photograph me while performing a spreading. Following the shot, he asked a few questions about my friend, so I told him the story of Jack's short life and the influence he had on my youth. I asked where he was from and he said, North Carolina. I asked where and he answered, "Nowhere you'd know." "Try me," I said. He replied "Morgantown," and I told him I had driven through it on motorcycle trips to avoid I-40. We laughed at the small world, and he talked about his love of the Blue Ridge Parkway. I explained that my friend, the one's ashes I just threw in the air, had owned a B&B off the Parkway in Bedford, Virginia. Describing it, his face lit up, and he told me that he and his wife had spent two days there. He said it was many years ago and recalled meeting the owners. What a coincidence! It seemed the more I traveled the world, the smaller the world got.

From Bryce, I directed Brother to Kanab in southern Utah situated between Bryce, Zion, The Staircase, and the Grand Canyon. I had mail waiting at the post office—my first pick up since setting up residence in Texas. The process was simple and made my nomadic life easier. Kanab, another small town settled by Mormons, had an inviting atmosphere and I was looked forward to settling in for the evening.

Locals refer to Kanab as, "Little Hollywood." A moniker due to the incredible number of movies and TV shows filmed around the town. In 1924, Hollywood cowboy star Tom Mix chose the area to shoot his first western. After a series of movies, two local brothers were inspired to start a limousine service, delivering actors and crew to film locations. The service was so successful they built the Parry Motel in the early thirties to host the cast and crew of over one hundred movies and TV series such as *Mackenna's Gold, The Outlaw Josey Wales,* and the TV series *Branded* with Chuck Connors. At the motel, I got the Omar Sharif room with a framed photo of him on horseback over the bed.

Zion became my last and favorite park in Utah seeming to encompass some of every park—a common denominator of buttes, spires, cliffs, amphitheaters, terraces, and towers. It was a half mile deep with a drive down that made me feel small, insignificant, and aware of how I, at times, took myself too seriously.

I returned for another night in the town of Kanab. The Parry Motel was full, so I found another motel. I laundered clothes, downloaded pictures, wrote in my journal, then researched Kanab's history. I read about one interesting item about a man named Freddy Crystal who spent over ten years in the area searching for the Treasures of Montezuma. Freddy had been struck on the head by a crowbar causing him to have "panoramic visions" of an area in southern Utah. He saw images of petroglyphs on canyon walls directing him to a hidden bounty of jade, turquoise, gold, and silver. His vision brought him to the Mormon town of Kanab where everyone was trying to scrape out a living by farming while establishing an outpost for the Church of the Latter Day Saints. They thought Freddy, who arrived on a bicycle with stories of Montezuma's Gold, to be strange. They abused and belittled him with nicknames and ridicule. For two years he combed red rock canyons searching for clues on petroglyph-carved cliff walls. He looked for anything that might match the images in his visions. Nothing was found, so he went to Mexico for six years, returning with a map he found in an old church. The map showed the Aztecs coming to southern Utah and seven layered mountains with a staircase leading up a cliff, then to a cave where the treasure was believed to be buried.

Freddy returned to Kanab with the map, which inspired reluctant town's people to take an interest. Every man in town stopped what he was doing to help Freddie to wildly dig for gold in cliff walls from his interpretation of the map. Finally, a cave was discovered that Freddy felt confident was "The One." The cave entrance was covered with a flat rock. Rolling it away it was a booby trap—a boulder tumbling to entrap Freddie's leg. He was freed, but the incident made the Mormons reluctant to assist Freddy in further pursuits.

Montezuma's treasure was thought to be huge, yet no one could be sure since it was never found. It was Montezuma II, the Emperor of Tenochtitlan at the time of the Spanish Conquest in the 1500s by the Spanish conquistador, Cortez who was last in possession. Before his murder, it was thought that he had hidden the treasure. Many were tortured by the Spanish in an attempt to know the whereabouts of the bounty, but none spoke. American Indians in the Southwest say the treasure remains for the ancestors of the Aztecs, but it is not yet time to uncover. Many feel there is a curse surrounding any search and the closer people get to finding the treasure the more fatal the curse becomes.

About sixty years after Freddy Crystal, others pursued attempts to dig where he left off, only finding old moccasins, a conquistador's helmet and a pot of turquoise beads in front of what was called the "Sacrificial Stone," similar to that used by Aztecs for gruesome sacrifices. There was a spirit of excitement, but not enough to keep people engaged, so once again, they retreated in frustration.

Years later a local farmer had the hunch that the treasure was buried in a cave in a lake located on his land outside of Kanab. So he hired divers from San Francisco with equipment to perform a search below the surface of the water. They encountered multiple issues with their breathing apparatus, ghostly figures in the water and one man experiencing strangulation. It caused such fear of subsurface exploration they hired a team from Wisconsin to drill above where they assumed the cave was located. Once they did, they pulled the bit up to discover gold flecks on the dirt suggesting treasure beneath. That night, the man who operated the drill died of a heart attack.

Following that episode, the farmer hired a group to use seismic tools to probe the earth hoping to provide some direction for a successful dig. Walking the area above the cave, to investigate with his laptop he became violently ill and passed out, then suffered multiple heart attacks to eventually fall into a coma—another incident to validate the curse surrounding the quest for Montezuma's treasure.

In more recent years another attempt was made to enter the mysterious, cursed cave below the lake. Scuba diving to the entrance of the cave was impossible, due to thick silt that obscured visibility. A pump was employed in hopes of providing clarity but with no success. So they considered pumping the lake dry. An effort that was quickly stopped by the government game and fish agency who threatened heavy fines if any harm was brought to an endangered species called the Kanab Ambersnail. Ironically, the Ambersnail is known in Mexico as the "Gold Snail.

14

STAGE XI: Miles 6,787 - 6,959

Grand Canyon - Flagstaff to Sedona
Kingman Pacquiao Robbery

*"If we wait until we're ready, we'll be
waiting the rest of our lives."*

—*Lemony Snicker*

AT THE RANGER station in Zion, I asked if the north rim of the
Grand Canyon was open. "Not until the fifteenth of May" I was told—
two weeks out. It was what I expected, but unfortunate, wanting to go
to the side I had never seen. The north rim had a different ecosystem
and different views. From Utah, I dropped south to Fredonia, then Jacob Lake at the north rim canyon entrance finding a restaurant appear-

ing to have been built at the inception of the park. Inside there was a counter with red padded stools and the rich smell of greasy cooked burgers. Pine paneled walls were darkened by age to the color of maple syrup to make the interior feel like an episode of *The Twilight Zone*. Hikers sat at the counter, voraciously eating burgers like they were tired of trail mix. I put my order in for a grilled cheese sandwich with sliced tomatoes. The waitress looked like a high school student and wore an outfit as old as the facility: red apron top with a large bow in the back. I finished my lunch and stepped out to Brother, feeling as if I had escaped a time warp.

The day was crisp, clear, and chilly for my long ride to the south rim of the canyon. It was nearing two months since leaving Virginia Beach, and I was conscious of my time for good reason. Having worked all my life, I no longer marked my time by satisfying the obligations of a job. Now my obligations were reduced to boarding a ferry in Bellingham, Washington on a scheduled date.

I rode easterly below Vermillion Cliffs National Monument near the town of Marble Canyon at the confluence of Colorado and the Little Colorado River. From there you could launch a boat for a rapid ride through the canyon. Crossing the steel structured Navajo Bridge, I looked south to see the beginning of the Grand Canyon far in the distance.

It was in September of 1540 that Garcia Lopez de Cardenas along with Hopi guides and a small group of Spanish soldiers traveled the south rim of the Grand Canyon. It was during the Coronado Expedition in pursuit of the Seven Cities of Gold.

Years after the Spanish left, the Mormons came to settle Utah. A trail that once existed south of Vermillion Cliffs was called "The Honeymoon Trail," named so by the Mormons who traveled the path to reach the temple at Saint George to get their marriage sealed. Now there is little accessibility through Vermillion Cliffs, named for brilliantly layered colors.

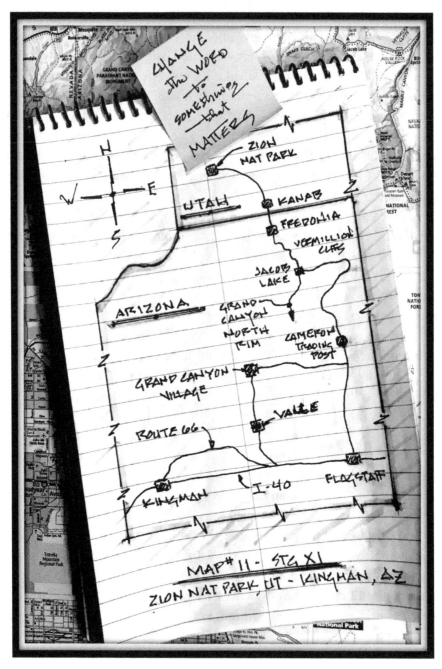

MAP #11 – STAGE XI
Zion National Park, UT – Kingman, AZ

From Marble Canyon I headed for the Grand Canyon, a hundred miles away making a side trip to Tuba City, the largest city in the Navajo Nation, with more multi-colored landscape of the Painted Desert. It was appropriately named because it appeared to be hand painted—granulated yellow, red, and blue bands on gentle, soft, sloping hills. The color granulation was made from petrified wood, fossilized bones and plants, looking like something a baker created.

In 1956 Tuba City became a boom town for uranium mining under the direction of the Atomic Energy Commission. The objective was to collect radioactive material for armor piercing ammunition and fuel for nuclear plants. The drilling continued into the nineties, and now, its just a crossroads town with a few casinos, fast food joints, and all that exist in every small town.

Continuing to Cameron, I crossed a sway back suspension bridge over the Little Colorado River with a view of the Cameron Trading Post and motel; a historical landmark dating back a century. I stopped for the night wanting to see the Grand Canyon fresh.

The Trading Post began with the Richardson brothers in 1916 as a place to trade wool, blankets, and livestock to the Navajo and Hopi Indians for dry goods. I got a room in the back on the first floor with a view of the river and bridge. I sat at a table with my computer and the door open. A roadrunner in the parking lot came to peer in. I got up for a closer look which scared him away. A Native American lady with a cleaning cart told me it was good luck to see a roadrunner. Could I be any luckier?

Leaving for the Grand Canyon, I recalled being there forty years ago. Considering that length of time caused me to ponder my mortality. Would there, could there be another forty years to my life? After all, I was carrying the ashes of a man that died five years younger than I was. I felt like the constructs of modern man had been restrictive, with life stages that we were conditioned to honor—birth, school, career, marriage, retirement, death. Now, at the end of those stages, I wanted to add new stages for the remainder of my life—wanting to see my life like the weave of a rope with multiple stages flowing concurrently. I did not care to think that I was at the final stage before the boneyard—having someone spread my ashes.

Many Americans think of the Grand Canyon as a necessary destination in their lifetime. I would be so fortunate as to go twice. Along the south rim, there were numerous overlooks with views down to cascading flat rock surfaces and severe cliffs like staircases to multiple canyons to finally reach a depth of one mile at the river. Staring across the canyon to the north rim was a distance of eighteen miles at places. The massive canyon is a geological wonder that continues to recreate itself as it has for about seventy million years.

I recall a movie from the eighties entitled *Grand Canyon* starring Danny Glover and Kevin Kline. The character played by Danny Glover said that no matter how bad things got all he had to do was remember looking out at the Grand Canyon to make his life issues seem trivial. There are really no words to convey the depth of emotion that occurs while standing cliff side and trying to comprehend the vastness of that natural wonder.

It was explained to me that the Grand Canyon was carved out of the surface of the earth by the remorseless erosion of the Colorado River on the Colorado Plateau. The idea made sense. Although staring down at the massive canyon, past layered cliff edges, straining to see the tiny sliver of green water at the bottom, it was hard to imagine something so narrow carving something of such breadth. To a geologist the Grand Canyon offered a perfect slice of the history of North America revealed in sediment displayed on rock walls that had been carved away by the relentless river.

Much has been learned from relics found in the canyon that predate the occupation of early Pueblo People of the Anasazi age, 1,200 years ago. The canyon is a preserved timeline for geologist, anthropologist, and a history of man and earth from the earliest known periods.

The early Pueblo People have a history of beholding the Grand Canyon, believing it to be a "Holy Site." It was a place of pilgrimage for the early tribes living on the Colorado Plateau. In learning that I had to compare the Native Americans with present-day Americans that feel they must do the same.

At an overlook, I saw a young man with an older gentleman that looked to be his father. He was in his mid-thirties and wore a bright tie-dyed T-Shirt. I asked that he photograph me tossing my friend's ashes into the big canyon. He said "Sure Thing," and grabbed my iPhone while I walked to the railing at a cliff edge, and he athletically jumped up on a rock for a shot to capture the canyon. After taking the photo, I asked where he was from. "San Diego," he told me, then said he had just finished Army Ranger training and was off to the Middle East soon. He confirmed my hunch that the man with him was indeed his father who had wanted to see the Grand Canyon with his son before his deployment. He asked a few questions about Jack and about his life and death. I explained my ten-year period of close acquaintance and then explained how I was traveling North America on my motorcycle, spreading his ashes along the way. Now an Army Ranger, he looked the part—in shape, strong, and I could tell, educated. It was impressive to meet someone at the beginning of their life and then learn they had made a choice to head off into harm's way for their country. It had a way of shining a light on my youth and my age, causing a sting of regret for not having done more. I felt a chill because I would share photos on Facebook, almost daily, of men and women who selflessly gave their lives in service to their country. He let me take his picture at the overlook while I was absorbed in the disturbing thought of how the vibrant young man looked so much like those in photographs I would post—proud, ambitious, and happy.

From the Canyon, I rode south to Flagstaff, Arizona, a town named for a ponderosa pine flagpole that was placed in the ground during a Centennial celebration in 1876. Twenty miles into my ride I saw a couple on a Triumph Scrambler 900 in my side view mirror. As they passed, I noticed they were as loaded as I was. We pulled into a gas station and parked side by side in an unspoken act to check out each other's bike and all the farkles—add-ons to make our bike our own. Making introductions, I learned they were from Banton Rouge and had been living on the road for a month. I explained my life on the bike and my divestment. They both lit up, telling me it was what they both want to do—eventually.

The first thing I noticed on the Scrambler was the custom panniers which were military ammo cans cleverly and creatively attached to the bike. I was impressed and told him so. Then I saw his tires and was curious knowing I would be shopping for off-road tires before I got to Alaska. He was excited about them and told me about the German brand new to the states. The tread pattern was unique, and he told me it offered an excellent highway ride and good traction on gravel. Hearing his infomercial, I knew they would be on Brother before the Last Frontier.

The way the couple dressed and the way they wore their hair they looked like cast members from the movie *Road Warrior*. His wife was goth—black clothes and dyed black hair. Her husband wore a brown leather jacket appearing to be a WWII German relic. His boots were the same as mine only higher, just below the knee with his pants tucked in. His hair was an exaggerated mohawk that stood about nine inches tall. He got excited and began detailing their time in Death Valley and how they spent a week off- road while primitive camping. I explained that I was heading there and it had been high on my list since leaving Virginia. Their excitement was infectious, and he left me energized, and I rode from the gas station with a full tank and full in spirit, having met fellow gypsies that knew the thrill of the open road and the value of freedom.

Continuing south, I passed the San Francisco Peaks with Humphrey Peak at 12,633 feet, the highest point in Arizona. From the mostly flat Colorado Plateau, I was traveling a road flanked with the ragged lines of high mountains on both sides. Flagstaff, once a lumber town, sits contiguous to the largest ponderosa pine forest in the US. My plan there was to get a much needed front tire. The penny test on the tread was showing too much of Abe's hair.

I found a cheap room run by a family of Asians two miles from downtown and, like so many motels in the west, it was across the street from railroad tracks. So many towns were developed for the railroad, in this case for logging.

I did a quick search for motorcycle shops and set up an appointment for the morning. I showered and enjoyed the long walk into town for food and drink. The streets were filled with college kids cut'n loose on a Friday night. I ate sushi in a European-style restaurant with day glow lights. I found the oldest tavern in Flagstaff and sat at a horseshoe bar next to a young lawyer who was back in college to get his master's degree in English literature. We talked about authors, writers, and the Beat Generation while drinking Coors in cans having to yell over a loud jukebox.

The next morning I took my bike to the shop, then walked to a nearby restaurant for a late breakfast while they changed my tire. I sat at the bar, read, ate, and drank coffee to pass the time. Sitting a few seats down was a woman drinking a Bloody Mary and on her way to intoxication. She made attempts to engage, but I ignored her. Then she got loud, obnoxious, making harsh and ugly comments aimed at no one, in particular, using profanity in a hostile rage, coming from a fight with her own demons. The manager came out and asked her to leave, and she did, but not without a fiery exit. Once out the door, there were chuckles and humorous talk about her. I ignored the slander and tried to read while thinking about her instability and the pain of her mental anguish, wondering what could possess one to require such a release. She was afflicted without a wheelchair.

By two in the afternoon I had a new front tire, so I decided to take an impromptu ride to Sedona—a New Age town with five energy vortexes at pillar rocks. Its red rock country and a magnet for the spiritual and mystical. There is an energy that surrounds the so-called energy vortexes, invisible to the eye with the only sign to suggest the energy exist are pines twisted in odd shapes close to the pillars.

It was a beautiful day for a dream motorcycle ride. The road to Sedona twist turns and climbs a narrow two-lane along cliffs with vistas of rock formations and ponderosa pine that decorate sunlit canyon floors. My panniers were stowed in my motel room, so Brother felt like a Mustang. As advised I took it easy with the new tire, but the bike felt nimble and being on the motorcycle made me feel high as if we were one—me and my most prized possession.

Main street Sedona was filled with everyone from gnarly motorcyclist to golfers in convertibles. I saw a saloon, parked Brother and walked in to be greeted by a tall buxom bartender wearing a black T-Shirt with something about a Sedona motorcycle rally tightly stretched across bulbous breasts. She was friendly, relaxed, bossy, yet accommodating. I ordered a beer and asked a question that I had been asking others "What do you think of Las Vegas?" I had been weighing the option to make a visit but was having mixed feelings. I had never been and was curious but thought I might find it abrasive being too commercialized for my taste. Her response was "Yea, I like to go, walk the streets, see the sights, do some gambling." It was a predictable answer, so I told her "The idea of the place kind of turns me off, but I would like the experience." She said "Go to Freemont Street and see the original Las Vegas. Watch the wacky people, enjoy the street art." I took note.

From Flagstaff I head to Kingman, taking in a small taste of Route 66, beginning at Seligman. The old road wiggled southwesterly through tiny old towns that looked like movie sets that once thrived off the historic route but now survive by selling memorabilia to weekend sightseers.

I stopped at an old cafe with a row of motel rooms at the back. A young boy got me black coffee then I sat beside full-size cardboard cutouts of Elvis and Marilyn near an antique jukebox. Photos from the fifties decorated the walls—remnants hanging onto a dead era. The interstate put an end to what once had been prosperous businesses along the old highway. Now it was sad, like something dead, but not buried. The owner came out, introduced himself and told me his rooms were twenty-five dollars in a desperate voice. I was tempted but found the place depressing, so I excused myself with a white lie about having to be somewhere by nightfall.

The town of Kingman is in the Mohave Desert. I settled for a cheap motel with a dirty carpet, depressing dark paneling and fogged sliding doors. I remembered there was a big fight that night between Manny Pacquiao and Floyd Mayweather—a fight with a lotta hype and little chance it would be aired so close to Las Vegas where it was taking place.

Walking the street in search of dinner I found a motel bar lit up with blue lights and the parking lot filled with classic cars reflecting the neon lights off buffed shines. Inside a gregarious bartender greeted me so I ordered a Heineken and pessimistically asked where I might see the fight. He pointed across the bar at a man I would learn was Jamaican, leaning against a pillar starring at his a cellphone. "He's watching it right now," the bartender said. I walked over to be greeted with an inviting grin. In front of him was his cellphone leaning against a basket of condiments. I told him that all the talk about how hard Mayweather trained had made me a fan. He told me how much he hated Mayweather and explained how the boxing commission was in his back pocket and that he was crooked and would win. That was—unless Pacquiao knocked Mayweather out. The fight went all twelve rounds with the decision going to Mayweather. My new friend with the cell phone said: "See." I nodded and bought him a beer.

15

STAGE XII: Miles 6,959 - 7,375

Las Vegas Dilemma - Death Valley
Lone Pine - Big Pine

*"Do novel things, you may react in novel ways.
Pay serious attention to those reactions—
they're telling you who you are."*

—Harry Brown

FROM KINGMAN, I could either take I-40 south to Needles, then to Barstow, a hundred miles through the Mojave or US 93 north to Boulder City. I chose the later for my next destination—Death Valley. I continued to struggle with my decision about Las Vegas while waiting for some truth, some clarity, some "divine intervention." The thought of that particular city made me cringe, while I continued to consider it.

It was Sunday and very hot—the hottest since Big Bend the Mexican border. Before Las Vegas, I took the turn for the Hoover Dam for a quick circle around the dam built during the Great Depression and the FDR presidency. An effort that employed thousands and resulted in the death of over one hundred men. The dam impounds Lake Mead on the Nevada-Arizona border and is the largest reservoir in the US. It was a magnificent display of human engineering and man's ability to contain nature as a resource. It was far too crowded to get off the bike, so I continued west with my dilemma chewing at me as the city got closer.

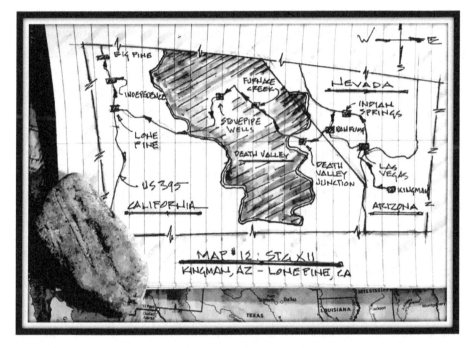

MAP # 12 - STAGE XII
Kingman, AZ - Lone Pine, CA

From I-15 I sped towards Las Vegas, riding a taupe-colored cement interstate. The pale color of the highway, the monotone haze of the skyline and tint of the desert landscape set an eerie discomfort as I entered Las Vegas through a thicket of suburbs.

Las Vegas is and has been one of the fastest growing cities in the nation. It's sprawling, flat, and as unappealing and uninviting as the image, I had painted in my mind. Closer to the city center I saw big casinos and motels in packs then the turnoff for Freemont Street—the area recommended by the Sedona bartender. Nearing the exit, my mind directed me to begin my move towards the ramp, but my arms did not respond. There was a turmoil between my mental intent and my physical body, with my body acting on behalf of some inner direction—the "divine intervention" I was waiting for. Brother never turned as I passed the exit and continued at eighty miles an hour.

Through miles of suburbs and brown desert haze, I passed clusters of high-rise hotels and casinos. Now I was on the other side of the city and a decision I had struggled with far too long. I stopped for gas and to hydrate, asking a guy how far west I would have to go to find a town with a motel. He pointed saying "Indian Springs, about twenty miles." From I-15 I picked up US 95 out of the city and on a straight two-lane in the open desert. I was riding the east side of the Spring Mountain Range with a view of Mount Charleston at 9,000 feet. A heavy thermal wind from the desert floor filled my helmet and lifted my head before reaching the empty town of Indian Springs where there were no motels or gas stations. I continued with no idea where I was going, at one point questioning whether it would be wise to head back to Las Vegas. Looking at my map, I saw little in the direction I was traveling. What an odd twist of fate it would be to end up back in Las Vegas.

I saw a sign for the town of Pahrump, so made the turn to take the gamble with hopes to find gas for another two hundred miles. It was an open backroad with desert horizons in all directions. After ten miles of flat tarmac, I saw a road with a sign for CRYSTAL NEVADA. Under that sign, another for SHORT BRANCH SALOON and below that another that said 5 MILES. All three aged, faded and weathered. The idea of a saloon in such remote and desolate country piqued my curiosity. I was truly "out in the middle of nowhere." Off Brother to stretch my legs I sipped hot water from my Nalgene bottle. Standing at the crossroads, I looked in every direction and saw or heard no one or no thing—no cars, no people, no airplanes in the sky, no bird sounds or birds flying, only a silence you could hear.

Down the straight road, I saw what must have been the Short Branch Saloon; a rustic wood construction with a hitching post out front to mimic a saloon from the old west. At the corners stood mannequins of nude women which gave me an odd feeling—one of caution, aware that I was somewhere I should not be. It was obvious I was at an abandoned brothel. Down the road, I encountered another closed brothel named The Cherry Patch. I experienced an eerie, nasty mood from the two places I stumbled upon—curious underbelly I wanted to get away from.

I reached Pahrump and for miles, while entering, passed low-income, asbestos-sided, single story houses that looked to be from the fifties. Their existence suggesting there once was an industry to support the town. I passed a sign for Death Valley wondering if it was the only entrance. I continued with hopes of seeing in more in Pahrump than what I was seeing, finally seeing casinos, motels, and stores, so I got a room.

A cold beer, a shower, and into a casino restaurant bar and like usual, I brought a map. I ordered a salad and asked the bartender where to enter Death Valley—Ah, she used to be a beauty. But now, in her mid-sixties, she worked hard to maintain her Las Vegas glamour look. She referred to me as "hon" and called someone over to assist with directions. A waitress stepped up with her boyfriend, both robust and eager. The boyfriend took charge while pulling my map over so we both could see. During our initial exchange, he learned I was on a motorcycle which caused him to hand me a card with a motorcycle club insignia decorating the front. He boastfully explained that he was the chapter president of the club. The only thing I could think to say was how much I enjoyed *The Sons of Anarchy* series. That comment inspired him to share tales of his association with infamous motorcycle gangs such as the Vagos and the Hell's Angels. He looked like a well-fed "happy go lucky" plumber—too docile to be a threat in a motorcycle gang type of way. With what I was doing with a motorcycle, he and

I shared no commonality other than riding on two wheels. However, to get directions, I had to endure his lengthy braggadocio.

A night in Pahrump, a hot breakfast, and then retracing my entrance where I took the turnoff for Death Valley. It was desolate and brown and real desert—an unfamiliar landscape for me.

Growing up there were several black and white westerns on TV. A favorite of mine was *Death Valley Days* sponsored by Twenty Mule Team Borax. Episodes dealt with the hardships of making it through the rugged and harsh terrain of Death Valley in a wagon train. Tales portrayed early settlers passing through the extreme desert climate as black and white images magnified the sensation of sweltering heat and people appearing near death as they pushed through what resembled a hell on earth. Ronald Reagan was a host on the show, also performing as an actor; his last acting job before moving into politics.

Borax, aka sodium borate, came from dry lakes in Death Valley. It had many uses, detergent being one. It took a "Twenty Mule Team" to haul heavy loads of Borax from low levels of Death Valley to rail depots in the Mojave Desert. Before entering the National Park, I passed through the tiny town of Death Valley Junction and saw a mysterious white stucco motel with dusty blue trim that appeared abandoned. In the front a gravel courtyard with roses—leggy, withered, and brown. Cast iron ornamental chairs, tables, and benches were scattered under an overhang where three young bicyclists sat; two guys and a girl. They appeared to have been on the road for a while, judging by the haphazard arrangement of their loaded bikes—similar to the way I was packed. Time on the road causes attempts to keep things neat and orderly to be abandoned.

They passed around a loaf of bread and jars of peanut butter and grape jelly. I said hello, and we began a friendly conversation. They were from Chapel Hill, North Carolina, having flown to Key West, Florida, with their bikes and were now in route to Fairbanks, Alaska. It was impressive, and I admired how they appeared to get along so well. Two had careers which they would return to, and one was going back for more school.

The girl cyclist asked me if I knew about the hotel and the opera house. The hotel and theatre hall was built in the early twenties by the Pacific Coast Borax Company and comprised of twenty rooms, a dormitory, and a small store. It was originally built to service the needs of the town and used as a recreation center and a church.

In the mid-sixties, a lady was traveling with her husband through Death Valley, vacationing from New York City. A flat tire forced them to Death Valley Junction for repair. The lady, Marta Becket, noticed the old hotel and theater and was taken by the possibilities. Marta was a ballet dancer and performer having danced in Radio City Music Hall and in the Broadway production of *Showboat*. She convinced her husband to stay and, through negotiation, they rented the entire site from the town, cheaply. The motel and theater were known initially as Corkhill Hall.

Marta and her husband renamed it The Armargosa Opera House and Hotel and performed there from 1968 until 2012, entertaining locals and curious tourists. Marta still lived in the hotel, and a biography of her life was written entitled *To Dance in the Sand: The Life and Art of Death Valley's Marta Becket*.

Entering Death Valley, my first stop was Furnace Creek, two hundred and eighty feet below sea level; the lowest place in North America. The location also held the record for the hottest place in North America at one hundred and thirty-four degrees. Hot, where you see the air in wavy layers like western movies with a cowboy walking the desert after his horse died. Thermal winds howled with dry, hot air. All the vents on my pants and jacket were open, which did little unless I was moving on the bike. The lowest and hottest place in North America was just eighty-five miles from Mount Whitney, the highest point in the Lower Forty-Eight at 14,505 feet—two landscapes, so diverse, in such close proximity.

I was in Badwater Basin, which ran north to south between the Amargosa Mountain Range and the Panamint Mountain Range—rugged and uninviting. But I found the land fascinating, much like the couple I encountered from Banton Rouge.

I stopped at a diner run by the park and got a greasy cheeseburger and fries, the heat having made me ravenous. Then I began my ride through the rolling mounds of sand. Within a few hours, the road climbed to an altitude with temperatures that cooled my hot and sweaty body. The view from the top was expansive and beautiful with vistas as far as could be seen. I saw what looked to be a dark row of clouds in the west to eventually realize it was the Sierra Nevada Mountains spread in a north to south direction.

I stopped at a gas station for a cold drink and sat outside on an old-fashion porch glider. The decor was a peculiar arrangement of old motors and compressors that circled the property. Lying next to me on the dirty pavement was a snakeskin of considerable length. I felt very much like I was...somewhere else.

I will use the word spiritual again to describe the road out of Death Valley to US 395 that paralleled the Nevada-California border to the east side of the Sierras. Spiritual is a placeholder for the unexplainable. The unexplainable was how awestruck I was during the dramatic transition from low desert to high mountains—the sight one of the more precious gems from the road.

On the map on the top of my tank bag, I saw Lone Pine, Big Pine, Bishop, Mammoth Lake, and Yosemite. Riding along the high Sierra peaks, I kept glancing over in search of Mount Whitney. It was nestled over there somewhere in all those equally overwhelming gray monoliths.

In Lone Pine, I found a room, unloaded fast so I could shower from the hot and dusty day. I took out on foot and found a bar offering Happy Hour. My first cold beer went down easy while getting advice from locals about a road up to Mount Whitney and the Bristlecone Pines. I chose a taco truck in the parking lot for dinner.

I was excited about the next day but slept till ten, tired from my rough and dehydrating ride through Death Valley. I left the motel and headed thirteen miles up to Mount Whitney, having been told they served breakfast at the top of what was called The Portal Road. The ride was steep, twisty, with broken pavement and loose gravel. The south side of the road was treeless with open vistas that became more stunning the higher I climbed. Five miles up, I saw Mount Whitney through openings in surrounding peaks. In 1864 the mountain was named after Josiah Whitney, California's leading geologist, who discovered the high peak in the Lower Forty-Eight.

The Portal Road ended at a small house nestled in large pines and a gathering of gray boulder rock. The air was pine-scented and chilled by high altitude with a bright sunny blue sky. Everything felt perfect, so I took a moment to be conscious of how all was so good.

The house served as a store and a restaurant, surrounded by a deck with tables. Walking inside I was hit with the familiar smell of cooking hamburgers. They sold an eclectic array of products from backpacking equipment to books, stickers, and T-Shirts. A young outdoorsy type was behind the register where I ordered a BLT. I told him I would be on the deck, choosing to sit in the crisp air and enjoy the smell of pine instead of grilling beef. Over my shoulder was the big mountain. In front of me, through hanging limbs, I could see all the way to the high mountains of Death Valley where I rode yesterday. I wondered why a pass had never been cut through the Sierras, linking the east side of California to the west. Than thought was interrupted by the delivery of my BLT. While grabbing half of the sandwich I, again, made myself conscious of the perfect moment and how far I had traveled in less than two months.

16

STAGE XIIV: Miles 7,375 - 7,704

Gunga Din - Bristlecone Pines - Yosemite Slavic Party

"There is only one success—to be able to spend your life in your own way."

—Christopher Darlington Morley

HEADING DOWN THE Portal Road, I had views from heights I had not seen since The Valley of the Gods in Utah with endless vistas to landscape stretching before the Sierra Nevada range. The ride was golden with untouched land and no signs of humanity, enveloped in quiet calm. I pulled off and got off Brother to take in the breathtaking views—trying to make the morning last.

From the bottom of the thirteen-mile ride down, I took a turn towards a wilderness area that invited exploration. One sand road enticed me, so I took it to thread my way through a short canyon of scattered palomino-colored boulders, strewn throughout the cascading drop of the high range of peaks where ancient geological debris gathered over millions of years. I approached an unusual stand of rocks, arranged in a prominent pile as if assembled by humans. They were smooth and appeared scorched by fire. I turned through a canyon enclosed by other collections of rocks sixty feet in height enclosing a sand-filled area. I parked Brother to walk the area and discovered a pass to open landscape while keeping a keen eye for rattlesnakes. In the center was a white, rectangular stone monument with a bronze plaque mounted to an angled face. The plaque stated that the location was where the 1938 movie *Gunga Din* was filmed with the California landscape serving as a stand-in for the mountainous region of India where the story took place.

The 1939 movie *Gunga Din* was based on a 1890s Rudyard Kipling poem about an Indian water bearer who desperately wanted to be a British soldier. William Faulkner was the first screenwriter on the preliminary script for the movie, which starred Cary Grant, Douglas Fairbanks Jr., Joan Fontaine, and Sam Jaffe as Gunga Din.

The landscape I looked out on doubled as the Khyber Pass of northern India. The plaque stated that the area, during filming, was covered with elaborate sets, hundreds of horsemen and tents for cast and crew. Now, almost eighty years later, I stood at the lonely spot where it all took place lucky to have found the obscure location. No one was around to hear me sing Bob Dylan's *You Ain't Going Nowhere*— "Cloud, so swift the rain fall'n in, Gonna see a movie called Gunga Din." Was I crazy to be standing in a canyon singing in the open air? No! Crazy is sitting in an office looking at a computer, then your watch, ticking the minutes of your life away until you get off work.

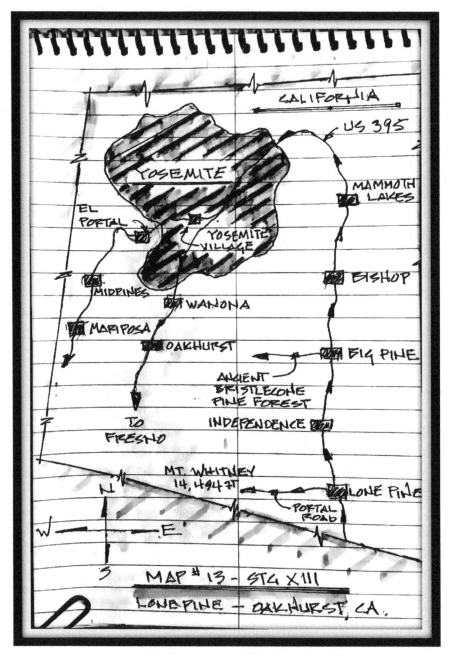

MAP # 13 - STAGE XIIV

Lone Pine, CA - Oakhurst, CA

Back to Lone Pine, I continued north to Big Pine and further, passing through the town of Independence where the Manson Family was incarcerated. My secondary objective was to visit the Ancient Bristlecone Pine Forest, located twenty-four miles up and into the White Mountains. The Bristlecone pine is considered the oldest living organism in the world, dating back over 5,000 years.

The twenty-four-mile ride to their location was one of the more amazing rides I had experienced on a motorcycle—winding, twisting, uphill, steep, open to cliffside views at 8,000 feet. At the top was the Bristlecone Forest, with ancient remains of trees and trunks. Having once been a cabinetmaker, I wanted to lay my hands on the old wood.

It was a hike up to where they stood, through a valley covered with short grass. The wood of the ancient trees was rich and shiny, and palomino colored like the *Gunga Din* boulders. It looked like it had been sanded and shellacked and was dense, seeming impenetrable like a stone.

Lone Pine, Big Pine, and Bishop are all in a row, located on US 395. Each about the same size and occupying both sides of the two-lane road. In Bishop, I chose a motel that looked like a German ski lodge with tacky baby-blue trim cut to look like a gingerbread house with little appearing maintained. Walking in the lobby, it looked more like the living room in a slummy neighborhood—two sleeping dogs, a cat, and several guitars on a nappy couch and smelling like pot. A teenage boy worked the front desk and wore a toboggan pulled over his long hair, his eyes barely visible through bangs. Checking me in he told me there would be coffee and breakfast in the morning. Obtaining the key, I asked myself why I had not searched for another motel.

Parking Brother I encountered groups of humans that showed too much curiosity to my presence at a place they called home. A few made gestures in an effort to make contact, which I sensed as predatory. The thought of such nature threatened me, frustrated me, and made me a bit angry. I removed my panniers, brought them in the room and slammed the door. I chose to honor my instincts—my gut, over any idea that my perceptions were wrong.

The name Yosemite means "Killer," as named by the Miwok Indians, a tribe that was shoved out and annihilated by the California State Militia, known as the Mariposa Battalion. Mariposa was a town to the east and was being preserved to eventually become a National Park. The militia was formed in 1851 during the American Indian Wars and the movement west to obtain land that had been occupied for 3,000 years by the Ahwahneechee Indians, said to be related to the Paiute Indians. They were pushed to an area near Fresno, California, a barren place in the heat. American Indians were looked at like animals and were either extinguished or herded away.

In 1864, Abraham Lincoln signed a bill to protect the area of Yosemite, an act central to the future development of the National Park system. Yosemite is known for high granite cliffs, and flowing waterfalls, constructed by glacier ice thought to have been 4,000 feet thick. The park was home base for the Scottish naturalist John Muir who hiked every area of Yosemite and climbed most of the difficult peaks. From his love of the area came the National Park System, with the aid of Teddy Roosevelt, who would often join Muir to hike and camp. In 1892 Muir founded the Sierra Club to developed concepts for environmentalist today. Muir is a hero for his efforts to establish and preserve national parks in American history. Today, Yosemite is one of America's most visited National Park although the center of recent controversy regarding overcrowding, crime, and troublesome bears.

Yosemite was packed, compared to any other National Park I had been to, the roads crowded with more sports cars than RVs. The park was beautiful with high granite cliffs, but the crowded highway was hectic with pushy traffic—a tight single-file ride.

I parked Brother by a small lake in front of a magnificent granite wall. Then grabbed the container of Jack's ashes and stood on a walking path like a panhandler, waiting to solicit a photographer. A thin woman wearing a burgundy beret walked by, and I asked if she would take the picture. She spoke broken English, so I asked where she was from. She said Italy and was traveling with her husband, pointing to an RV where he stood. She took the picture and returned the camera. I asked if I could take her picture and she agreed. She was frail, pale, and looked very foreign with a shy nature like someone you would see in a WWII newsreel. Saying goodbye I turned to look at the surrounding granite wall mirrored in the lake with a perfect blue sky in no hurry to get back to the crowded road.

Turning from the lake, I contemplated a change that had occurred since leaving in March. Without an acknowledged attempt, I had reached a stage where I seemed to be comfortable without a schedule. My day began with no thought of where I would be that night or when a meal would come. I climbed on Brother with a grin that turned to a contented chuckle, knowing soon I would be standing at the Pacific Ocean.

Heading south towards Wawona, Oakhurst, and Fresno the road was a series of twists and drops with departing congested traffic from the park. I stopped in the charming town of Oakhurst, finding a motel run by a pleasant family from Pakistan. Rain was in the forecast, so I paid for two nights, liking the idea of a few days off the road, wanting to fix and waterproof a pannier I busted in Texas.

I choose dinner at a small, family-owned Italian restaurant located behind my motel. Entering, I knew it was a good choice when I saw authentic checked tablecloths and a statue of Michelangelo's *David*. I passed a table with a party of ten who spoke ragged English, with breaks as they abandoned the King's language to yell in a Slavic tongue. The waitress sat me in an alcove where I could vicariously observe the party table. In a booth near me was a couple that seemed bothered by the party noise filling the restaurant, complaining in a British accent.

The group that sounded Russian was hammered drunk, talking over each other with manic energy while passing around a bottle of clear liquor. From the short time since walking in the mood had gone from festive to ballistic and too funny for me to be annoyed by—I was digging their good time. A cosmetically enhanced woman kept glancing back at me. My meal came, and I kept my head down to not engage with the lively party, not wanting a fisticuff with an intoxicated Russian because his woman had a wandering eye. They wrapped things up, paid the bill and stumbled out. The woman stared over her shoulder in my direction while her man kept her propped on her feet.

Once they were gone, I heard the English woman sigh in relief while saying something in my direction about the noisy group. I responded, "Seems like they were having a good time." The waitress came by and told us they were all from Albania and live locally. I began a conversation with the couple learning they lived in Portsmouth, England, so I asked if they were near Bognor Regis, causing surprise that I knew the area. They spoke with that stuffy, proper English tone, sounding like characters in a PBS series. They brought up American politics, asking me questions as if I was an authority on what took place in the White House. I surrendered my ignorance to politics, choosing not to banter over what I considered a broken system. They ended up being good people, so we talked about being in similar life stages while sharing thoughts on retirement. As with so many, they were perplexed with the indecision of giving up their occupations, having a fear they would become bored without a reason to wake up each morning. It was an honest and candid concern for both, so I shared my perspective on how I approached the dilemma—jumping in, diving off the cliff, going for it, dealing with negative ramifications when or if they occurred. Where the English couple was fearful of the unknown, the unknown was appealing to me knowing it would provide excitement and freedom. I knew I would rather wake up in five years with regret of retiring than to wake up in five years with regret of not retiring. They nodded in affirmation like I made sense, but I felt sure they would continue to wrestle with their dilemma.

17

STAGE XIV: Miles 7,704 - 8,064

Coast to Coast - PCH - Surfer Savior

"He has the most who is most content with the least."

—Diogenes

OAKHURST WAS AN excellent place to spend a rainy day. Repeated thunderstorms with torrential downpours were relaxing while I researched my California map to decide where I would hit the coast. Highway 1, the Pacific Coast Highway, the PCH, was to be my reward for crossing the Lower Forty-Eight on a motorcycle. After my day of research, I picked Morro Bay, about two hundred miles to the southwest.

The next morning the rain had ended, and the skies were blue. The route I planned took me through Fresno and then through country that made me think of John Steinbeck books and Woody Guthrie songs. The and rolled softly to both sides of the two-lane highway with tan-colored wheat, sparsely patched with groupings of trees—the land that greeted so many who escaped the Dust Bowl in the early thirties.

I got caught in some stalled traffic and watch a Harley Sportster pass everyone on the shoulder like they had special privileges. Then I saw he was wearing a sleeveless denim jacket with a patch on the back——"HELL'S ANGELS." I knew I was in California now.

On to Morro Bay, the road weaved downhill to a tidy waterfront area with docks and restaurants in the foreground of Morro Rock and the Pacific Ocean. I had just crossed the United States of America on a motorcycle, and I wanted the completion to feel special—but it didn't. It was anticlimactic, and I felt indifferent. My cross-country achievement was just one of so many boxes.

I would check. I gave myself a pat on the back and parked Brother with the blue Pacific in the background.

Morro Rock or, as the locals call it "The Rock," is a massive five-hundred-foot volcanic plug—the remnants of a volcanic eruption where the only thing left was solidified lava from the interior. The process of such erosion takes millions of years. The plug stands as a monument of the erupted volcano. Morro means "crowned shaped hill" in Spanish. It's round and coarse and protected by the state as a bird sanctuary—a reserve for the peregrine falcon. It's worshipped as a holy site by the Chumash People. Once a year, during their winter solstice ceremony, they are allowed to climb the rock—the only day the rock can be touched. The Chumash People were here during the discovery of the California coast in 1542 by Juan Rodriquez Cabrillo, considered the Christopher Columbus of the west. September twenty-eighth is Cabrillo Day in California, in honor of the day he first set foot on soil at Point Loma, San Diego.

Staring at the Pacific Ocean, I massaged my ego while considering my 7,893-mile, sixty-two-day circuitous route that got me there. I savored the moment, forcing myself to accept some self-praise for turning a three-thousand-mile ride into almost eight thousand miles before arriving at the West Coast.

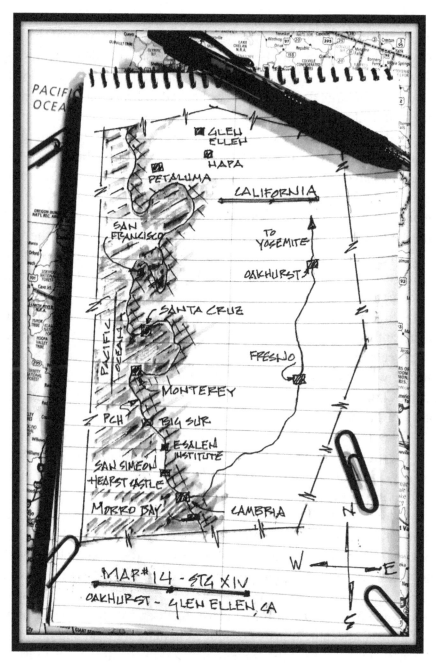

MAP # 14 - STAGE X

Oakhurst, CA - Glen Ellen, CA

I circled the waterfront breathing in the smell of salt water. It was so appealing, and I knew I would want to spend several days in the relaxed little town. Up the hill, I found a comfortable motel run by a family from India. Their children were precious with their curiosity of me through large dark eyes. Once checked in I relaxed with the door open to fall-like temperature.

I showered and took out on foot to the waterfront, finding an Asian fish market on the wharf. Behind a display of filleted fish and oysters in shaved ice were draft beer spouts, so I surrendered to a frothy amber. Outside was a fire pit surrounded by wooden benches, with a couple embraced to keep each other warm through the chill of dusk with the sun dropping behind Morro Rock. I joined them for the heat of the fire. They ignored me, and I gave them privacy. The buzz of the beer on an empty stomach made to flatter myself with kudos for crossing the country on Brother.

Three nights in Morro Bay made the town a favorite with the waterfront village atmosphere. It was a comfortable mix of restaurants and an eclectic number of bars with live music. I took time to check where I was with my Nomadic Experiment, pleased to know that as much as I liked the town of Morro Bay I had not had my fill of the open road—or the next place.

The next morning I pointed Brother for the Pacific Coast Highway. My plan was to parallel Sonoma, Petaluma, Glenn Allen, the Wine Country, then turn inland to visit a long-time friend from my twenties while living in the lower east side of Manhattan.

Along the PCH, trees grew at high cliff edges, twisted and deformed from a life of struggle against heavy winds off the Pacific. Looking down, waves crashed abruptly on a rocky shoreline. Multicolor wildflowers decorate cliff walls down to the ocean. I passed protected lagoons with emerald green waters. God was in a creative mood when he put the California coast together. My attention required a balance as I became transfixed on the challenging road and the magnificent vistas. Taking in the endless views of the Pacific, I was twisting and turning on the cliffside highway while I felt rich in soul, present in the moment, and meditative with the mind-blowing experience. I knew what I was seeing was without a doubt the most beautiful thing I had ever seen. Like Monument Valley, the California coast is known through iconic calendar pictures and commercials. The PCH is miles of cliff-side road at heights that put a lump in my throat and a knot in my stomach. In Mexico, they say the Pacific has no memory. At least that's what Andy Dufresne said in *Shawshank Redemption.* Somehow, the comment made sense as I looked out on the gray-blue slate-like ocean rolling over the curvature of the earth.

The dangerous, twisty, corkscrew road was filled with sports cars on Sunday joyrides, no doubt following a brunch that included Bloody Marys or Mimosas. I pulled over to a northern elephant seal rookery. Elephant seals are so named because of their size, males reaching fourteen feet in length and weighing up to 5,000 pounds. They make a distinctive barking sound. The species was polygamous, and a male could mate with up to fifty females a season. I enjoyed watching the lazy animals at the water's edge flipping sand on themselves, having to undulate to move. I had to breakaway finding their laziness infectious.

North, through the town of Cambria, the PCH skirts the inland towns of Paso Robles and Atascadero. In the town of San Simeon, I passed Hearst Castle high on a hill. Looking up, I could see a line of eucalyptus trees obscuring the view of the clustered mansions. That's what the castle is—a cluster of mansions designed by the San Francisco architect Julia Morgan for William Randolph Heart, the famous San Franciscan newspaper magnate. Morgan was initially called upon to design a bungalow, but during a thirty-year period, Hearst and Morgan collaborated to build a sprawling complex that exceeds 60,000 square feet in what has been referred to as a "Pastiche of Historical Architecture Styles." Building continued from when she was hired in 1919 until 1949—an experimental cash cow for the architect—a lavish, ornate, and opulent home to host movie stars, authors, painters, and politicians for Hearst.

The estate was the inspiration for the castle "Xanadu" in Orson Welle's epic movie *Citizen Kane;* an adaptation of the life of William Randolph Hearst. The story was a revelation of a man who had obtained everything only to confess that the single most important thing in his life had been his boyhood sled, as he whispered the sled's name on his deathbed—"Rosebud." I was glad I did not wait until my deathbed to realize what was important in my life.

I traveled through Big Sur and ninety miles of coast from San Simeon to Carmel. Big Sur is Spanish for Big South, referring to the coastline south of Monterey. The construction of the Pacific Coast Highway was instigated by Dr. John L.D. Roberts in the 1890s. A resident of Monterey, Dr. Roberts was the first to survey the area by horseback. He estimated the road could be built from Monterey to San Luis Obispo for $50,000, a price that included the construction of numerous bridges. Funds were finally appropriated in 1921, thirty years later. The State of California used unskilled labor from San Quentin Prison to perform road and bridge construction, paying the men thirty-five cents a day and reducing their prison sentence. Local author John Steinbeck assisted the effort. The construction was a part of FDR's New Deal in response to the Great Depression. Completion took eighteen years and required building thirty-three bridges, finally opening in 1937.

I found an overlook that jutted out proud of a cliffside with views east and west of ocean crashing into jagged rock. Shoreline waters were tropical green with surging kelp beds. Numerous people stood to stare, and breath deeply as they gazed over the vast ocean. I had the container of Jack's ashes in my hand while selecting a photographer.

A man stood near where I parked, leaning against his Jaguar. He was in his mid-fifties and wore a newsboy hat and a burgundy Member's Only jacket—a conscious fashion statement to look sporty like his car. I approached him with the request and knew right away he was a bad choice. He seemed confused, holding the iPhone like he had never seen one. It took several explanations to convey how a phone camera worked with the one, two, three, toss the ashes in the air instruction. His eyes were glazed at my careful explanation, and he failed to coordinate the shot. It would have been a great picture as the wind caught the ashes and carried them out before the Pacific. Handing the camera back he had a confused look. Pulling up the picture, it was a shot of my boots and parking lot gravel. I thought it possible that he was a "trust fund baby" having known little responsibility in his life—a narrow-minded frustrated assumption on my part. I chose to push forward asking the man to take another shot. The container empty, so I explained how I would mimic what I had done on my first attempt, taking the shot on the count of three, feeling the directions necessary to repeat.

The second photo was a shot of me twisting the top off the container—a bewildering outcome. I gave the iPhone back to him and began explaining my next desperate plan, which was to stand like a statue, hold the open container in the air as if tossing the ashes so he could photograph me at his own pace. This attempt was a success, and the man was quick to hand me the iPhone and scurried to the security of his sports car. I offered a faint, insincere thank you over his shoulder.

I directed Brother towards Monterey through Carmel by the Sea and the town of Big Sur, the home of the late author, Henry Miller. Miller moved to the coast to escape what he called the "air-conditioned" world of civilization. I was a fan of his books in my twenties: *Tropic of Cancer, Tropic of Capricorn, Black Spring;* autobiographical accounts of Miller's bohemian and sexual life while living in Paris. His book *Big Sur and the Oranges of Hieronymus Bosch* detailed comparison of his city life to the natural life while living in Big Sur.

Jack Kerouac visited Big Sur during his failing years, drinking himself to death at the age of forty-six. He was visiting his friend and fellow writer Lawrence Ferlinghetti at his cabin. The result of his visit was one of Kerouac's last books entitled *Big Sur*—a sad book with Kerouac honestly portraying himself as a burned-out drunk. Being such a fan of the author, it stung to read his words of self-deprecation as he compared himself to Ferlinghetti—in shape, alive, the owner of his own bookstore, and Kerouac—washed up, lost, with little to show from a life of writing. His cathartic words bled truth as he detailed his demise with painful confessions.

Passing Esalen Institute, the road paralleled the coast with the campus located cliffside. The movie *Bob, Carol, Ted, and Alice* came out in 1969 starring Natalie Wood, Robert Culp, Elliott Gould, and Dyan Cannon. The movie begins at the Institute during a retreat with two couples from Los Angeles sitting on the floor with a Gestalt therapist. Considered a comedy-drama, the film dealt with the era of "Free

Love," and the retreat was about getting in touch with emotional honesty and embracing complete openness with your partner. The couples returned home enthusiastic with their new found philosophy but eventually experienced negative impacts on their infidelities of swapping partners and experimenting in an open lifestyle.

The Institute was established in the early sixties by Micheal Murphy and Dick Price, each with psychology degrees from Stanford. Both focused on alternative humanistic education and exploration in what the English author Aldous Huxley called "Human Potentialities," a philosophical concept derived from the Human Potential Movement that began in the sixties; a concept to cultivate extraordinary untapped human potential, an attempt for social change and blend into the New Age movement. Gestalt therapy gained popularity during this period and allowed a person to become free of engrained blockage that inhibited growth to their natural path. The therapy pointed out that our lives were a result of past relationships and the only possible way to know oneself was to know oneself through the relationships with others—a concept resulting in the "Empty Chair" experiment with a client addressing the issues of their past as they addressed an empty chair. Gestalt Therapy forced a person to become aware of his own actions resulting in shift and change—a shift from the Freudian world to the Jungian.

Aldous Huxley lectured at Esalen just before his death in 1963. Huxley was the author of such books as *Brave New World, Doors of Perception, and Point-Counterpoint.* Jim Morrison named the band, *The Doors* after Huxley's novel. In the book, Huxley described his experimentation with psychedelic drugs. He was a man considered ahead of his time with progressive and experimental thought. Also a supportive member of the Institute.

Passing through Monterey caused me to remember Steinbeck's novel, *Cannery Row*—a book that opened my world to reading. In my early teens a friend loaned me the book and it, with other books of fiction led me to choose English literature as my college major. The novel was about a group of bums who lived along the wharves of Monterey. My new love for fiction was a threat to my father, as it announced my interest in the direction of the arts and denounced a direction to engineering.

From Carmel, I continued onto Santa Cruz, once was a quiet seaside town with a surfing museum. Now, the city was sprawling and the most sought-after real estate in California. I entered a seedy part in the city that appeared a little dangerous in regards to petty crime. Cheap motel options were on both sides of the road, along with dive bars, diners, and tire shops. It had a vibe of California authenticity. My guard was up, and I was conscious of watching my back, sensing that anyone new in the area would be a target.

The motel I chose was run down but not deplorably so. I walked into the office to the smell of pot with a teenage boy wearing a toboggan pulled over long hair; *deja vu* of my check-in in Bishop. The room I checked into was old, with few working outlets and a TV that did not connect to channels. Neighbors appeared to be calling the motel home with kids playing between two rows of rooms—pitiful to think of children growing up in such a manner and hopeful for them that it was temporary.

With the idea of a nice dinner, I began my walk in the direction of the beach. It was two miles through downtown neighborhoods that looked lifeless and dark, appearing to have changed little since the sixties. Homes looked sad, like something described in a Tom Wait's love song about the collapse of romance and the white picket fence. I was a voyeur in my slow stroll and in no rush to get where I did not know where I was going. I stopped and looked at the calendar on my phone and felt good to see I had three weeks until the Alaskan ferry. Looking up I saw a Ferris wheel to give me bearings for my oceanfront direction. I walked into a bar attached to a bowling alley, forced to step across a stage floor lit by a disco ball with a woman singing karaoke. It was a Kenny Rodgers song, and she was quite serious about her performance. I ordered a draft from a tall brunette sharing as much cleavage as possible. Drinking my beer, I watched people fulfill their need to make fools of themselves by singing poorly. I did not understand.

I left in search of food, seeing that much of the area was closed. Through the glass front of a pizza restaurant I saw a row of seats at a bar filled with guys staring at a football game on TV. One seat was left so I ask if I can take it. "It's yours man," a guy said. He looked to be the archetype for the California surfer—lean, long blonde hair, now in his sixties. I order two slices, a draft, and forget about my objective for a nice dinner.

The surfer dude and I began small talk about bad referees and football. He was sitting next to a Hispanic friend that looked like he would own a "low rider"—authentic California Hispanic pride. The surf guy was sharing a phone pic of a long breaking wave with him. I caught a glimpse and asked where it was taken, and he nodded his head in the direction of the beach through the pizza kitchen. He said it was one of the longest left breaking waves he had ever encountered. I told him that I had surfed Pavones, Costa Rica numerous times, the second-longest left-breaking wave in the world. He told me he had been as well but never caught it epic. We were in a surf conversation twisting and turning the way surf conversations do. Both of us, at our age, still held excitement while sharing our surfing history. Once my life was all about surfing. But now it was more a part of my past. The surf guy was a lifer, with no career or family commitments. Careers don't do well with committed surfers. Wives don't either. Waves come and when they do commitments are jettisoned to satisfy a surf addiction.

Back and forth the conversation went—surfing, surf breaks, board sizes, and board shapes. Much of what we shared was similar—a cross-pollination. He confessed in never having had a good surf experience on the east coast, as I offered a few locales I considered incredible surf spots. He negated them in a stubborn, unwavering, California-is-the-best-coast, snobbish manner. I let it go. Then the conversation took an abrupt turn from surfing to the subject of his life and what a mess it had been telling me how much money he had lost to his ex-wife and kids. And how if it weren't for the Lord Jesus Christ he would be nowhere. He spoke about his salvation and his peace and how when he died he would be with his Lord. I didn't see it coming—but when do you? People who want to witness have a dialogue scripted in their head and when they start talking it's like they chase you into a box canyon and fire from above.

Then the question came that I knew was coming. "Do you know the Lord Jesus Christ as your personal savior?" I saw the Hispanic fellow lean forward in his seat and stare past his friend, curious in my response. I tried to deflect the question by saying that I was raised Southern Baptist and I knew Jesus Christ. He was not satisfied with that response, so he restated the question in a controlling manner: "But do you know the Lord Jesus Christ as your personal savior?" My response: "I think Jesus of Nazarene is one of many exceptional manifestations of God." He offered Bible quotes, then talked about the Blood of Christ and how it cleansed his soul. I did not want a religious argument, knowing I had never had a religious or political discussion where I felt any resolve. Religious and spiritual beliefs are personal and, I felt, should be respected as so. I was not only raised Christian but had studied the history of religion in college, and later spent time in Jerusalem. There I witnessed layers of historical confusion and torn to pieces by religious strife—a place that was supposed to be a place of peace.

Several times in our conversation I gave affirmation, telling him that I was happy he found Jesus. But each time he came back with "It can change *your* life too." Again, I would explain how I was content with my beliefs and chose not to favor one manifestation of God over another. The Hispanic friend shook his head in disgust while I wished I had eaten wings at the bowling alley bar with the waitress and her cleavage.

The more I talked with the man, the more I learned. He no longer had a job, or a family, and lived on a friend's couch while struggling with a drinking problem. I believed he was a Christian, but felt he was using his faith as an emotional crutch which gave him an excuse to live the way he was living. His knowledge of eternal life and Jesus taking care of him gave him a free pass to ignore his responsibilities on earth. He may trust his savior, but he didn't trust himself.

I was held hostage for another half hour until the bartender began swatting our feet with a push broom—the universal sign for "get out, we're closing." I walked out with the old surfer to his beach cruiser. His parting words were about how he would pray for me. I thanked him, saying I could always use prayers. Then I headed back to my drab motel room.

On the two-mile walk back I gave thought to my undefined god. Ironically, my undefined god was significant in my existence. I knew his spirit, saw his creations, but sought no reward and feared no punishment. Following a lifetime of religious questioning, I came to a pragmatic agreement with myself that it would be impossible to conceive of a god with my limited capabilities as a human. I felt my soul was intact and the Surfer Savior had no impact on my comfortable and trusted relationship with my nebulous deity.

18

STAGE XV: Miles 8,064 - 8,374

Golden Gate - Artsy Friend - Fort Bragg
Weekend Motorcyclist

*"Whosoever is delighted in solitude is
either a wild beast or a god."*

—*Aristotle*

LEAVING SANT CRUZ, my plan for the day was to cross the
Golden Gate Bridge—a much-anticipated ride. Since leaving Virginia,
I contemplated the crossing of the historic bridge in a manner similar
to my apprehension of Las Vegas. I thought about the height, the steel
structure, the heavy winds, and thick pushy traffic, and the experience
of being dwarfed by the immense size and openness. Unlike Las Vegas,
I knew crossing the Golden Gate on Brother must be done.

By midday, I found my way to Nineteenth Street in San Francisco where I first saw signs for the Golden Gate. San Francisco was a favorite American city, but stopping was not in my plan. I had dinner plans in Petaluma with a friend.

Nineteenth Street is where the cable cars ran, so I had to be conscious of weaving around the pavement cut for the rails. On a motorcycle, you're always thinking.

It was windy, typical for the city, and I knew there would be a stiff wind coming off the San Francisco Bay once on the big bridge. I wound my way to a ramp, and the road funneled traffic to the bridge on six lanes of sand-colored pavement. Now moving with traffic, the speed stepped up, and soon I lost the blockade of high trees I had to accept open gales coming off the bay. The wind robbed my attention from anything other than to maintain a heavy lean on the bike against repeated gusts while staying centered in my lane and maintain the speed of surrounding traffic. I wanted to look up to the high cables and the massive vertical uprights, but I did not. I was too alive with raging adrenaline and focus.

The Golden Gate Bridge is an engineering marvel and declared one of the Wonders of the Modern World. It's the most photographed bridge in the world. It's a suspension bridge, held by vertical woven wire cables attached to two large wire cables that drape from two tower structures, supported deep in the channel floor of the bay; a channel a mile wide and three miles long. The two huge cables supporting the spanning bridge are thirty-six inches in diameter, each comprised of 27,572 single wires. The concept of woven wire originated from the design of the Brooklyn Bridge, by John Augustus Roebling.

Because of the proximity to the San Andreas Fault, close inspection began before the turn of the twenty-first century. As a result, the bridge underwent a retrofit to better resist seismic events. The expensive retrofit was completed in 2012, with the inspection of over one million steel rivets that held the bridge together. Most were replaced due to sheering and damage in tension from the moving structure during earthquakes since the bridge opened in 1937.

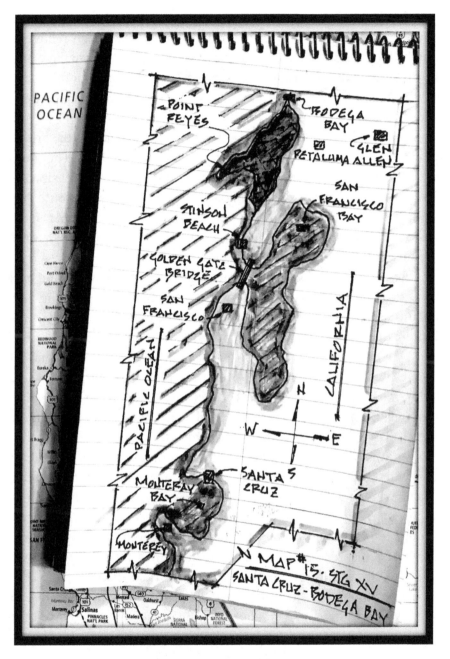

MAP # 15 - STAGE XV
Santa Cruz, CA - Bodega Bay, CA

The bridge has suicide issues to offset its superlative accolades. From 1937 to 2012 an estimated 1,600 bodies have been recovered from the bay; the second largest number of bridge suicides in the world. The first—the Nanjing Yangtze River Bridge in China with more than 2,000 deaths. Efforts have been made with the Golden Gate to prevent jumpers but to no avail.

The wind was howling through the channel and across the bridge, forcing me to use all my concentration to stay in my lane. The traffic was fast, and I felt entrapped by steel rails at both sides. Occasionally, I looked up to vertical cables attached to massive suspension cables looping down from monolithic towers — quick, short glances causing my stomach to turn. The bridge was a little over a mile in length—ride felt much longer.

Just off the bridge, I took a ramp for Stinson Beach heading back to the PCH. It was a corkscrew with a ten-minute twist at the edge of Muir Woods. I was engulfed in foliage; redwoods and eucalyptus. Through the forest, I caught a glimpse of the Pacific, stretched before a blue sky with trees to block the strong wind. I was rich in spirit and felt present, aware, and conscious—proud for crossing the Golden Gate. During most of my time on Brother there was a dialogue taking place in my head; one—an endless chatter of ideas, the other—holding the reins. Today, the two were aligned, in unison.

In Stinson Beach, I stopped at a restaurant tucked in a cluster of trees with tables below an awning. I wanted to relax, reflect, and relish my achievement. I had an omelet while listening to the Mamas and the Pappas, enjoying the California vibe, then took out to look for a route inland. I found a road to Point Reyes Station where I got gas—a small town that appeared to have changed little since the thirties. I found a route to Napa and Glenn Ellen where my friend lived. I planned to stay in Petaluma, considered the most beautiful small town in California with the Sonoma Mountains setting a backdrop. Because of its All-American appearance, the city has been used in movies such as *American Graffiti, Basic Instinct,* and *The Tree of Life.*

Brielle and I made arrangements to meet downtown at an Italian restaurant with starched white tablecloths—a bit upscale from my road dining. We sat in a booth and talked for hours about travel plans and experiences. It was comfortable to be with someone who understood my reasoning to abandon all for travel. For the past decade, Brielle had done much of the same. Divorced and divested, she had lived in a makeshift manner while working as an artist in Manhattan. A job opportunity brought her to California, so she bought a house with thoughts of slowing down. In her own manner, she had been performing her own Nomadic Experiment, but now was changing her life of impermanence to be more grounded following six years of global vagabonding. The transition was stressful and was wearing her out.

She shared tales of being deported to Turkey and being stuck on an obscure island in the Mediterranean without transportation and intimidated by traveling youths circling the globe on their wits and thievery. I was in awe of a woman in her late fifties who took off to see the world with a backpack filled with art supplies. Now turning sixty, she was skeptical of her nomadic lifestyle and thoughts about buying a cinderblock structure in the Bahamas or living on a barge in Europe, floating from town to town on a canal. She kept one foot on the nomadic road while wanting domesticity, contradicting herself with ideas of continued travel. Her comments made me wonder if, in time, I would encounter the same conflicted struggle.

Hearing my friend speak made me recall the Bob Dylan lyrics: "She's got everything she needs, she's an artist, she don't look back." Brielle was an artist, but much of what she said indicated that she did not have everything she needed and she was preoccupied with looking back in question. I tried to put my finger on the essence of her struggle—being pulled in two directions the way she was. To choose one life, she was forced to dismiss another—a truth I had been forced to acknowledge. With each path you choose, you're forced to ignore others. There was a certain entrapment with that acknowledgment that taught me to choose wisely and trust my choices—and own them. It's impossible to have everything so you either accept your sacrifices or you moan.

I spent three enjoyable days with my friend, sharing stories and an array of life observations. One day we drove to Point Reyes along

Tamale Bay, an area of tranquil landscapes and rich verdant country sides. At night we ate in local restaurants, paying too much for diminutive portions with lengthy descriptions. I enjoyed the culinary experience compared to nights of trail mix and beer. At her house, we continue free-flowing conversations while passing a ukulele back and forth pretending to know how to play the instrument. Obscure chords filled the backdrop of our conversation like the soundtrack to an Avantgarde movie— silly, childish fun between two friends who valued a similar approach to life.

I left Glenn Ellen with a positive outlook, riding west for Bodega Bay, the location of Alfred Hitchcock's movie *The Birds*. In town, there was an old general store with a mannequin of Hitchcock on the porch. I parked Brother and had my picture taken with my arm over his shoulder.

It was forty years ago when I was last in Bodega Bay, and it brought back memories. Thinking of forty years was like rising above my time on earth to look down omnisciently, tying all the events of my life together——like a chain. I felt like I could see my history since birth in a short film, weaving a tale of self-absorption and regret. I shook the moment off and got back on the road, reminding myself there was not yet a conclusion to my story.

I was hoping to find a room in the quaint town of Mendocino. On the way, I passed through the town of Sea Ranch, which stirred a ghost that had been buried deep. I knew if I rode through the area there would be an emotional sting that involved a girl, her family, conflicted emotions, and poor decisions from an immature mind. A time that resulted in a pinnacle change in my life. And a period of time I try my best to ignore. Riding through, I recalled my time spent along the lonely coast and cringed. I've turned the page, but the chapter remains in my book. A phase of my life that ceased without closure. Not all things that end have closure. Most of the time we just move on.

The San Andreas Fault was just to my right. A transform fault and the most prominent showing of the tectonic boundary between the Pacific Plate and the North America Plate. Further up, in the town of Gualala, I remembered an old western hotel with a wood bar like something from the "Days of Forty Nine" so I stopped for coffee. Walking inside I could see, like so many places, it had changed. Where were the smoke-stained walls? The painting of the reclining nude looking over her shoulder? The tables in the adjoining restaurant were now Victorian with polished oak claw feet and the walls a cappuccino color with wood trim sanded and smooth. And numerous stands for potted ferns.

The bartender came up and threw his hand over the bar for a crushing handshake. I told him how I noticed the place had changed. He said he just bought the place and the remodeling was completed last week. He smiled proudly for having ruined the historic bar.

Riding to Mendocino, I enjoyed the open views of the ocean. The town was originally a logging community, later settled by Portuguese fishermen then immigrants from the Canton province of China. The Chinese built a Taoist Temple in the town in the 1800s; the oldest Chinese temple in California. There was an abandonment in the early forties but was rediscovered and redeveloped as an artist town in the fifties. It was the filming location for the Hollywood movies, *The Summer of 42* and *East of Eden,* James Dean's second movie.

There was no vacancy in Mendocino, so I continued to Fort Bragg. I was of the impression that there was a military installation in the town. And there once was, but no longer. The town was established in 1857 as an army outpost in service of the Presidio in San Francisco. Its purpose was to oversee the Mendocino Indians. The fort was named after Braxton Bragg, a Confederate Army General. Fort Bragg, North Carolina, was also named after Bragg, a native of the state.

Parking Brother in front of my room, I saw two Harleys and a BMW parked nearby. Once inside I looked out to see two guys milling around my bike—two who owned the bikes I saw. I stepped out, and we chatted, and they asked that I join them for a drink on the patio. All three were from LA, the two Harley guys owned a hair salon. The other, who owned the BMW R1200 said he drove a lot, causing me to think he was a truck driver. I later found out he drove to obscure locations to produce automobile commercials, or "shoots" as he called them. All three were good conversationalists and welcomed me into their fold, showing curiosity about my life on a motorcycle. In the changing colors of the sunset, we enjoyed our drinks, then took out for dinner.

Hiking unlit roads down steep hills, we found a seafood restaurant with a halibut special. We sat for two hours and talked about life, motorcycles, and retirement. They were curious as to how I pulled off the manner that I was living. All three were ten or more years younger than me and, of the three, two were thinking about retirement. The younger of the three had just remarried a woman with children and admitted he would be confined to a working life for some time. The two ready for retirement had children to get through college before shutting down shop. I felt for all of them and realized how unusual I was next to those that had wives and children.

But, this freedom thing is fickle in its own way. People tend to think that if you are free, as I was, that you remain in a constant state of euphoric glee. Freedom comes with its own cost. To be free and nomadic as I was, you had to know how to be alone. And if you had not cultivated a comfort level with being alone before taking off by yourself, you would not last. There's a big void when you take away your job. Before you consider retirement, it's best you have an objective.

I left dinner feeling fortunate and flattered by these three who envied my life. It gave me a deeper appreciation of my freedom and validated the person I had created to live in such a manner.

19

STAGE XVI: Miles 8,374 - 8,869

Humboldt - Into Oregon - Gold Beach
Weekend Bikers

"Forever is composed of Nows."

—*Emily Dickinson*

WHILE DRINKING COFFEE in the motel lobby to the babble of CNN, I heard my three dinner partners start their bikes. It was the two Harleys I heard. Like Brother, the BMW made a low throaty purr. They passed the motel entrance, not noticing my thumbs up through the window. They were focused on finding a real breakfast and not the doughnuts and cereal the motel offered. I took advantage of the free breakfast before heading toward the California-Oregon, border with plans to visit Jedediah Smith State Park.

Forty miles from Fort Bragg I encountered steep inclines, tight turns, and spectacular views of the Pacific. Pillows of fog floated low to create a mysterious atmosphere. Turning on US 101 I headed inland through dense woodlands toward Eureka and Arcata.

Between Garberville and Fortuna, I saw signs for the Avenue of the Giants, located in Humboldt Redwoods State Park—a thirty-one mile scenic drive through massive redwood groves established in 1960.

Redwoods ranged up to two hundred and fifty feet in height, and nine hundred and fifty years of age, the tallest named the Immortal Tree. Once it had been even taller, near three hundred feet but was struck by lightning in 1908, removing the top fifty feet. I spent midday riding through the big redwoods, awestruck at their massive trunks. The road was carved through the groves sparing little room between the two-lane and the ancient trees. The area was cool with the smell of evergreen and the forest looking like a medieval fairy tale. The high canopy made the

road dark except for regions where sunlight found its way to create abstract patterns. I parked at a pull-off for a short hike through the forest. Fallen trees had been cut away to allow passage on the trail, allowing me to stand against the enormous diameter and ringed surface of a cut redwood. The mood and atmosphere in the canopied forest were relaxing, mysterious, quiet, and soothing, like a secret room in an old mansion.

Humans were responsible for cutting down over fifty percent of the old growth redwoods. Settlers coming to the northwest saw the big trees as no more than a motherlode of construction material and showed little respect for their magnificent size or age—mentality similar to the slaughtering of the American buffalo. The naturalist John Muir gathered like-minded people to protect the great treasures with the protection of the national parks system.

In Arcata, I began to look for a room while seeing "NO VACANCY" posted at every motel. Asking what was going on, I was told it was graduation weekend at Humboldt State University. Arcata is a naturalist wonderland, so I knew campgrounds would be filled with ultra-hip aging parents of their graduating granola kids.

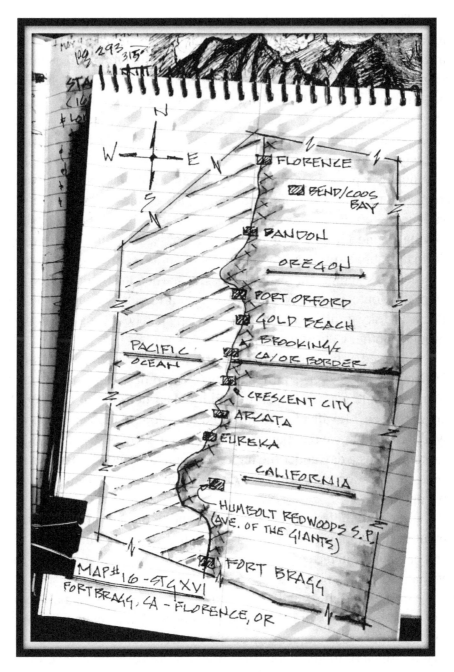

MAP # 16 - STAGE XVI

Fort Bragg, CA - Florence, OR

The Humboldt area is full of tree huggers with the college having an acclaimed School of Botany. Many students spent their spare time hunting for the tallest redwoods in surrounding forests. The tallest range close to four hundred feet, having germinated at the time the Parthenon was constructed, 447 BC, over 2,500 years ago.

Crescent City was seventy-five miles away with small towns between Arcata and there. I planned to visit Jedidiah Smith State Park the following morning to see where the most massive redwoods lived. For ten minutes I passed Humboldt Lagoon, an enormous body of water connected to the Pacific. Through rolling hills and big cedars, the sky darkened to produce a steady drizzle. Four lanes dropped to two while moving inland through a denser forest. I passed a field with grazing elk that grabbed my attention—long enough to look back at the road and see two standing elk ready to cross. It startled me. I considered the alternative outcome to my safe passing with the idea haunting me for hours. The sky turned a dark gray with wispy patches of fog as I moved through another California climate.

I passed a dive motel like something from a horror film. Out of desperation for shelter, I turned around. The office was closed with a poorly scribble message taped to a filthy glass door—"Go to Room 8 for assistance." I walked over, knocked on a door that opened to wild-eyed barking curs and a man in a sleeveless T-shirt, greasy from what I assumed was a day under the hood. The quick encounter made up my mind, so I pardoned myself knowing I did not want to sleep with one eye open.

In twenty miles I reached Klamath and found a room across from an interesting looking bar. The lady checking me in said the bar had the best hamburger in the country. I stepped over for a beer and to see if the woman was right and she was.

In the morning I had my continental breakfast in a small room with a lady and her young daughter. There was a piano against the wall, and the child was banging away on it with her mother in some euphoric glee of "modern motherhood" so I took my free breakfast back to my room to review my route to Jedidiah Smith State Park, looking forward to more redwoods.

The route took me through Crescent City, home of the legendary surfer and big wave pioneer Greg Noll, aka "Da Bull," a moniker he acquired because of his size and the way he would charge a wave. In 1957 he surfed a thirty-five-foot wave in Waimea Bay—a sixty-foot face. Noll was the first to surf big breaking Waimea which was thought to be impossible. The photo of him standing at the shore, starring at the surf with his ten-foot surfboard in his black and white prison striped trunks, is iconic in surfing history.

The rain was gone, and the sun was bright on the road meandering through groves of redwoods. Once again, giant redwoods were up against the road, with views deep into the canopied forest. I passed the crystal clear water of Smith River then got off Brother for a stroll into a gathering of redwoods, feeling like I was stepping into a cathedral with a purifying and ethereal silence. The massive trees with their thick burnt umber bark looked unworldly. The bark is considered insulation for the tree, preventing devastation during a fire with the heat from the fire incubating the seeds.

Near Patrick Creek, I discovered an old lodge tucked in thick trees that oozed history and character, so I pulled in for coffee. Inside it was dark and cozy with an atmosphere similar to the canopied forest. A long bar had windows looking outside and next to a porch restaurant under thick tree coverage that kept the room in a dim gloom. The bartender got my black coffee while I looked out at Brother. She asked where I was traveling so I gave her my *Reader's Digest* version as a waitress came up to share in the small talk. I made the off comment that the area would be an excellent place to hide. The waitress responded, "There's a lady that lives down the road that was a member of the Manson Family." I told her I just read *Helter Skelter*, the story of the Manson family then thought about what your life would be like after involvement with such a deranged group of people. The dark and aged atmosphere of the lodge and the disturbing thought caused me to gulp my coffee and excuse myself for the sunlight.

Returning to the coast road, I crossed the border into Oregon on the way to the majestic town of Gold Beach. There was a chill in the air with a stiff wind which made the ocean rippled like murky corduroy.

Cliffs were high with wide, with empty beaches except for great promontories of stone along the shoreline. The Oregon coast is wild, making the California coast seem manicured.

I found a small motel a block off the beach run by an elderly couple who said they were motel-sitting for friends. The two had been together so long they looked like twins, both with a sweet whistle and carefully crafted sentences. I checked in and took out.

In a tavern I sat next to a man that lured me into a conversation that turned into his demonstration on how to scare a bear away; throwing his arms in the air while standing tall and yelling loud. I walked out before he entertained reason for another such display then ate Mexican food before going back to stare at my Oregon map.

To Port Orford through Brandon, along coastal Oregon, it was another incredible ride on Brother. Heading inland I made my way through Coos Bay, then North Bend, and back to the coast road. It was Sunday, May seventeenth, and three weeks before the Alaskan ferry. Closer to the date, the more finite my scheduling had to be. Florence was next, then inland to Eugene, for an anticipated visit with my uncle.

On such a beautiful day I saw a lot of motorcycles. Just before Florence, I stopped for gas. While standing outside warming my face in the sun up drove a group of four Harleys; three guys and one gal, the guys had their "old ladies" on the back. They looked like the real deal, in particular, the single woman—aged, weathered leather over an athletic body with a dirty blond single braid that hung to her belt. I was fascinated with West Coast Harley groups, especially the authentic ones. Not the weekend outlaw types who return on Monday to a job. This bunch was the deal—the sell drugs, steal cars, dabble in prostitution type.

Brother was parked beside the Harley group, and they did not acknowledge me as a fellow biker which I knew would be the case. They were too caught up in their own camaraderie and a cigarette break. As with the group at Gouldings in Utah, there was a particle of me that envied what they shared. But I knew I would not last with my introverted nature that could be unwavering to compromise with my plans.

There was a carnival in Florence causing congestion on the coast road. The pretty town is located at the mouth of the Siuslaw River, with a marina situated along a bulwark. Spotting a motel I got a room, unpack and waited for the traffic to subsides. After an hour I walked down to the marina seeing carnival tearing down. The town looked dated, like the era of the forties with wooden, whitewashed buildings—a Norman Rockwell look.

Walking the sidewalk, looking in storefronts and bars, I reconnoitered the length of main street before making my choice. I stepped into a bar-restaurant with a live band and fell into a shoulder-to-shoulder crowd crossing the dance floor to the bar. The group was playing traditional blues-rock with couples dancing in the late afternoon. I was in no mood for the ruckus, the crowd, or the garage band. I felt contemplative and cerebral, so I pushed through the thicket of people to a back deck that overlooked the slow flow of the river with a setting sun—better suited my mood.

There were two tables, one with a couple and the other with a group of three; one of them a motorcycle guy dressed in full Harley regalia. He wore a long, sheathed knife on his belt like Jax Teller in *Sons of Anarchy*. While leaning against a deck rail, I was fixated, aware that I was staring at the unthreatening man. He was the polar opposite to the bunch I saw earlier in my day making me question if he was aware of what a pretentious poser he was with his narcissistic image. His clothes look new, even his square-toed motorcycle boots without the usual markings from a shift lever. How could someone create such a caricature of themselves, I wondered? His hair was long and perfectly groomed, and he had a studiously trimmed beard, styled somewhere between a goatee and a Fu Manchu.

My fixation annoyed me, so I turned to stare at the mirrored reflections on the flowing river. To my right was a truss bridge across the Siuslaw River with two half crescent structures supporting a rusted span. The sun was setting with colors of orange and gold on a beautiful night that inspired me to think about all I had done and everywhere I had been. Closing in on 9,000 miles since leaving, I continued to appreciate never knowing what would be down the road.

20

STAGE XVII: Miles 8,869 - 9,710

Master Beekeeper - Crater Lake Let Down
Bend Heavy Metal - A Friend of a Friend - VFW
This Old House - The Great Columbia

"I'd like to be here more all the time."

—Bill Murray

ROUTE 126 FROM Florence to Eugene is postcard beautiful. The road rolls, twists, rises and drops through a thick forest of tall Douglas fir and craggy mountains of gray rock. The road follows the Siuslaw River until intersecting Wildcat Creek with the two merging into a fast flow to create rapids impacting boulders in crystal water, while raptors drift overhead. It's pure Oregon—wild, untouched, and exciting. It passes through logging towns that reminded me of Ken Kesey's second novel, Sometimes a Great Notion, written in 1964. An epic American novel. Kesey claimed to be his, magna opus.

The novel is about a logging family mired with a conflict between brothers from different worlds having to work together to hold onto a logging business. Images from the book came to mind while staring at the majestic Douglas fir on the ride.

The wild country caused me to recall the rambling mentality that possessed me in my early twenties; a mentality ignited by Jack Kerouac's On the Road. His main character in several novels was based on close friend Neal Cassidy, i.e., The Angel. Kerouac's writing inspired the Beat Generation and the beatniks of the fifties. Kesey followed to vanguard the hippie movement of the sixties. Both men were pinnacle forces to cause change and create countercultures. Neal Cassidy, friends with both, served as a bridge between the two generations and used as characters by both writers.

Pulling into his uncle's driveway the garage door was open with a clearing for Brother. We shared a big hug with the honesty of being glad to see each other. He's my mother's younger brother from the Texas side, also the uncle to my new found cousin in Farmersville, also possessing wild Texas stories of crazy cowboy madness. He was eight years older than me and had been my hero while growing up, though rarely seeing him. He joined the Navy in his teens, rose to the rank of chief boatswains mate then transferred to the Coast Guard to serve on an icebreaker and made numerous tours to Antarctica. He retired from service in his early fifties then went on to graduate from a local junior college where he learned carpentry and started his own business.

After giving him a tour of my motorcycle, he invited me to join him while he inspected his beehives, an inspection he performed every ten days. It was timely since I intended to see his bees. Beekeeping was a hobby he began since my last visit,—a hobby that was now a serious passion. He taught classes, was featured on radio talk shows, a local celebrity, and the "go-to guy," if you had questions about bees.

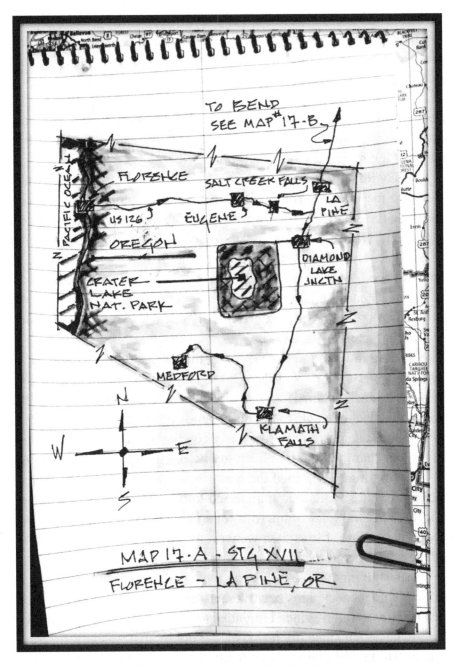

MAP # 17-A - STAGE XVII

Florence, OR - La Pine, OR

He handed me a beekeeper's veil and jacket, then stepped into his beekeeper's jumpsuit with a head veil. At the side of his house were three hives stacked in a row under a slanted cover. He gave me a tin container with a squeeze handle like a caulk gun; a contraption that blew smoke from burning cedar chips to calm bees in flight. Then he instructed me when to send smoke to the hives once he opened the boxes. He pulled out what was called a brood frame which was where the bees made honey. With the box top removed I was amazed at the number of bees, appearing to be a thousand. I was too interested to be afraid as he scraped a build-up of substance from the frame periphery explaining that he was removing mold that may result in bacteria to spoil the honey. The bees swarmed around us as he performed his task thoroughly and with loving care. With each question, I asked I got a well versed and articulate answer. He pointed the queen out, and I saw she was the largest, and my uncle explained the only reason the males were there was to impregnate the queen and then they would die. The inspection took about an hour, and I felt I had just watched a Discovery Channel episode.

I spent five days in Eugene, following my uncle through his day-to-day life. He was curious about my travels, plans, and how I was adjusting to my nomadic wanderings. He, like many men, said he understood but was no fit for his stage of life. Following his full life and having had his own adventures, he was good with his bees, his garden, his music, and woodworking. He had reinvented himself several times and had always been an inspiration.

Brother had a maintenance appointment in Seattle to get off-road tires for Alaska. My uncle was excited hearing I was going, having been stationed there while in the Coast Guard. Putting our heads together we arranged a meetup time, reserved a room, and got Mariners tickets for some fun "Bro Time." Then I took off to travel more of Oregon and Washington until my appointment.

From Eugene, I directed Brother towards Crater Lake National Park, mid-state. Taking Route 58 southwest, I went through Oakridge and then an open road in a dense forest. High peaks were in view; Diamond Peak at 8,744 feet and Mount Thielsen at 9,182 feet. Leaving Eugene the sky was a cloudless blue. Closer to Crater Lake the sky thickened with gray clouds. Before turning to the park entrance, I entered Diamond Lake Junction—a crossroad with a depressing dive motel at one corner. People sat outside on white plastic chairs smoking while children played in a muddy parking lot. Across the street was a greasy spoon, so I pulled in for coffee. Inside a group was clustered in the back that looked to be Oregon's version of West Virginia hillbillies and a comment on obesity in America. A heavy-set, heavy breathing waitress walked up in a frantic huff, to leave frustrated for my meager order of black coffee. I sipped and surveyed the glum surroundings that were pulling me to a morose mood. Before I let it take hold, I gave the waitress three bucks for the over-stewed tar and got out the door.

Near Crater Lake, the sky was a thick pelt of gray, adding to the mood from the crossroads—a maudlin emotion. I engaged in self-consultation to turn things positive. I had learned to monitor my moods and to grab myself by the collar and jerk myself back into shape.

I had heard about the beauty of Crater Lake and was anxious to see it. Crater Lake was the opposite of Morro Rock, which was a volcanic plug. It was formed from the eruption of Mount Mazama, a part of the Cascade Mountain Range—a caldera, formed in the collapse of the volcano. The eruption left a massive basin to naturally fill with rain and melting ice. The lake is 1,943 feet deep, the deepest in the US. And the color is known for being a striking blue.

I got in line at the entrance station, waiting to enter the park. I put Brother in neutral and dug out my senior's pass while watching cars coming up to the ranger and then making a U-turn, which gave me a sinking feeling. At the window, the ranger said: "The lake is clouded over with no visibility." Then added, "I especially would not want to be up there on a motorcycle," his delivery, blunt and professional. Disappointed, I made my U-turn to head back to the nasty crossroads. In the parking lot of the greasy spoon, I grabbed the Oregon map to consider my options. Medford or Klamath Falls—a coin toss.

Back to Oakridge, I saw a sign for Salt Creek Falls; a plunge waterfall, at two hundred and sixty-five feet, the second highest in the state. The falls are fed from Salt Creek, a tributary of the Willamette

River. I took out on the three-mile hike that climbed four hundred feet up for viewing, with hopes to clear the blues from the ugly crossroads, the gray skies, and the Crater Lake disappointment.

The trail meandered through a forest in the moist, cool air, a characteristic of the Northwest. Cedars, firs, and gray boulders accented with moss decorated the forest floor covered with conifer needles and decaying limbs. You could hear the waterfall throughout the hike—a pounding, dynamic splash. Once there, I stared at the hypnotic flow mesmerized in a relaxed trance. I stopped for a moment to clear my mind, to just be, taking a break from making plans. I reminded myself of there being no demands, other than food when hungry, a place to sleep, and a ferry date in Bellingham. The flow of the waterfall became an allegory to my treatment of timed my expectations. I saw a need to adjust.

I was heading to Medford and in search for a room. Motel after motel displayed "NO VACANCY" signs. Asking why "It's Memorial Day," a desk clerk said. Like Easter, I had no idea. It was hot, and the thought of camping was not appealing. I continued my search, eventually renting a room under construction at a discounted rate, happy to have a place to spread a map, while feeling Crater Lake deserved another shot.

The next morning I began a route for Klamath Falls, to the west of Upper Klamath Lake. I passed signs for Crater Lake with the sky still overcast, so I drove through Diamond Lake Junction, hopefully for the last time.

In Bend, I found a "mom and pop" motel, unpacked and took out on foot to explore downtown. I passed a microbrewery, a few nice restaurants, and then one that called to me with a European look. I sat at a horseshoe-shaped bar, ordered wine and an appetizer. Two couples sat nearby making me aware of how oblivious I had become to always be alone and rarely craved social interaction. I was comfortable in my own skin, regardless of the situation.

Roaming the streets, I found nothing to pique my interest, so I headed for the motel. Originally a pioneer town Bend is where the Cascade Mountains turn to high desert. Oregon has a great deal of desert landscape, mostly high desert located on the eastern edge of the Cascade Mountain Range and the Deschutes River. The name Bend comes from "Farewell Bend," referring to a fordable bend in the river. Established as a logging town and now modernized, its economy relies on the constant flow of sports and outdoor addicts from rock climbing to golf.

A mile from my motel I heard heavy metal music throbbing from a small brick building that looked to have been a barbershop. A glass door was covered with posters of heavy metal musicians in contorted positions, bent screaming with faces in the lens, mouths wide opened, obnoxious, repulsive, irreverent. A chalkboard advertised the band playing; something like BLACK EARTH MOAN or DESPERATE FETUS. Out of curiosity, I walked in, knowing I would probably be perceived as an undercover narcotics agent. The band was in the corner near mismatched tables and chairs with eight or so people holding PBRs, rocking their heads to the reckless pound of a bass guitar and the unpolished thrash of an electric guitar. Two guys raised fists in the air and bellowed a low, YEAAAAHHH. At the bar, people sat with heads rocking fore and aft repetitively to the ugly sound.

Finding an open space at the bar, I ordered a draft from a young female bartender dressed in black leather, distressed stockings, and rag wrappings. Initially, she's cold. Next, to me, a guy covered in tats in a plain white T appeared as if he was going to explode. He gave me the "What are you doing here?" look. I nodded, which I knew was abrasive to his counterculture mentality to exude hate. I noticed the bar girl having an issue with him, having cut him off. I thought it odd, in a place where everyone was hammered drunk. He argued, and she became adamant—she was no pushover. Then she engaged me in conversation, and I discovered the young lady very much had her life together, contradictory to looking like a heavy metal mistress. She was in the Army Reserves while working her way through college. And she was not the first person who surprised me with their life structured, contradictory to their appearance. My perceptions could be wrong. Why shouldn't a goth, heavy metal mistress be successful?

Studying my Oregon map over breakfast, I saw an area called the John Day Fossil Beds National Monument. There are three locations spread about twenty miles apart in a triangle. I made it my plan for the day.

It was arid desert; dry, brown, harsh, yet scenic and inviting. The sun was bright, temperatures were mild, and it felt good to be on Brother. I was on my way to the furthest fossil bed; the Sheep Rock Unit, west of the town of John Day.

John Day was an American trapper that received some notoriety in Oregon. He moved west in 1797, from Culpeper, Virginia, signing up as a hunter for the Pacific Fur Company's Overland Expedition, also known as the Astor Expedition. He was the first person of European descent to set foot on the river, now his namesake. It's located at the confluence of the Columbia River, near the town of Biggs Junction. The Astor Expedition was financed by John Jacob Astor of New York City, at the time the wealthiest man in America. He made his money in the fur trade which decimated the beaver population, all for fashionable hats sold to elite city dwellers.

The route of fur traders like John Day eventually became the Oregon Trail. Naming the river after John Day followed an incident where he was caught by Indians and stripped naked. Then, the town of John Day was named after the river along with the three fossil beds.

Heading to the Sheep Rock Unit, I passed a lone bicyclist wearing neon yellow, climbing a steep hill along with me. I admired the cross-country cyclist I passed. We exchanged a wave as I noticed he was not a youngster.

Nearing the first fossil bed, the landscape changed to rich green grasses growing in patches on dry brown hills. I read that there were over eighty different soil types to make up the fossil beds. Interpretive signs explained the history of the sediment of the land dating back to the Eocene and the Miocene periods, forty-five million years ago. I found it hard to comprehend someone so confident to date anything that long ago.

I pulled into the dead town of Mitchell, stopping at a general store appearing to be the only surviving business in the old town. Off

Brother, I heard "Triumph huh?" I turned to see the man in the bright cycling outfit that I passed earlier. He was friendly, curious, and I

learned he was sixty-five years old, which impressed me, knowing he was bicycling those hills at that age. He explained how he flew his bike to Astoria, Oregon, and was riding back home to New London, Connecticut. "Wow," I said while congratulating him then I told him what I was doing with my motorized two-wheeler. We laughed about me giving up cycling for motorcycling. I told him I had a friend in Groton Long Point, near New London and mentioned his name. His face lit up as he proclaimed "I married his ex-girlfriend." We both shook our heads in shock.

To cool off, I removed the Gore-Tex from my jacket and opened the vents. The next fossil bed was the Painted Hills Unit, and I got there fast, rode the trails, and stopped at a picnic table to enjoy the surroundings; a blend of dry desert and thick greenery. Hillsides were variegated with colored layered soil types with a few tall conifers that looked out of place. The landscape was unique, oddly inviting and confirmed to me how subtle places could be as magnificent as those touted as being grand.

At the last fossil bed, the Clarno Unit, I was fossiled out. I rode through the area quickly, finding it similar to the others and ready for a room and a meal, so I head for the town of Condon, thirty miles away.

Condon was arranged around grain silos with a lifeless main street. I got gas and inquired about motels and restaurants learning the only restaurant was closed, and there was one motel on the edge of town. Condon was withered in decay and no more than a shell of what remained from a more prosperous past. It was a farming town, named after the lawyer Harvey C. Condon, the nephew to Thomas Condon, responsible for preserving the three fossil beds was also an Irish Congregational minister and a famed geologist and paleontologist. He was the first professor of geology at the University of Oregon. It was fascinating how history weaves and intertwines with people and places. Like meeting a friend of a friend earlier in my day.

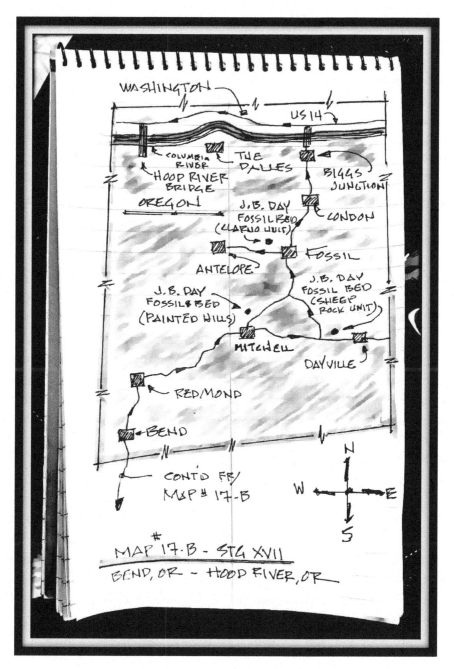

MAP # 17-B - STAGE XVII
Bend, OR - Hood River, OR

Past the silos and down a gravel road, I found the motel, literally on the edge of town at rolling green plains. Into the office a lady behind the desk spoke to me like we were old friends, handing me the registration clipboard before I asked for a room. Inquiring about food, she said the only place would be the VFW (Veterans of Foreign Wars), a big white building on Main Street. Then she told me to make sure to have breakfast at the diner, "The cook is from Seattle," she said. I unload Brother and put off my shower to find the VFW before it closed.

I retired from a career working closely with the military. Much of that time my association was direct, working on-site where the military operated. Through my profession, I had become aware of how the American veteran was devalued despite the enormous sacrifice they made with their lives. So many civilians I knew were oblivious to their sacrifice and gave little gratitude for their service. They did not connect the freedom they woke to each morning to the sacrifice of those serving in the armed forces. Soldiers continued to die on foreign soil with most of America taking the human loss for granted.

The Veterans of Foreign Wars is an American veterans organization, established in 1899 and consists of veterans of all armed forces who served in foreign wars. The intent of the organization was to speed rehabilitation of the nation's disabled with the camaraderie of fellow brothers in service. To be a member, it is required that you be active military or honorably discharged. For a small fee, a civilian may eat and drink at any VFW location.

I saw a Harley parked next to the white building—an American flag attached to the sissy bar. Inside, three guys were at the end of the bar, one obviously the Harley rider, with a long white beard, leather vest, and unapproachable. Two men near were ranchers. I could tell by their loud conversation about hay, feed, and deliveries. Mid-bar sat an elderly couple, the woman had hair a pale yellow from years of bleach. It was teased to the consistency of cotton candy. The man was crumpled, lifeless, and near the end. Everyone except the two ranchers was smoking.

From the kitchen bounced out a girl in her twenties; thin and vivacious. She asked if I was a member. I said no, so she grabbed a register and told me it would be $1.98 and asked that I write my name and where I was from. Now a member, I could order a beer and any item from their xeroxed menu. I made the bold choice of bratwurst with wasabi sauce. Looking around I thought about how I would not be experiencing this side of America without traveling in my nomadic manner to wander and accept where I landed—the VFW just another obscure fiber in the fabric of America.

I was up scrambling to get to the diner before they stopped serving breakfast. Walking in I saw the cook and the waitress were the only two in the place and talking through a window between the counter and the kitchen. The interior was chic and a contrast to the farm town of Condon. She spotted me and advanced while talking about something the cook said as if I was acquainted with the two while handing me a menu and suggesting the special: a western sandwich with avocado. So that's what I ordered then pulled out my map. She came back and sat across from me at my booth asking questions, interrupting as I tried to answer. I let her talk and was quickly exhausted with her flow of unrelated nonsense, wondering if she was on amphetamines with the spill of energy that was disrupting my morning calm, my gathering of self, the start of my day. The bell rang for my breakfast sandwich, and she returned with more questions that she never let me answer. I left thinking how lonely it must be in Condon.

Out of Condon on US 19, I turned north for Biggs Junction, sixty miles away. It was there I could cross the Columbia River for my ride west to the Pacific. The landscape took an immediate change as I drove away from Condon and the weather was perfect. From a hill, a curve descended to an expanse of open, rich green plains, that looked more like Nebraska than Oregon. There was a soft and gentle roll that connected layers of shadowed greens at the cleavage of joining hills. People are drawn to the plains— infinite and majestic as the ocean. I had acquired a taste.

Halfway between Condon and Biggs Junction I saw an abandoned house and thought the location peculiar, which drew me in. I parked Brother and stepped over a broken fence into the property. Since Condon, there had been no structures or evidence of life, present

147

or past. Now there was what looked to be a one-story English cottage standing alone in the expanse of the open plain. The architecture style and carpentry were impressive with an attractive stoop under a portico. Moldings were rounded, giving a soft look. Formerly painted, it now held onto chipped flakes, faded by time, weathered, and speckled with debris from high winds. Windows were broken, allowing views to the interior with floors mostly open to the ground and littered with scribbled graffiti and gunshot. I could only imagine that someone, many years ago, enamored with the tranquillity of the open plains, built the home midway between the two towns to enjoy majestic views of open rolling land. A place of seclusion under a massive night sky filled with stars. Now it was no more than bones in decay, someone's abandoned and obscure dream.

Biggs Junction is a crossroads near the bridge over the Columbia from Oregon to Washington with a small gathering of stores, restaurants and gas stations. The view looking downhill was of the steel arched suspension span over the deep cavity; the Sam Hill Memorial Bridge, also known as the Biggs Rapid Bridge. What a sight it must have been coming up the Oregon Trail and seeing the Columbia River after a lengthy and dangerous trek by wagon train. A view that must have been both spectacular and menacing. Crossing the bridge, I turned west on Route 14, now in Washington. Small signs displayed silhouettes of Lewis and Clark, the trail a part of their expedition.

Riding the north side of the Columbia offered views unlike anything else you will see in America rivaling the Grand Canyon. Cliff walls are high, like the Cliffs of Moher in County Claire, Ireland. The enormous chasm was formed by the broad flow of the river; a multilayered series of severe changes in the climate of the world that included volcanic eruptions and periodic floods that took place twenty to sixty million years ago with the earth in a state of continuous flux. Excessive flooding occurred in what geologist considered in recent years: 13,000 to 19,000 years ago, a time frame I found comprehensible. It was during a massive meltdown in the Ice Age, discharging more combined flow than all the existing rivers in the world over thousands of years. The Columbia River was formed by the melting of the Missoula Lake, located west of the Great Lakes. The Lake was huge and dammed by a massive ice bridge. Constant melting of the lake and the ice bridge at a high elevation carved the Columbia River Gorge while flowing into the Pacific.

Across the deep gorge, I saw the city named The Dalles. Before 1957, you could have looked across the Columbia to see the massive Celilo waterfall, outpouring at the breadth of the Long Narrows River. Along the waterfalls, edge existed the oldest continuous inhabited settlement in North America, dating back 11,000 years. The Native American village of Celilo was an accumulation of tribes; the Yakama, the Nez Perce and the Confederated Tribes of the Umatilla Indians, comprised of Cayuse, Umatilla and Wala Wala. In 1952, the Army Corp of Engineers began construction to wall the Celilo waterfall to satisfy an initiative by the Federal Government to harness the fast flowing waters for hydroelectric power. The project took five years to build and was filled with protest for what would occur when the dam closed off the Celilo waterfall to flood the Celilo village. Protests were to no avail, their land was flooded, and they were forced out. The village was where large gill net stands draped the river to catch salmon, sturgeon, and steelhead with a trading post to smoke and dry fish. With the completion of the dam, the floodgates stopped, and all that had been stopped.

I continued to the Gorge National Scenic Area with a distant view of Mount Hood on the horizon. Cliff walls heightened as the river widened dramatically. The Columbia Gorge is a geological wonder with depths of four thousand feet. The length is eighty miles from the Cascades to where the mouth of the river empties into the Pacific. Annual precipitation ranges from ten inches a year at the eastern end to one hundred inches to the west—a unique ecological change, a diverse and dynamic transition from dry grasslands to a temperate rain forest. The atmospheric pressure differential between each end of the canyon creates a wind tunnel effect through the deep gorge to generate winds up to thirty-five miles an hour, making it a mecca for windsurfers.

I spent hours riding Route 14, along the massive river and dramatic cliff walls having been through many changes since my breakfast sandwich in Condon. Maybe I was a little cold to the chatty waitress. Or perhaps viewing the gorge was just making me sensitive, and introspective. Heading back to the Hood River bridge I hoped to find a better menu than my previous night at the VFW.

21

STAGE XVIII: Miles 9,710-10,275

Hood River - The Shining – Astoria
Mystical Sequim - Port Townsend Unitarian

"Don't compromise yourself, You are all you've got."

—*Janis Joplin*

I CROSSED THE Hood River Bridge over the Columbia and into Oregon. Glancing in each direction, I could see the environmental differences with clear skies to the east and windswept clouds to the west. I took the ramp on I-84 for Hood River. I hate interstates, even for a short distance. They're a jolt back to modern life after farmland and wilderness. On the interstate, you get chain restaurants, outlets, motels, fast food, all the same, all over America.

Along the Columbia River, I found a cozy family-owned motel and got a room in the back with a spectacular view of the river. Pulling the drapes open I saw a park-like setting and the river wind rippled and peppered with speeding windsurfers.

Hood River is about the size of Morro Bay, small and manageable. I found an English pub with an outside patio and sat next to a party of men. Parked in the next lot were restored sports cars; Triumph, Austin Healey, Spitfire, and an MG. It was a car club that met for a pint or two after a weekly ride through the beautiful countryside. The pub was a real English establishment, the furnishings possibly shipped to the states and reassembled. A husky bartender stepped up in a jovial manner, and we exchanged a few words while she drew me a Guinness. I went back to the deck for more of the crisp late afternoon. Finishing my Guinness, I decided to have another, not so much for the beer but for more time with the clear skies and the mountain views.

The following morning I force myself out of the comfortable motel. Leaving, I found a breakfast spot that exuded the laid back flare of the town. Maybe it was the Northwest that resonated with me or perhaps it was Hood River. I left confident it was a place I would return to.

I found a road south to the Timberline Lodge, fifty miles from Portland. From Hood River, I enjoyed stunning views of Mount Hood; crisp, clean, massive, and snow-covered before a blue sky. The road was curvy, rising and dropping through hills for views of the ominous mountain on my way to Mount Hood Scenic Highway. Climbing higher, blue skies became overcast.

At 11,249 feet, Mount Hood is Oregon's highest peak and said to be the loftiest mountain in the US. Lofty, due to its overwhelming prominence. It stretches out in breadth three times its height and hosts twelve different snowfields and glaciers.

I saw the sign for the Timberline Lodge and turned in past its elaborate stone-structured entrance. The lodge was significant to me because it was used as the lodge in the movie *The Shining*, with Jack Nicholson and Shelly Duval, and directed by Stanley Kubrick. It came out in 1980 and made quite an impression on me, having been a Nicholson fan since seeing *Five Easy Pieces*.

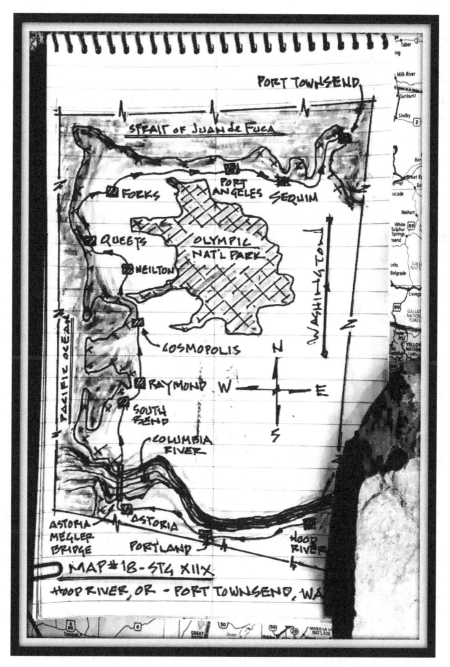

MAP # 18 - STAGE XIIX
Hood River, OR - Port Townsend, WA

It was an impressive structure, nestled up to the snow banks at the timberline of Mount Hood. Standing close I looked up to the peak that was pillowed in clouds. Before entering the lodge, I stepped over to view upper-level rooms at the exterior. I saw a window that I was sure was where Shelly Duval was trapped with her son as Nicholson bashed through the door with an ax, sticking his face through a broken panel with a crazed look, yelling "Heeerrreeeesss Johhhhnnnyyy." No doubt, a Nicholson ad lib.

In the movie, the only real shots used of the Timberline Lodge were the aerial views. I remember seeing those shots as the troubled family drove to the lodge and my thoughts were of how I had to see that country, certain it was in the Alps or the Canadian Rockies. I recall having to tame my wanderlust as I struggled with my travel gene. I had recently started a job that would become my career after years of vagabonding in my twenties. It was time to "pay the piper," settle down, get serious, be responsible, and plan for my future. So I ignored the urge to bag it all and take off—an urge that would nag me throughout my career.

Walking into the big entrance, I expected the grand open room that was in the movie, with big fireplaces, Native American wall hangings, and huge windows that looked out to a snowy wilderness. I expected to see the big desk where Nicholson sat with his typewriter during a slow progression to insanity. Instead, it was a cramped lobby with displays detailing the history of the lodge.

Leaving the lodge, I made a choice to ride right through the belly of Portland, atypical to my norm of creating some circuitous stage of interconnecting roads to avoid the entanglement of a city. On the outskirts, I reached the town of Sandy pulling into a filling station for a cold drink, something to curb afternoon hunger pangs and directions to the coast through downtown.

Stop and go, stop and go, city center Portland, knock off traffic, texting, talking, mindless drivers, passing streams of slimy bars, convenience stores, and all the monotonous stuff to service a mass of humanity. Following the tension of the city center, I searched for the interstate. City streets or interstate, I knew I would be in the throes of commuters—angry, disgruntled, and impatient. At the Willamette River, I picked up I-84 west for the coast. After ten minutes, at eighty miles an hour, traffic peeled away to off-ramps, leaving me an empty road. In the act of spontaneity, I twisted the throttle to hit a hundred on my speedometer—an expression of relief, of freedom. The landscape was open and vibrant green with orchards, wineries, and farmland; picturesque and relaxing. I caught a second wind.

I was excited about going to the coast. I saw a country store with a gas pump and parked Brother to stand and stretch after sitting through the long ride through the city. My lower back and legs were stiffs, so I walked a circle to stretch. Looking up the road, I saw a tunnel of trees that looked mysterious and inviting.

I drank a half liter of water-thirsty from the hot day. I asked a teenage boy how far to the coast. "A few hours," he said. I was ready to lay down. Outside, I turned the corner to see three guys standing around Brother next to their parked dirt bikes covered in mud. One of the three spoke for the others, asking about my bike—there's always a spokesman in a group. They were reading the stickers plastered on my panniers while the spokesman told me about their off-road day. They all looked like lumberjacks with matching jeans, jean jackets, high lace logging boots. They headed back to the pumps, and I mounted Brother for that inviting tunnel of trees.

I was heading to the town of Astoria with a chill coming from the coast and overcast, with a fog bank. The terrain had changed from forest of fir and maple to coastal oaks and beach grass. I was back on 101, the coastal road paralleling the shoreline. I stopped off to snap in my Gore-Tex lining and swap mesh gloves for a heavier pair.

I rode north through Cannon Beach, a vacation spot with rental cottages, seafood restaurants, and all the trappings for tourists. I was worried about the dense fog, hoping I could be seen. I passed through Seaside then Warrenton at the confluence of the Columbia River and the Pacific Ocean. The fog was settling along the ocean and the river, creating a surreal atmosphere. The ride inland along the southern edge of the Columbia had overwhelming vistas with land sloping from high cliffs at the northern side of the gorge. It was where the great floods of the melting Missoula Lake drained to find the ocean—repetitive surges for thousands of years. And now we fret evolutionary change during our brief period on earth. My rambling thought pointed to my fatalistic view of the future of the planet and my low expectations to see positive change. I even questioned the longevity of our species, wondering if our fate would mimic the dinosaurs with some event to cause total annihilation and extinction.

Entering Astoria, I saw a long green bridge spanning across the Columbia, an imposing structure, high and eerie. Downtown felt as if it was frozen in the fifties. I found a room near the bridge and the wharf area. Astoria had a pace I favored, so I chose to spend two days relaxing. The climate was cool and overcast, with an occasional cloud break to offer a bright blue patch of sky. The town was at the end of the Columbia River that originates in British Columbia and terminates its 1,200-mile length at the Pacific. Standing at the wharf, you could look across the river to the state of Washington, past anchored tankers and container ships. Pilot boats stayed busy to manage the arrangement, ingress, and departure of vessels.

Lewis and Clark made the location their final stopping place. The expedition, officially named the Corps of Discovery, left Saint Louis in current Missouri, in May of 1804, and did not return until September of 1806; a two-year, five-month perilous journey commissioned by Thomas Jefferson. It followed the Louisiana Purchase and had multiple objectives: to explore the west, find a route across the continent, and to establish a presence in western territories before European countries established a foothold. They also studied plants, animals, established trade relationships with Indians and explored the Missouri, Colorado, and the Columbia rivers. On their return, Jefferson and Clark unrolled maps from the expedition on the floor of the presidential office and, on their hands and knees, Clark explained the route. Lewis was commissioned to deliver a document detailing the particulars of the exploration, but fell sick with deep depression, never fulfilling his obligation to Jefferson before his mysterious death.

The expedition reached the end of the Columbia where they built Fort Clatsop, located at modern-day Astoria. They intended to board a boat and head east, but no watercraft ever came, forcing them to hunker down to survive the cold, wet winter. It was a struggle with illness, hunger, and living off of dried whitefish exhausted from their arduous expedition.

The city got its name from John Jacob Astor, a New Yorker and owner of the Pacific Trade Company. The company had a short life, beginning in 1809, to establish their home base at Fort Astor in 1811. The war of 1812 forced the company to dismantle due to conflicts with the British, the Spanish, and the Indians—territorial rights for the border between the United States and Canada. Astor was so enamored with the life of trappers that he called on his friend, Washington Irving, to write about the period directing him to mythologize the men. Irving wrote the book, *Astoria* and in the book refers to the men in the fur trade as "Sinbads of the wilderness."

Fort Astor, established in 1811, was the first permanent US settlement on the Pacific. Because of deepwater ports and the fishing industry it attracted immigrants from Finland who came to fish and Chinese came to work at the canning companies.

The Astoria - Megler Bridge crosses the Columbia River near the mouth with distant views to the Pacific. The bridge enters Astoria at what used to be Uniontown, once populated with Finnish immigrants. It enters the state of Washington at Port Elice, near the town of Megler. I found the bridge addictive and spent time in Astoria beneath the high span, staring up at the complex and orderly matrix of steel beams. It is the longest continuous truss bridge in America, stretching almost four and a half miles; a cantilever truss bridge, anchored at each end. The vertical supports are massive cement pillars, supporting the span at two places in the river, similar to the Golden Gate Bridge. Construction began in 1962 and was completed in 1966 and is an eye-catching marvel.

On my first night in Astoria I had dinner along the wharf then walked the downtown streets staring into glass-front novelty shops. On a side street, I heard a cacophony of loud talking, rock music, and motorcycle engines seeing a club where people gathered—finding the underbelly of Astoria. It was a bar with a stage and chairs and tables strewn in disorder. I got a draft and sat to observe the unusual dress, the posters, curious artifacts decorating the walls, then examined the interaction of the subculture, fascinated by those who dressed to express anarchy that I knew was mostly fashion. Behind all the bravado, there was insecurity. I found it ironic that those who shelter and insulate themselves in groups were the ones that voice so much about independence, seeming to swap one social order for another. Or maybe it's all about the camaraderie; a brothers, sisters thing. With so many rebelling, rebellion now had little impact—a convention worn thin.

The next morning I had some trepidation about crossing the impressive bridge. I knew there would be no problem, but I wondered how much was grated if any. Once I headed up and over it, it all went too fast, with no grating, sorry it ended so quickly. Views from a thousand feet to the mouth of the Columbia at the Pacific were terrific.

Into Washington, I was heading to Olympic National Park and leaving the cool, cloudy Astoria weather for some inland heat. I stayed on Route 101 until South Bend then turned towards the logging town of Raymond and then through Cosmopolis at the mouth of Gray's Harbor. Passing an odd looking coffee and tea shop, I stopped to check it out. Inside I was greeted by a warm and jovial woman looking like a Canterbury Tales character; robust, rosy cheeks, and all. I asked what she had brewed, and she described her dark roast. I grabbed a seat and pulled out my journal to document my morning route. Sitting my coffee down she asked where I was heading. Her smile and her eyes told me she was intelligent, open, and a giver. I opened up to her positive nature explaining my time on the road and my plans for Alaska. She listened intently as a man walked in that she introduced as her husband, then got him up to speed on our conversation. He told me about buying the city municipal building, turning it into their home and business and explained how they left high paying jobs in Seattle, sick of the rat race.

I found their choice admirable and a brave move to risk change to better their lives. Now, he said with pride, they were raising their kids in a small town without the bad influences of the city with the whole family breathing better. I connected with the two like kindred spirits, knowing that we made choices to reinvent ourselves, hoping to get closer to that very slippery concept of happiness.

Walking out the door they mentioned a rain forest in the park. I asked about motel options, and they directed me to the town of Forks, a hundred miles up, saying it was the filming location for the TV series *Twilight*. I had never heard of it continued on 101, through the town of Humptulips and Neilson at the southwest corner of the Olympic National Park when the road turned west, hugging the coast for twenty miles, then inland to Forks. I saw the sign for the rainforest but thought it too late to investigate, so I rode on to find a room.

The town of Forks originated as a logging town, but since the filming of, *Twilight* it had become dependent on tourism. I found a bar and grill looking to be the place to be on a Friday night in Forks. It was packed and alive with jukebox music and the jubilation of ending a work week. Walking to the bar, someone turned the music off so they could begin Karaoke. I ordered food and settled in to observe a gargantuan former football player get up to entertain. Having no appetite for karaoke, no matter how good it was, I went back to read in bed.

I continued north until the road hooked east to Port Angeles, on the Strait of Juan de Fuca. I was going to the town of Sequim (pronounced SKWIM), to visit a friend of my sister. She was an author, a painter, and a progressive thinker. At her home, she showed me how she was creating her own translation of the sacred Hindu scripture, the *Bhagavad Gita*, or *Gita* as it is called in Sanskrit. She spent some of her adult life in India and was knowledgeable in Eastern religions and philosophy. Her insights were fascinating as she conveyed ideas without being didactic. She had worked to remove as much of her ego as possible; an effort at the core of Eastern thought.

She called my sister before me arriving to get my birth date and place and time of birth. In a matter of fact manner, she said she had prepared my astrological reading. It would not be my first, but her reading was the best and highlighted characteristics of my makeup that rang true. Many snub their nose at astrology, thinking it as ancient black magic performed by charlatans—a Pagan ritual. I had no trust for daily astrology readings found online or in newspapers. What drew me to astrology was the people I have known that so closely matched the makeup of their particular sun sign.

I left Sequim the following morning after coffee and conversation. Her astrological reading surmised that I was living exactly as I should be living—a life suited for who I was at this stage of my life. I knew it was more than motorcycle travel she referred to. It was my transition and how I was choosing to fill the void of my home and career.

I had devised a schedule to get to Seattle wanting to avoid the entangled network of heavy traffic. From Sequim I rode to Port Townsend and found a room, wanting to catch the ferry to Whidbey Island the following day. Port Townsend was said to be a delightful town on the water with a wooden boat-building school and the main street with bars and restaurants.

It was Sunday so much of the town was closed. I saw a dark wooden staircase and walked up to a restaurant with an outside deck overlooking the water. Nearing dusk, the air was calm, and the bay was smooth with translucent clouds nearing a colorful sunset. I was among a few who leisurely sat, making it contemplatively quiet. I ordered a beer and clam chowder. It was perfect; the view, the air, the chowder, and the relaxing beer. While I was mopping the bowl with sourdough bread, the waitress asked if I wanted dessert. Taking my last sip, I raised the mug up to indicate I wanted another.

A middle-aged lady came and sat at a table in the path of my view to the sunset and apologized, which opened a conversation. I asked if she was from the area commenting on the impressive small town. She said she lived in town, but was moving to Colorado. I asked about her occupation, and she said she was the minister of the Unitarian Church, having been a biologist for the Bureau of Land Management before she answered her calling. I told her that the Unitarian Church was the only church I had darkened the door since attending the Baptist church in my youth. I explained how I was fond of the Unitarian concept the way it embodied the essence of other religious beliefs. It was serendipitous to meet the woman after leaving so many discussions in Sequim about religion and spirituality. Was it coincidence, synchronicity, or the universe taking control? I've heard there is no such thing as a coincidence.

We talked, and I was impressed with her energy as she turned the conversation more in my direction, asking what I was doing with my life. I explained my retirement, my divestment, and my travel, and she spoke about her transitional phase of leaving her field of science to go into the ministry. Her presence seemed to exist on a plane of calm that I found infectious. And like my new friend in Sequim she displayed little ego and evoked a radiant presence, a testimony to her faith. I was most impressed that she asked nothing about my beliefs and did not serve witness to hers. It was admirable and a contrast to my encounter with the surfer I met in Santa Cruz. Where he spoke of his faith to suggest there was only "ONE WAY" in a tone to offer an ultimatum, the lady I spoke with radiated a nature to serve witness to her own spirituality, making me feel positive and aligned and when I left I felt confident it was not an accident that I met her.

Years ago I was in a car with a new friend driving to the Outer Banks chasing some sizable surf. We met through work and once discovering we both were surfers, we made plans to head south the next time there was a swell. The ride was an interview of getting to know each other; upbringing, college, hobbies, marriage, work history. At one point, he looked over at me and asked: "Who's your team?" In my ignorance, I answered, "Team?" "Yea, your team?" he questioned again. I gave him a puzzled look and once more, he said "Your Football Team?" "Oh," I said, "I don't have a team." Like the surfer in Santa Cruz, he shook his head.

22

STAGE XIX: Miles 10,275 - 11,343

Triumph Seattle - More Uncle Time
The Yanks - Shakedown Ride - Lake Diablo Bellingham

"A man is a product of his thoughts.
What he thinks, he becomes."

—*Gandhi*

IN PORT TOWNSEND, I waited for the Whidbey Island ferry. Research from the night before set my plans to tour the island, then catch another ferry to the mainland above Seattle and find the main artery to my motel—The Marco Polo.

Looking at my mileage logbook, I saw that between Forks and Sequim, I passed my 10,000-mile mark since leaving. Ten thousand miles and still in the Lower Forty-Eight with no regrets and a mentality that continued to look forward. My friend in Sequim was correct when she told me I was doing what I was supposed to be doing—to make a plan and point Brother.

Boarding the ferry, I was in the company of other bikers. One a Harley guy, another on a Harley knock-off and the third, a Honda Pacific. I found the Pacific curious, with the motor enclosed by sheet metal. Jay Leno, talk show host, and motorcycle collector said: "You're supposed to see through a motorcycle." I think he was referring to the Pacific.

Harley guy looked to be a thirty-year-old lumberjack and very curious about my loaded bike. Almost three months of stickers on my panniers invited questions, so I gave him a capsulized story about my retirement, my divestment, and taking to the road. He said it was what he wanted too, but it was a long way off—one of many I encountered with a wanderlust soul but their life in the way. Newly married, a job, there was no taking to the road for him. Marriage, children, job; the natural progression of human existence was not compatible with a no-madic life on a motorcycle.

Harley lumberjack was helpful, giving me directions for cruising the island out to Point Deception. Through misting rain, I rode open farmland that looked like Ireland; lovely, quaint, rich green fields, with translucent fog. I passed through the town of Oak Harbor, on my way to the other end of the island. Seeing Point Deception was worth the ferry ride over with the fast-flowing brilliant green water through the pass from Puget Sound to the Strait of Juan de Fuca. There were two bridges, one across Point Deception, the other over Canoe Pass, both built-in 1935. Each, a steel cantilever bridge with an arched truss and painted the same green as the Astoria - Megler bridge.

Whidbey Island is known as "The Rock." The island, originally inhabited by Native American tribes and first visited by the Spanish in 1790. Two years later the English expedition directed by the Royal Navy officer and explorer, David Vancouver made the landing. Two officers serving under Vancouver, Joseph Whidbey and Peter Puget, were the first Europeans to explore the island, the island taking the name of Whidbey and the Sound, the name of Puget.

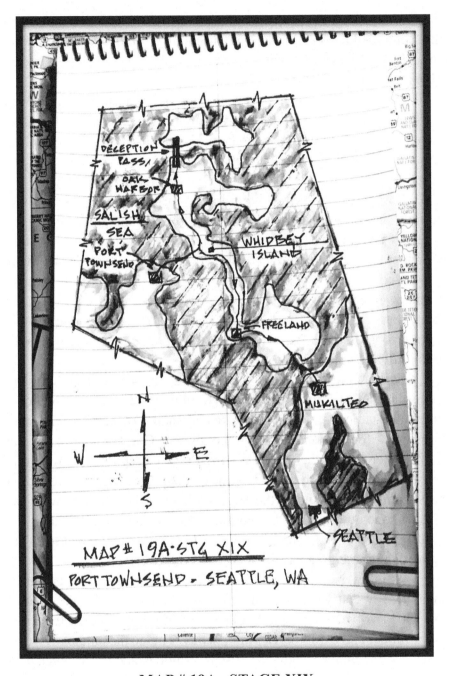

MAP # 19A - STAGE XIX
Port Townsend, WA - Seattle, WA

I barely caught the ferry as I rolled over the ramp into the well deck for the short ride to the mainland or, as the islanders called it, "America." I rolled off in the town of Mukilteo having reserved a four-night stay at the Marco Polo Motel in Seattle. My uncle was arriving the next day. In Eugene, when I told him I had reserved a room, he said: "Dude, there's a Seattle motel where I always stay." He retrieved a postcard, not remembering the name, the card, a picture of the Marco Polo. I told him that was where we were staying—we high-fived.

The motel and the Triumph dealership were both on Aurora Avenue, about three miles apart. I checked in, unloaded and walked to the area of Freemont. From a walking bridge then downhill I arrived at the quaint hipster area with a bohemian atmosphere of trendy restaurants and bars. In an Irish pub at an old oak bar, I ordered a Guinness. I pulled out my Washington state map to study roads east of Seattle. Once Brother was out of the shop, I had a week before boarding the ferry for Bellingham. I had been researching routes to Idaho seeing that from Seattle I could head to Lake Chelan, the Grand Coulee Dam, then the Cascade Mountain Range. Hovering over my map, as usual, up walked someone curious, inquisitive, and ready to help. An open map at a bar is a magnet for those who want to give directions and talk about their favorite place you should visit. "Where ya head'n?" he asked—just a normal dude with a beer in his hand. "Heading east, then back during the next week," I told him. I explained what I had done to get to the place where I can live so free on a motorcycle. "WOW," he said, then slid a pointed finger over the map to get his bearings while saying "Man, you've got to go here, Lake Diablo." I was happy to see it was in the Cascade Mountain Range. He said "It's the greenest water you'll ever see. Don't know what makes it so green, but it's amazing." I circled the spot.

I slept late, waiting for my uncle to roll in then laid in bed mindlessly relaxing. With so much time on the road, when I got a chance to stop I relaxed into the downtime if only to stare at the ceiling. It was entertainment to be calm—motionless. My uncle arrived, so I had him follow me to the Triumph dealership to drop off Brother.

The Seattle Triumph dealership was big, clean, and the personnel, smart, and helpful; motorcycle shops are not all the same. I gave the go-ahead to look over the bike for potential problems and hoped they would not take advantage of the open door. They understood how I was traveling and my plans for rough Alaska roads. The staff was all impressed and envious of my plans to ride the Dalton Highway past the Arctic Circle. At the time it was my trepidatious intent. Before getting there, I would wrestle with the idea again and again.

We get to Safeco Field pregame for the Yankees-Mariners game. Our seats were up above the first base line. As we sat down, they rolled back the roof for a view of the Seattle skyline.

Out came the Yankees, to a cacophony of boos. There's a lot of hatred in Seattle for Alex Rodriquez, aka A-Rod, who left the Mariners to eventually end up with New York. Ironically, he was the guy I wanted to see. And seeing the Yankees would satisfy a long time dream. As a kid, I owned a collection of Yankee baseball cards during the time of Maris, Mantle, Joe Pepitone, Yogi Berra, and Whitey Ford—the whole team. I was amazed by how the players' names were still imprinted in my brain.

The game started as I overheard Seattle fans degrade their team with remarks about their losing streak. They knew there was little hope against the Yankees.

The Yankees were up first—three up, three down, getting a standing ovation. Then the Mariners—likewise—three up, three down. Yankees back at bat and there's action with somebody punching a line drive between first and second for a base hit. The next man up pops one short to the infield, causing a scramble, resulting in a man on first and a man on second. I heard harsh words from Seattle fans who cut their team no slack. You a season ticket, you expect your team to win. Bumbling an easy catch to let a man on base was unacceptable.

A-Rod stepped up to the plate for a standing boovation. I was thinking how that would hurt, no matter who you were. A swing and a miss. Then he passed up a breaking ball. Followed up with a lazy line drive for a diving third base catch off the bounce—tossed to second for the third out. A spike of action, deflated.

The remainder of the game dragged on with little excitement, tension, or fights; all the stuff I was hoping for. Seattle got a few men on base, and then a base hit to drive in a run. The Yankees got a homer and then a few anticlimactic runs. The score ended five to three, a Yankees win and to no one's surprise.

My Uncle and I hit the streets of Seattle with his guided tour from years of living in the city. I got him to take me by Touratech, a German company catering to the adventure motorcyclist. I got to meet the guys who took my over-the-phone orders during the past year. Then we stopped at one of his old haunts, ending our day in an upscale guitar shop.

On the fourth of June, my uncle dropped me off at the Triumph shop, eight days before the ferry in Bellingham. It was hard to say good-bye to one of my closest relatives. At seventy-one and me sixty-two, I realized the life stage we shared. It was not a morbid thought but an acceptance of the truth to know neither of us would get out of it alive.

They wheeled Brother out as I stared at my new off-road tires which made Brother look aggressive, serious—more Mad Max than before. Driving away, I noticed little change in regards to vibration or road noise.

To avoid interstates, I searched for Route 2 west for Wenatchee. At the shop I had a valve check, got new brake pads, a cracked clutch reservoir cover replaced, and off-road tires mounted. This was a "shakedown" ride for Brother before I got too far away from Seattle if I needed to return to the shop. I gave me eight days to explore more of the Northwest.

Reaching Route 2, the city was behind me, and I was headed for the western Cascades, through the Alpine Lakes Wilderness Area. Climbing Stevens Pass at 4,056 feet, I went from sea level to a high elevation. The area has the most rugged topography in the Cascades; rocky, with deep glacier-carved crevices, and over seventy lakes.

Following a coffee break, I was riding north to the town of Chelan, on Lake Chelan. Like much of Washington the area had been devastated by spring fires. Most of the landscape was brown desert grass and sagebrush on rolling mountains in the three-to-five-thousand-foot range. Closer to Chelan the mountains were black from fires that scorched dry land. I passed homes that were burned with cars burnt that were parked in the driveways. The area looked like it had been bombed.

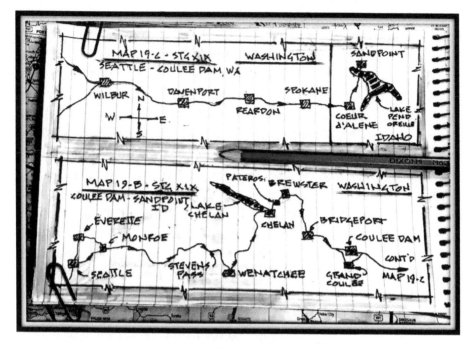

MAP# 19B – STAGE XIX:
Seattle, WA – Grand Coulee, WA
MAP# 19C – STAGE XIX:
Grand Coulee, WA – Sandpoint, ID

On the outskirts of Chelan, I saw flashing lights in my mirror. A police car—I was getting pulled. Parking roadside, I knocked down the kickstand, removed my glasses and helmet, and turned to see a young, stout Native American dressed in a short sleeve khaki uniform, exposing a tattoo on his forearm of a northwest tribal pattern. With hands on his hips, he peered through aviator sunglasses for a profile view of my bike. Before asking why I was pulled, he said, "You did nothing wrong, I just had to check out your bike." I laughed as I relaxed. Then he told me about his BMW GS1200 and plans for an upcoming trip to Southern California. I shared my excitement about the east side of the Sierras while giving my Reader's Digest version on what brought me to live off the bike. Hearing that, he threw back his head, turning a half circle to disguise his response of saying, "Shit." Then turned back to say, "Lucky Dude."

North of Chelan, the big lake became narrow for miles with high mountains to each side in places that looked like a fjord. I reached the small town of Pateros on Pateros Lake where the hills were more subtle, and the lake was like a great mirror, reflecting cliffside banks in a perfect image. Boats were floating on the calm water with reflected images to give me the sensation of vertigo. The lakeside town had only one motel with a parking lot full of old roadsters, with painted flames, shiny chrome, and open hoods. The desk clerk congratulated me for getting the last room. Inside I opened a back door to see a rich grass sloping down to the lake, edged with colorful river rock. From the town, I heard an acoustic guitar and saw people milling about but noticed an inviting pier with two bright red Adirondacks that I felt more inviting. I took a seat, mesmerized while looking at the reflective lake and listening to the distant performer sing a Jim Croce song.

The next morning I rode to Brewster, in search of the Grand Coulee Dam; an hour ride through dry farmland and another hot day. Following signs, I rode across a large gravel parking lot to an overlook to view the massive dam with distant vistas in all directions of empty, lonely landscape—barren, lifeless, and dry. The Grand Coulee Dam was built in 1941 and remains the largest cement structure in the US. It harnesses power at the confluence of the Columbia and the Spokane rivers to create Bank Lake. I left the secluded area pointing Brother in the direction of Spokane.

Through Wilbur, Davenport, and Reardon I surrendered to I-90 to make better time. Seeing the Spokane skyline, I continued into Idaho for Couer d'Alene, having heard it was a better option and to avoid Spokane. I was zapped by the heat and ready to kick back for some mindless TV and catch up with the world. A presidential election was in full swing with the country polarized on every issue. My nomadic life allowed me to be neutral and indifferent, choosing not to choose where I saw no choice.

I stopped to refresh from the hot day. In one of many small towns, I saw a tavern on an empty street except for two parked Harleys. Inside, a guy and a gal sat on bar stools, the only people in the place and as swelteringly hot as I was from riding in the heat. The waitress was friendly and asked where I was from. I shared travels stories and my new life. The bar was like so many; neon Bud Light and Corona signs and posters of NFL football, all placed strategically in a tacky attempt to decorate. All three reaffirmed what I had heard in regards to avoiding Spokane. They suggested the town of Sandpoint, telling me to make that my target. The motorcycle gal pulled out her phone to sharing an aerial picture of the town with a long bridge. I left to head in the direction of what excited them so.

On the Sandpoint bridge, I understood as I crossed over Lake Pend Oreille. The view from the bridge was the picture I saw on the woman's phone a few hours earlier; the water like a sheet of glass. I circled the town square twice until I spotted a group of adventure bikes at a restaurant, so I parked Brother. Inside a motorcyclist spotted a Triumph patch on my coat causing us to share motorcycle tales of travel. I found a table on the restaurant's deck overlooking the water in the relaxing afternoon breeze and used my map as a tablecloth while investigating my return route.

I enjoyed my evening in Sandpoint; the next morning leaving early. In a short time I was in rugged black volcanic hills on both sides of another long glassy lake; a finger of Lake Pend Oreille.

I know people will eventually ask: "What was your favorite place?" And I know I will have no answer. The United States of America is so diverse, with a range of landscapes making it impossible to single one location as a favorite.

Riding along the lake was dreamlike, with a sky showing a few brushstrokes of white clouds. The road was tight against the water's edge with rough rock strewn along the shoreline and one hidden curve after another, each around black lava cliffs. The lake was vast with vistas that cleared my mind to relish my freedom, Brother, the open road, and conscious awareness of how I now lived.

I was completing my third month since leaving and had a positive and clear mind, no longer riddled or encumbered with the conflict of responsibilities or obligations. I slept better and did not wake apprehensive about what could derail my state of mind. I felt I had turned to a new chapter. My career was not something I would regret—it got me here. As Hemingway said, "Regret is for people who think they have a second chance."

Through the North Cascades, I made it to Lake Diablo, a reservoir northwest of Diablo Dam. There was an overlook for a fantastic view of the unique turquoise body of water. It was as fantastic as the guy in Freemont said it would be. I read that the color was the result of crushed sediment from glaciers that flowed down from mountain streams—a surreal and mesmerizing color.

Up the steep road, I encountered a grouping of high-spired peaks appearing to be hard granite and as unworldly as Lake Diablo. It was Liberty Bell Mountain. At an overlook I wanted to spread Jack's ashes, thinking it likely that he may have passed this way on his travels to the Yukon. I saw what appeared to be college kids; hyper, playful, and goofy. I asked if they would photograph the spreading. They were quick to perform the act and on then be on their way, the act having no impact at all on any of them.

Into the town of Tonasket, I turned south and rode through more towns with Indian names like Omak and Okanogan. In Twisp I turned northwest, stopping at the attractive town of Winthrop in the Okanogan National Forest. I checked into a motel built like a log cabin. Entering my door, I was blasted by the heat, so I turned on a window unit. The sun streamed through glass doors, so I closed the drapes, making the room like a cave then stretched out on the bed for a nap.

Winthrop was settled by Native Americans that lived all along the Methow, Twisp, and Chewuch rivers. The first white men were French trappers. It was beautiful country, but winters could be hard with heavy snows and harsh conditions. I read that few trappers made it through their first winter, many dying of dysentery, caused by extreme dehydration, the result of excessive diarrhea, a demise more common than bear or Indian attacks.

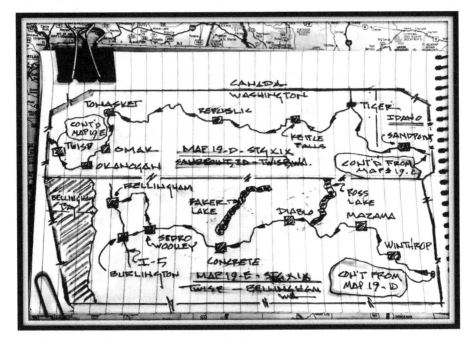

MAP# 19D – STAGE XIX:

Sandpoint, ID – Twisp, WA

MAP# 19E – STAGE XIX:

Twisp, WA – Bellingham, WA

An interesting tidbit I discovered about the town was that a Harvard graduate named Owen Wister had his honeymoon in Winthrop around the turn of the twentieth century. The town inspired him to write the novel *The Virginian,* considered the first-ever western book. I remember the TV series *The Virginian* starring James Drury as The Virginian. He wore all black, all the time, just like Adam on *Bonanza*. I favored the idea. It was simple and deleted one more decision to clutter your day.

Winthrop was an old western town and restored with wood plank walkways and storefronts like a cowboy movie. I found a restaurant with a deck along the river but the flies were so bad I sat inside at the bar. I took a seat next to two young girls clothed in tiny tank tops and shorts. They were covered with cryptic tattoos and what appeared to be painful piercings. Both looked unhealthy in a drug-user way. The bartender was prissy but spoke with a macho tone, an attempt, I surmised, to impress the girls. Inquiring about the beer selection, he spouted too quickly to understand. I asked for an Amber, so he rattled off several names, so I just told him to just pick one. I sulked a bit, drank the beer, and left to walk back along the river to my wooden cave.

I was heading to Bellingham and anxious to get there and wait for my ferry boarding. I had reserved a room and took the ride back through the North Cascades with a view of Mount Baker at 10,781 feet; the third largest mountain in Washington and the second most active volcano to Mount Saint Helens. Baker was supposed to be the next to erupt, but rumors are how Mount Rainer may surprise.

Route 9 north paralleled I-5 to Bellingham. The brush along the road was in reach, and I exhausted myself scanning for deer. I kept my fingers crossed, having heard stories of deer jumping into the laps of bikers in such close environments.

I liked what I saw as I rode into downtown Bellingham—an old town with steep hills and cobblestone streets. My motel backed up to I-5 with the roar of steady traffic. Kicking back on the bed I relaxed, no longer anticipating my arrival. It was June ninth, and I had the room for three nights before my boarding on the twelfth. I had time to get supplies for the three-day ferry ride, launder clothes, and arrange my luggage, discarding what I had not used since leaving. It is my nature to be anal and control an outcome to avoid a crisis. Many confuse worry with preparation. I think of scenarios that may occur and attempt to minimize what might blindside me. I'm proactive.

Brother was stripped down, and the panniers were in the motel room. The nimble feel of the bike made me want to ride, so I chose what looked like a backroad to find myself in thick, thick forest, and high mountainsides, amazed at how close such wilderness was to the city. At a filling station, I topped off my tank, not knowing where I would land in Alaska. I read about long stretches between fuel in The Last Frontier. The statement "If you see gas, get gas" was not a joke.

I slept well the night before the ferry and woke relaxed and ready. I felt a similar excitement as I did with my fourth-grade field trip to Colonial Williamsburg—a rare thrill in adulthood. I drank motel coffee and packed Brother getting to the ferry terminal to settle in a cafe with outside tables three hours before check-in, so I got a breakfast sandwich, nursed a coffee, and tried to read with my busy mind. Back to Brother, I grabbed my mileage log. Below the name, "Bellingham" I wrote "11,348 miles - VB to Ferry." I was surprised to calculate that my mileage since Virginia Beach was almost that of crossing the United States four times. Wow—what a trip it has been.

23

STAGE XX: Mile 11,348 – 11,348 (no gain)

Four Ratchet Straps - A Ferry Tale
Haines Arriving

"No matter where you go, once you get there, there you are."

—*Anonymous*

AT A CAFE near the terminal, I sat drinking coffee with an hour before check-in. My relaxation turned to shock when I remembered I had my ratchet straps buried at the bottom of my panniers. Booking the trip, I was told to bring my own straps to secure my bike down in the loading bay. So, I packed four ratchet straps, separated in two groups, each neatly rolled in baggies.

Stepping out to Brother I began an effort to remove items in my panniers—an ever-changing arrangement. Finding both sets, I put them in what I referred to as my "Possibilities Bag," a term I took from trappers who carried a small bag for their flint, powder, and miscellaneous items for quick access. The bag was red, waterproof, rollable, and about sixteen inches wide. Because of the bright color, I kept it strapped to the back of my luggage for visibility.

Before tossing the straps in the bag I held them in my hands, recalling something that riddled my body with a quiver, causing my eyes to well with emotion. The straps were a gift from my father over thirty years ago. I remembered unwrapping the Christmas present to see the four straps, enclosed in elaborate commercial packaging of hard plastic and cardboard and being puzzled. I looked at my Father, thinking the gift odd then asked: "What am I going to do with these?" "You'll find something to do with them," he said, shrugging casually. I rolled my eyes while tossing them in a chair. Looking back now, I realize I was an ungrateful jerk. Once home, I placed them on a shelf in the garage, forgetting about them for years. Eventually, there was something I thought I would use them for, so they made it out of the package. As I recall, they did not satisfy my intentions, so they ended up in a coffee can with nuts and bolts. Time passed, and through multiple moves, I filtered through my belongings to weed out what was needed and what was not. Because they were a gift from my father, I always kept the ratchet straps through multiple moves and my divestment.

I remember the day I was instructed to bring my own ratchet straps. While on the phone I glanced to an adjoining room in my beach cottage and saw the straps laying on the floor. I could not help but smile at my father's words: "You'll find something to do with them." Now I was preparing to strap Brother down on a ferry on my way to Alaska for the greatest adventure of my life. I wished my father was alive to share this. Just so I could see him shrug in the same casual manner, he did when I asked what to do with them. It would have been one more "Gotcha" moment for him.

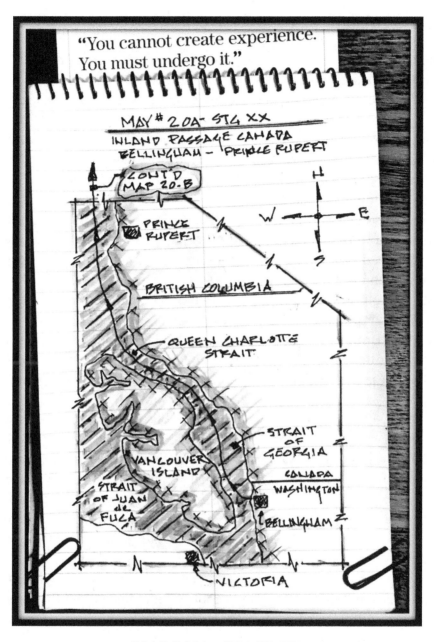

MAP # 20A - STAGE XX

Inland Passage Canada

Bellingham, WA - Prince Rupert, BC

I headed to the terminal for early check-in. I thought I was over-loaded but parked in a group of bikes making me look like I was packed light. They were loaded all over and, on some, the back seat was free for a significant other. Seeing the heavily loaded bikes made me feel good. Too many times on the road I had heard "Man, you're loaded."

At the check-in window, I waited to get my ticket and instructions for boarding. To the back was a food bar looking out to the water. Not sure when I would eat again, I ordered a sandwich. Taking my coat off, a guy came up noticing the Luckenbach T-shirt I was wearing; a souvenir from the Texas Hill Country. He began a conversation, asked questions, only so he could talk, with no room for answers. His stories began mid-topic and made little sense and were impossible to follow. I had a good vibe going, but his rattling flow of nonsense was disruptive and annoying. I ignored him and disengaged eye contact. Those that rob your time, your attention, your good vibe, are pickpockets—they're energy vampires.

On Brother, I made my way to the lane for motorcycles, passing through a ticket stand where I was directed to join a large group of bikes. I was a gathering with everyone looking over each other's machine. I was in no mood to be checking out farkles.

Finally, they directed the long line of bikers to board. We crossed a steel plate ramp onto the ferry deck, while an attendant arranged us between the hull side and a stairwell. We were instructed to use our side stands, and not the center stands, which I liked, knowing how loaded Brother was to lift. I began attaching the ratchet straps, two places each side, hearing we would pass open ocean and pick up rolling swells. Following a career of working with small boats, I knew how to tie the bike down for rolling seas.

I secured Brother and began unloading for my three-night stay. I got a key and directions to my cabin. Several bikers said they were camping on the fantail. I could have as well, but it was my retirement gift to myself to have a cabin.

MAP # 20B - STAGE XX
Inland Passage Alaska
Prince Rupert, BC - Skayway, AK

Once inside, I found the small cabin had all that I needed—nothing luxurious; aluminum bunk beds, a sink, a small table for luggage, two aluminum chairs, and a bathroom with a toilet and a shower. I made it comfortable for my three-night stay, moving the luggage table in front of the cabin window, placing my canvas rack-pack on top to serve as a platform for my laptop. In Bellingham, I purchased small containers of wine, so I chilled a few in the sink for sunset. I was looking forward to the changing scenery that would parade past the cabin window. I pulled out my Alaska motorcycle travel guide to begin my initial research, feeling I had been delinquent in preparing for the most anticipated part of my adventure.

The ferry was a big ship named the *Columbia*, after the Columbia Glacier, an Alaska glacier named after Columbia University. The ship was four hundred and eighteen feet in length with a fifty-nine-foot beam, a gross tonnage of 3,946 and a service speed of seventeen knots, designed to carry four hundred and ninety-nine passengers. Commissioned in 2007 by Governor Sarah Palin and looked new. For the money, I was paying it was a good deal. People taking Alaskan cruises were paying three times what I paid for the same route. The amenities were not comparable, but it was where I'd rather be.

I immediately felt at home and enjoyed running into fellow bikers. Some were riding as couples, using their vacation time, hard charg'n their way to the Dalton Highway to cross the Arctic Circle. I was still clueless as to my path other than I wanted to see Alaska. I read about the Dalton, or the "haul road," as it is referred to, named so for trucks running to Prudhoe Bay and Deadhorse. The road had a reputation for being the most dangerous road in North America, and for that reason, it was sought out by the adventure motorcyclist. I questioned whether or not I should ride the demon road, having read details about the dangers. Dangers to the point of making sure your insurance policy would cover the cost to medevac you out and such. Bikers spoke about riding the desolate gravel road with a lot of bravadoes. "What's it like?" I'd asked. One said, "Man, there's eighteen-wheelers passing you at ninety miles an hour, spinning rocks off their wheels as big as your fist and the whole time you're dodging huge potholes while your bike gets caked with calcium chloride that will never come off. And then there's the wildlife."

I would be a liar to say it did not scare me. But at the same time, it intrigued me, and I saw it as a challenge that I may choose. I would quickly learn that each biker either exaggerate the dangers or play them down. Taking off solo on the road like the Dalton was nothing a sensible person would do. But then again, someone would not think a sensible person would choose to live off a motorcycle—would they?

The most interesting person I met on the ferry was an eighty-one-year-old man named Alden; a retired orthodontist from Northern California with a Kawasaki KLR 650 dirt bike. When talking to him about his bike he would reply "It's just a Mule." He was tall, lean and sophisticated in the manner he carried himself. He looked as if he should be stepping out of a black Mercedes and reminded me of the Swedish actor Max Von Sydow. My first encounter with Alden was while we were securing our bikes to the loading dock. He asked me if we should leave our helmets with our bike. My answer was casual, "Why not?" I asked Alden where he was heading and he told me, "Up the Dempster Highway to Inuvik." I had recently read about the road as another way to cross the Arctic Circle, with less truck traffic but tougher gravel. The road begins thirty miles southeast of Dawson City, Yukon Territory and about the same length as the Dalton. Hearing Alden say he was heading up the Dempster caused me to give the Dalton serious consideration.

During my time on the ferry, I would run into Alden, and we would share small talk. One evening we were watching the brilliant colors of the setting sun from the fantail where he was camping on a lounge chair. The colors in the sky, while traveling north, intensified and became more magnificent. I shared my plans with Alden, so he invited me to take a seat and discuss them with a map of Alaska. While unfolding the map, he peered over his reading glasses and said with a pleasant smile, "Many years ago, a buddy and I came to Alaska on our bikes, and I have to tell you, going through Thompson's Pass on your way to Valdez will be something you will never forget." I got a chill of excitement, knowing the road was a planned ride.

While navigating a narrow pass, the ferry slowed to a near stop. We stood and walked to the railing to observe the large ship in a severe turn while twisting through channel markers. There was an abrasive sound from the strain of opposing props that created a tense atmosphere during the struggling tight turn. The land was closer than it had been since leaving Bellingham. While casually standing together, Alden turned to me as I was watching the water muddy from the churning props. In a raised voice he asked, "Have you ever been married?" I thought the question odd, but said: "Yes, twenty years, divorced now for thirteen." He paused, then in a confessional tone said: "I have been married several times and for that, my life has not turned out as I would have planned." I gave a nod as we continued to watch the ship struggle as props growled, racked, shook, to vibrate the deck.

With Alden, everything was a matter of fact. He had grown old gracefully, while still nurturing an adventurous spirit. He reminded me of a few simple Dylan lyrics from a song I identified with "...Just keep on, keeping on." I liked his style, his quiet approach, and how little I saw of his ego for the incredible thing he was doing. Earlier, a younger man was describing the treacherous details of the Dalton Highway with bowling-ball-sized potholes and fist-sized rocks—all so dramatic. When I asked my new eighty-one-year-old friend about the Dempster Highway his remark was simple, "It's a gravel road." There was a message there—build things up in your mind, and they'll be bigger than they are, minimize things, and you'll find them manageable.

It was the fifteenth of June and my last day on the ferry. We were making stops in Alaskan ports, and the skyline changed, now filled with snowcapped peaks like I had never seen before. How much of what I was seeing was untouched—unexplored? It gave me a better understanding of the term "The Last Frontier."

The first stop was the town of Ketchikan and then Wrangell. With so much time on the ferry, people were antsy to get off the bike if only for a moment. It was early morning when we arrived in Ketchikan, and I was still in bed to fill the vibration of props as the captain pulled to the dock. I got up to look out the cabin window finding it odd to see a pier after days of seeing nothing but open waters and remote landscapes.

On my last night, I had a buffet dinner in the dining room with a view across the bow of the cruising ship. The meal was like a company Christmas party with lines of people self-serving roast beef, mashed potatoes, broccoli, and yeast rolls, from steel trays under a sneeze guard. Following dinner, I strolled the outside decks to enjoy the sunset. With two days on the ferry, everyone shared cordialities, acquainted by face if not by name. People pointed at bald eagles overhead as small commuter airplanes flew in various directions. Eventually, the sunset colored the sky like a bonfire with a chill in the air to make me feel like I was in Alaska. I held the moment and squeezed it tight then went back to my cabin and poured a glass of wine.

On June fifteenth I disembarked in Haines, Alaska, with the ferry ride feeling more like a pleasure trip than transportation. After so many miles on the road and constant day-to-day travel, I was ready to get off and back to the road.

An intercom announced "Haines, Arriving." Down to the well deck, I was glad to see Brother. I loaded and rolled my ratchet straps for my ferry ride to Skagway, the next day. My friend Alden was next to me loading his so-called Mule and very focused. "Good Luck," I told him, but there was no response. I put my hand on his shoulder with a pat for good luck—more for me than him.

Into Haines, I saw a small, pretty town on the water with snow-capped mountains in every direction. I got a room at the only motel I saw—my first experience with elevated prices in Alaska. The town was set back in time, nothing modern, just essential; grocery store, post office, library, school.

One morning, while in Huntsville, Alabama, I woke to stare at a map of the world mounted opposite my bed. I sat up to focus on North America to notice how far Alaska was from the Lower Forty-Eight. It was three thousand miles across the United States and another three thousand miles up to the far northwest state. Recalling my view of the map, I realized what a long distance I was from where I started.

In Hayes, I found a local tavern for a hamburger and a few drafts. I talked to the bartender about it being my first time in Alaska and where I had traveled from. The interior had dollar bills pinned on the walls and ceiling with names and comments printed in black marker. The history of such goes back to when men made their way so far north and would come into town before heading out to pan for gold. Leaving a dollar on the wall with their name on it would ensure they had money when they returned. The trend has undoubtedly been bastardized with odd, funky, and vulgar names on the bills that no one would return to get.

Back at my motel, I stood in the parking lot to view the area around the water. I could not believe my eyes when I spotted about twenty bald eagles swarming the shoreline like swallows. They were dipping down to the water's edge then back up high. With the big snow-capped mountains, the eagles, the crisp air, and the frontier town, I very much felt like I was in Alaska. I felt I had arrived.

24

STAGE XXI: Miles 11,348 - 11,883

In Alaska - Ferry to Skagway - Bear Spray
Klondike Highway - Dust to Dawson

"And those who were seen dancing were thought to be insane by those who could not hear the music."

—*Frederick Nietzsche*

MY CELL PHONE woke me on my first morning in Alaska by a friend from Virginia Beach. Once a colleague he was now a motorcycle buddy. Such a coincidence since I had invited him to join me in The Last Frontier. Because of work that wasn't going to happen. I owed the guy big. He convinced me to buy my Triumph, aware of my taste for long distant travel knowing the bike would be a fit. He was a research maniac and my sounding board for upgrades and add-ons for Brother.

"Hey man, where are you?" he asked. "Just got into Alaska," I told him. "No Shit" I hear, sensing envy

and disappointment. We went back and forth while I shared stories of my three-month adventure in the Lower Forty-Eight. Now in Alaska I was stepping up to another level and ready to use my adventure bike for what it was meant for. I felt bolstered by my friend's enthusiasm for what I was doing—a good dose of affirmation for my take-off into The Last Frontier.

I coffeed-up while loading Brother. The ferry terminal was a short ride away. I was two hours early with the ticket counter closed. So I stood in the sun and watched people read stickers on my panniers.

Boarding the ferry, I pulled out my ratchet straps to secure Brother. At the cafeteria, I got more coffee and sat with my maps and notebook to begin something new—creating my own map. In this case, a route from Skagway to Whitehorse, and then to Dawson City. I broke areas into mileage, marking towns as milestones. I initially was indifferent to traveling through the Canadian Yukon Territory, actually thinking it an interruption. My research on the ferry caused me to look forward to it—it gave it a face.

In Skagway, I saw two cruise ships docked at the port. I was warned about Skagway and it is filled with tourist. Mayhem was waiting, so I found a back street that kept me away from the crowds. Through cross streets, I saw Main Street was a sea of people. A group of Harley guys from the ferry pulled into a motel. I followed and went into a homey office to find a vacancy. The Harley group got rooms near mine with their Harley group attitude—a membrane of clannishness. I changed into street clothes and walked to town.

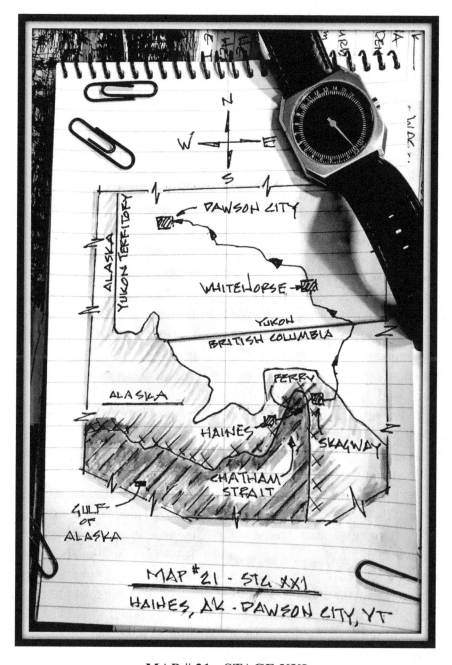

MAP # 21 - STAGE XXI
Haines, AK - Dawson City, YT

Skagway was created during the Klondike Gold Rush in the late eighteen hundreds. Areas for prospecting were five hundred miles into the Yukon Territory with Skagway the jumping off point for thousands who traveled the inland passageway by steamboat. The land was cruel, so many coming with dreams to make it rich and dying in their pursuit. The town was unimaginably corrupt, described by one Canadian Mounty as just a bit better than hell. A constant flow of men took on the rugged and fierce trek into the Yukon for their shot at fortune. Most lost their money to survive, many dying by extreme hardships, falling prey to the hostile surroundings. By the turn of the century, the town was mostly vacated. Now, the town is a tourist trap.

Skagway was packed, making walking difficult, so I stepped into a bar to nurse a beer until the crowds went back to the ships. Once gone, the street was deserted. Exploring Main Street I found a hardware store to buy bear spray hearing bears were not a joking matter in Alaska—that's what the academic man in Moab said. He spoke about bear etiquette and advised to scare a black bear you stood tall with a threatening presence and loud noises—an air horn was recommended. With a grizzly bear, those tactics would irritate the animal and cause an attack, and the best you could do would be to curl up, cover your head with your arms and hands, appear passive and hope for the best. The brown bear had a temperament between the two and could be unpredictable. Their uniqueness was their size. In Girdwood, Alaska, browns weighed up to 1,800 pounds.

From what I heard bear spray was my best option. My uncle carried a Mossberg shotgun while visiting Alaska. He loaded it with three different rounds, specific for scaring, slowing, and stopping the bear if he advanced; birdshot, buckshot, and slug. On man told me bear spray was more effective than a firearm. Bears have such a slow heart rate they could run through the gunshots without collapsing to continue and maul it's victim. Bear spray would cause the animal to choke, sting, stop, and retreat. In either case, an attempt to deter the charge of an angry bear was far worse than I could imagine.

The container of bear spray cost forty bucks. I bought it from some young kids working in the hardware store. I asked their opinion of bear spray, inviting a little fun, telling me I should buy three containers in case I was charged by three bears. I walked out mumbling "Yea, Yea, Yea" over my shoulder with one container while they chuckled.

I stopped in a pub and sat with my new purchase. It had an instructional pamphlet with a photo of the man who owned the company, after being mauled by a bear. It was a telling picture with his face and head bloodied with claw marks—obvious where his entrepreneurial inspiration originated. A few pages made me confident my money was well spent. The canister would shoot a blast up to forty yards. The instructions said to aim low, so the charging bear would run through a field of chemical fog the make his eyes water, sting, and he would halt. But once the bear ran away, you should too. He would lick the dried solution which was a likable pepper taste and return for more.

I had heard rumors that bear spray was more of a bear attractor and not a deterrent. Rumors that were silly, yet sad. The spray was attracting bear because idiots were spraying it on themselves like mosquito spray, thinking it was a repellant. Sprayed on the skin the substance would put out a pepper smell to attract a bear, similar to seasoned food, in this case, peppered people. The next morning I set out for Whitehorse. Thirty miles north I would be out of Alaska and into the Yukon on the Klondike Highway. A road that took eighty years to carve from the rugged wilderness. It paralleled the route used by Yukon prospectors during the 1889 Klondike Gold Rush. It climbed up and over White Pass, the challenging route used by so many brave people from Skagway to Dawson City in the Yukon Territory over four hundred miles away. From there I would come back to Alaska. My first stop was Whitehorse, the Capital of the Yukon Territory and the largest city in northern Canada and said to have the cleanest air in the world.

Up the Klondike, it was obvious why it took so long to build the road. The first part was steep, through an extremely craggy landscape of gnarly granite and thick black spruce. Reminding me of an area on the west coast of Ireland called "The Burren."

Along the road, I passed numerous rocks balanced in vertical arrangements. Rock balancing: the art of gathering stones and balancing one on top another, an act that can serve many purposes: decor, trail marking, or meditation.

I tried to put myself in the shoes of those adventurous souls who began to question their decision while making the arduous trek on foot. It was a single file flow while holding secured ropes for safety along the steep and rugged mountain, all loaded like pack mules. Usually, the trek was in deep snow during severe winters, the entire time reminding themselves of their objective—to become rich.

Once gold was discovered in the Yukon, there was a mass movement. The Klondike Gold Rush was the last gold rush, beginning in 1887, almost forty years after the California Gold Rush of 1849. Prospectors headed to Skagway for the long, dangerous trek over the Boundary Range. For seven years there was only one way, the Chilkoot Pass. A thirty-three-mile trail; steep, snow-covered, icy, and barely passable. Initially, it was a trade route for the Tlingit Indians, then traveled by more than 150,000 stampeders, as they were called. Canadian officials kept close oversight on those who chose the pass into the Klondike wilderness, requiring that each man have "one ton" of supplies, consisting of what was necessary to stay alive for the duration of their stay. Requirements were detailed down to the number of wool socks. A ton of supplies and no way to transport them other than a hand-drawn sled and a loaded back. Some men carried sixty pounds on their back with sixty-pound bags in each hand.

During the rapid progression through the Chilkoot, another pass was discovered at a lower level involving a political arrangement with the Chilkoot Indians. Called the White Pass, it was a favorable option to the Chilkoot—less steep and suitable for horse-drawn carts. A tramway was built—a crude pulley system operated by horses to pull loads. The pass got the name The Dead Horse Trail due to so many horses perishing along the way. It was still hellish, many dying of starvation, many forced to eat dead horses, and many going insane.

There were five small towns along the Klondike River, four of them no more than a trading post with a gas pump. They were infrastructure for the Tlingit and the Tagish peoples. The largest town was Carcross, originally named Caribou Crossing due to Caribou herds that migrated across the land bridge between Narse Lake and Bennet Lake. The Klondike Gold Rush caused the herds to dissipate. I stopped in the small town to stretch and meander the streets of odd houses appearing to have been fabricated from scrap wood with caribou racks attached to every structure.

Arriving in Whitehorse. It was an abrupt change from the wilderness to homes and paved walkways. Established during the Gold Rush, the city had a population of about 30,000. Near downtown, I crossed the Yukon River, again. The town took its name from White Horse Rapids—rapids that resembled the manes of white horses.

Whitehorse is a grid of streets and avenues and looked European with apartments, architecturally colorful with plate glass. It was an easy city to navigate, clean, well maintained, and simple.

I found a motel operated by an Asian lady and her daughter. My room was near three Harley guys who were sitting on the curb peering over a map. While parking Brother, one asked if I was going to Dawson City. I said yes, and he warned that accommodations would be difficult to find. The group seemed frantic to find lodging, saying the town would be packed. Their predicament was not mine. I was fine with camping.

Out to walk the city, I found it comfortable and attractive. I stopped at a trendy restaurant with an attached bar. I ate oysters then stepped next door to see someone hooking up a microphone while musicians and cool locals entered. Buying a beer, I got change back from an American twenty in Canadian currency. Looking at the money, I thought about how money from other countries was so much more attractive than US currency. The bills had beautiful colors and pictures of distinguished people, like the Queen of England. American money had portraits of dead Founding Fathers and dead presidents in dull green.

Up early I was ready for my long ride to Dawson City. I had trail mix and coffee for breakfast while loading Brother. With a full tank, I began clicking off the miles for what would be a long day. I was used to long days with cafe stops and conversation with locals. Meeting people was how I learned about a place. It required a lost art—listening. Listen to someone while they tell their tale. Then ask questions to make them aware you heard.

From Whitehorse, I continued the route of the Stampeders. The scenery changed from photographically picturesque to deeply wooded with the ubiquitous black spruce. The idea of traveling this far on foot was unfathomable and made my motorcycle adventure seem lame. I thought of men packed together doing what they could to help each other. I also thought about those who took advantage of the downfall of others. It was the survival of the fittest.

Along the road I would encounter like kind; adventure bikers in small groups of three or more, each asking if I was heading to Dawson City. On the road I was traveling, I had to be going to Dawson City. Roads were under construction with surfaces ground down to make gravel in preparation for paving. Flag people stopped traffic for twenty minutes or more. Roads were regularly destroyed during harsh winters, mostly by frost heaving; an upward swelling of soil beneath the road surface where water freezes and ice expands vertically to lift and crack leaving holes and broken chunks of asphalt. I heard there were only two seasons in Alaska and the Yukon—winter and road construction.

It was sunny and hot, and construction stops were sweltering and uncomfortable. At one stop I spoke with a young man who held a STOP sign. The conversation turned to wildlife and how the area was plentiful with bear. He explained how attuned they were to the smell of humans and how a little wind would carry human scent as far as ten miles. I mentioned my purchase of bear spray which he disregarded as not lethal enough, advising me to get a shotgun. Bears or not, I would not be carrying a shotgun on Brother.

He turned the sign from STOP to SLOW and said: "You're going to hit some gravel so take it slow." It was my first real encounter with gravel, so I tightened up. Taking off, I sunk in the deep gravel and was glad for my off-road tires while still experiencing the loss of control. The front wheel twisted while searching for a solid surface. Loaded to the back made the front wheel light. I eventually learned not to fight the front wheel and just let it do what it wanted—if I maintained a forward direction the back wheel would follow. Regardless, I experienced an uneasy feeling with my forearms tense, my jaws clenched, and my butt cheeks pulled together.

I continued to run into bikers heading to Dawson City. One asking if I was going to the rally. I questioned what rally he was talking about. "The Dust to Dawson Bike Rally" he barked. Then it dawned on me that my Alaska adventure motorcycling book detailed an annual rally for adventure motorcyclists in the town. It was a coincidence and an opportunity.

Dawson City was a well preserved, renovated town from the Klondike Gold Rush days. Between 1895 and 1905, at the height of the gold rush, the city was considered the Paris of the North. People from the United States and Europe made their way for what it offered; partying, theatre, prostitution, gambling, and prospecting. It was packed, and lawless, many having turned their lives upside down in pursuit of gold. Once the gold played out, there was a shift to Nome, Alaska, with rumors of gold. It left Dawson City to dry up.

The town of Dawson City looked as it did in 1905, with everything authentic from the Gold Rush days. I inquired about a room and was told by the desk girl what I knew—you will have no luck finding a room because of the rally. I asked about camping, and she gave me directions to the other end of town. The streets were filled with adventure bikes of all kinds.

Finding the campsite, I walked into the office to hear, "We're full" before having the time to inquire. "You might try the campsite across the river, but it's probably full too," she said. Now, I was feeling a little stressed. She pointing in a vague direction while saying "There's a ferry at the end of town."

At the northern part of town, the land sloped to the river, and the pavement turned to gravel. RVs, cars, and motorcycles parked in makeshift lines. A small ferry on the opposite side of the river was in the process of unloading. Once again, I would cross the Yukon. The ferry clumsily came to shore and dropped a steel plate ramp to the gravel. They boarded the RVs, then the cars, and then about eight motorcycles. On board, I got my kickstand down and supported Brother for what may occur during the rough docking I observed. Underway, I notice two guys on BMW adventure bikes. I nodded and saw they were eying my packed bike and the stickers on my panniers. One said, "Where you headed?" I explained my situation with no rooms and no space at the campground and hopes to find a place to camp. Without hesitation, the two invited me to their campsite saying they had plenty of space as the ferry throttled down to dock.

I followed them along the river bank through wild and charming wilderness beauty with tents pitched at comfortable distances. At their campsite, I saw that indeed they had plenty of room. I learned the two were cousins, Eric was from Seattle and Tony from California. Eric's brother Ted was across the river. Both were curious about my life and Brother. I barely answered one question before being asked another. For the most part, people tend to ask a question but interrupt during your answer, but it was not the case with these two. Eric was quiet, but the planner, the organizer. Tony was gregarious and social. I asked them to detail their plans for the bike rally, and they told me about poker runs to old mining camps in the morning. A poker run is an event where bikers visit checkpoints and draw playing cards with the objective to have the best poker hand at the end of a series of rides. While setting up my tent Ted, Eric's brother from Wasilla, Alaska, rode up. The three were a close-knit group of family members. There was talk about taking the ferry back across for dinner, but that never materialized. An unspoken agreement made it comfortable to stay at camp and eat what was available between the four of us.

By an open fire was a picnic table, covered with trail mix, beef jerky, nuts, and chips. I had a fifth of Jim Beam and passed it around. Eric and Tony, dead tired, crawled into their tents. Ted, who was my age, stood to stare at the fire and pull on the fifth with me. We seemed to connect with an energetic conversation in the glow of the fire and the buzz of the whiskey. There was a pause before he said, "You know, I think it would be a good idea for you to take the panniers off your bike and join us on the poker runs tomorrow." My immediate reaction was hesitation. I was reluctant, not wanting the three to nursemaid me through my lack of off-road capabilities. At the same time, I knew he was right, and I began to see the bike rally as a gift from the universe—

an opportunity to ride gravel roads with guys that came just for off-road riding. Following a pull off the fifth, I nodded and said "OK—I"m in!" It was a golden opportunity and a decision that had a slight push by the liquid courage.

We were all in our tents during what felt like the period of dusk, darkness only a few hours a night that far north at that time of the year. I slept but woke early to think about what the day would bring. Hearing someone stirring to make a fire I got up. We stood in a circle and drank coffee then took the ferry across the river where we each paid ten dollars for the day's festivities. We got a xeroxed map describing the four rides then went to a deli for breakfast sandwiches and more coffee, hanging out until the poker runs began.

Back across the Yukon bikes of all types were zipping in all directions, in disorder and confusion. Ted from Wasilla had the map with an understanding of where we were going having been to the rally several times. We gather at a gravel parking lot to begin. From there took out and I saw my new friends display confidence and experience with the speed and manner they operated their bikes in reckless abandon. They were out front, and I was just happy to keep up. Tony turned off his ABS so he could scratch off with his back wheel, tossing gravel when he took off or shifted to the next gear. It was apparent he had been raised riding dirt bikes. In route, motorcycles buzzed and passed at high speeds, most standing on their pegs while leaving trails of brown gravel dust in the air for me to pass through—and wear.

All four poker runs ended at old Gold Dredges along the Yukon, all national landmarks from their origin and role during the Klondike Gold Rush. They were like floating apartment buildings on barges, docked shoreside with cabling and rigging to crane hoisted sluice boxes.

Ted warned me about a portion of road that was heavy sand, telling me how to just throttle out of it. He had been king to share tips on road conditions and how to handle the bike. Through most road conditions I encountered, I found speed was my friend. From experience, I was gaining new confidence. I learned I could float my hands on the grips and no longer tense my forearms. Most of all, I was less apprehensive about things going wrong.

The last stop was at a gravel overlook high above Dawson City, set before layered mountains. We stood with the incredible view, taking turns to photograph each other as jubilant friends at the close of a great experience and a great day. Remembering I had Jack's ashes in my coat pocket I asked Ted to take a picture as I tossed them in the wind. The Yukon was once Jack's destination when he took out in his twenties with a group of friends in a laundry van they had converted to a camper. I thought it fortuitous that on such an exciting day I would remember his time as a young man to have come this far on his greatest adventure. Now he was returning. Maybe Nietzsche was right when he said "time is a flat circle."

25

STAGE XXII: Miles 11,883 - 12,322

Top of the World - Chicken - Tok in Smoke
Thompson's Pass - Valdez

*"Life shrinks or expands in proportion
to one's courage."*

—*Anais Nin*

THE NEXT MORNING we broke camp, packed our bikes, and took the ferry across the river for breakfast. We were all heading for the border of Alaska on our way to the town of Tok, by way of the Top of the World Highway; a much-anticipated ride. Past the border, we planned to stop in the tiny town of Chicken. The day's ride, about two hundred miles and would only be paved the last seventy.

We waited for the ferry while bunched up with a crowd of bikers leaving the rally. The ramp dropped to the gravel, and they loaded the bikers first, in multiple lines, arranging motorcycles in rows to board as many bikes as possible, packing us in like cordwood. One of the ferry crew climbed up on a gunwale and began to count the bikes out loud while pointing; thirty-five, thirty- six, thirty-seven, and then a loud, "Woooaaahhh." We clapped and shouted. Thirty-seven bikers that would fill a gravel road for Alaska. Ted briefed me on what to expect on the long ride. What I did not expect was the number of guys who would consider it a race.

The ramp dropped on the other side of the Yukon and bikes bolted off in a mad frenzy, scratching gravel back onto the steel deck. My friends tore out at a good pace, and I followed. We made it to the border fast then waited in a long row of bikes that turned into a testosterone-charged social gathering. Several questioned why I was packed so heavy, so I explained how the bike was now my home. All loved the idea of taking to the road—no destination, no termination.

From the border, we began the Top of the World Highway. The road, a mixture of gravel, sand, and dirt. My comfort level was to ride forty to fifty miles an hour, seeing guys doing seventy and higher. Views were to infinity and high above treetops far below, a layered verdant abstraction, as far as the eye could see making me feel like I was actually—on top of the world.

I read about the town of Chicken and how it was an authentic frontier existence, powered by gasoline generators. The town consisted of a restaurant, a souvenir shop, and an old pub, all in one structure with a porch. In the back—a row of wooden outhouses. From the border, skies got heavy and black. During the last few miles, I passed situations where accidents had occurred, one with emergency personnel assisting a biker twenty yards in the rough. I had to surmise it was bikers riding past their skill levels, following too close in packed groups, and someone catching a face full of gravel.

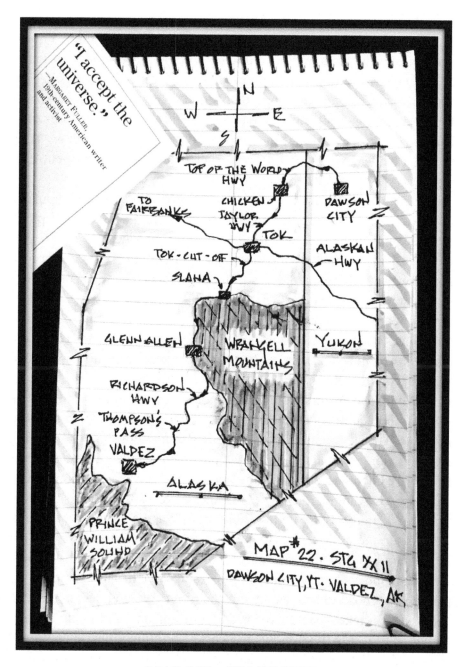

MAP # 22 - STAGE XXII
Dawson City, YT - Valdez, AK

Rounding a turn, I saw Chicken while getting hit by heavy rain-drops. Pulling into an already muddy parking lot, I dismounted quick and ran into the restaurant as a thunderbolt caused everyone to jump, as the bottom fell out with hammering rain. A line of bikers rolled up and scurried to escape the storm then stood in an open kitchen to order food—the special in Chicken, being chicken. The place was a buzz of chatter, milling about, and the constant slam of a screen door. They turned a heater on in an oddly constructed restaurant, more tent than structure. Many laid wet clothes out to dry.

The rain lasted for an hour, leaving deep puddles throughout the dirt parking lot. Back on the road, it was a mile of gravel until pavement began for the remaining miles to Tok. The ride was not so scenic, passing open fields with small, strangely configured black spruce that grew sporadically amid short, thickly bunched saplings. The trees looked weak, near dead, growing to heights of about twenty feet. Their tops curled down, looking deformed in a clustered garble, their color more black than green. Ted informed that the oddly shaped trees were black spruce and some were sixty years old due to deep snows provided a short growing season.

My friends wanted to be in Anchorage by nightfall. With the late sunsets, they could ride until midnight for the three hundred miles to get there. The sky continued to look threatening with shots of lightning sparking along our ride. Now on the pavement, we were faster. Closer to Tok, we encountered heavy downpours. Having been hot, I removed the Gore-Tex lining from my pants and jacket, so I enjoyed the cool soaking. I entered Tok with my friend from Wasilla, disconnected from his brother and cousin. We stopped for gas where Ted said he was not in the mood for the long ride to Anchorage in the steady rain. We both were beat and soaked. While filling our tanks, we discussed motels we passed and chose to rent an RV for the night. We grabbed some beer, checked in, kicked back, exhausted from our day and made another dinner of trail mix, beef jerky, and chips. Lightning flashes continued in sporadic directions. Ted called his brother to hear they were in a nearby campground, also choosing to forgo the idea of Anchorage. We spent our evening drinking beer and chatting to learn a lot about my new friend. Ted had a master's degree in psychology which opened the door to insights about people, past relationships, and jokes about ourselves. He left Seattle in his twenties and moved to Skagway to become a tour guide along the Klondike. Ted entered an Alaskan Land Lottery and won ten acres on a lake in the town of Wasilla, moved onto his new land, built a cabin, and started a window-washing business. He was an accomplished singer, songwriter, and acoustic guitarist. Heading off to bed my friend invited me to visit his home on the Kenai Peninsula, saying he owned an RV that I was welcome to stay in. He left the following morning, I decided to stay another night.

I walked to the office through a strong smell of smoke that colored the air. Paying for another night, I commented on the smoke, the proprietor telling me that lightning strikes set off over eighty fires yesterday. Asking if that was common, she said eighty was a lot.

Back at the RV, I spent the day at my computer, fortunate to have WiFi. I studied maps to create my own for my next stage of Alaska. The door was open, and the air continued to thicken with smoke to become more pungent. The atmosphere was surreal, and I could look directly at the filtered sun—a soft orange orb.

Tok was flat and wooded in all directions and, from the roadside, not at all attractive. A family restaurant was within view, so I walked over for an early dinner. Along the way, I passed an old saloon tucked in a wooded area. Nothing about the town inspired me to explore seeming like a place for someone in a witness protection program.

Following dinner, I went back to the RV to stare at maps. Getting bored, and to pacify my curiosity, I walked over to the saloon I had passed earlier, hoping to meet some local color. Approaching, I saw two trampy kids leaning against the building who appeared to be on the outs, possibly runaways. The boy was shoeless, and the girl had a dog on a rope leash. I walked in and saw a bartender with long white hair and beard, wearing a straw cowboy hat—a Deadhead look. There was one person at the bar who had his head in folded arms. He was skinny and very drunk. I ordered a draft and heard the man mumble something in my direction, assisting his inability to talk with flailing arms, then returning to his folded slump. The bartender said nothing and I said nothing, so I sat with maps and began jotting down routes heading south against my estimated timeline. I was planning a schedule to avoid winter, knowing I needed to be south of the Dakotas before October. Nearing July, I had three months to explore Alaska and Canada on my return.

I got another draft and relaxed into the dark and quiet atmosphere. Getting the bartender's attention woke the drunken man which inspired a rant spoken in tongues while he stood to pace in a frustrated tantrum. The bartender treated him with compassion, talking to him like a child wanting to call someone to pick him up. I thought how there may be a different mentality about issues of alcohol this far north. Those, this far away from civilization, endured long, hard winters, and drank to tolerate loneliness and isolation. They developed problems with alcohol. I recalled Jack London's book *John Barleycorn,* where London detailed the hooks of alcohol and his own struggles during his isolation in the Yukon.

While finishing my second draft, I asked the bartender about life in Tok. He mostly talked about the cold, down to seventy below at times with forty below, the norm. And that was with heavy snow. He laughed saying, if it was in the twenties, it was a heat wave, and you chopped wood in your T-shirt. Coming from Montana he made his way to Tok, telling me Montana had become a "rat race." So he came to Alaska to homestead—a choice for a hearty mentality and those serious about frontier life. I met very few native Alaskans, most were transplants that chose to abandon the "Mothership," the Lower Forty-Eight.

At the family restaurant, a motherly waitress took my breakfast order. It was a direct route to Valdez, about two hundred and fifty miles south. From Tok, I was on what was called the Tok Cut-Off, a road slowly built in the late forties connecting to the Richardson Highway, a hundred miles away. Tok lies on a vast flat alluvial plain between the Tanana River and the Alaska Range, an ideal area for the junction of various highways, the town located at the intersection of the Alaskan Highway, the Glenn Highway and close to the Taylor Highway. There have been Athabaskan settlements in the area for centuries. Flat, mountain-less and looked more like parts of South Carolina with black spruce instead of paper pine.

Down the Tok Cut-Off, I felt cheated by the smoke that obscured my view of the enormous Alaskan Mountain Range to my left, only seeing vague silhouettes of the big mountains. The road was well-paved asphalt, then stretches of heavily weathered, cracked, with broken chunks. Areas sloppily patched were of more concern than damaged areas. There was just so little good weather to repair damaged roads. Patches were a glob of asphalt rolled flat in a quick attempt to blend which left an abrupt and shocking bump.

The Alaska Highway from Tok continued northwesterly until intersecting the Richardson Highway. The ALCAN, as it is referred to, is the Alaska Canadian Highway. Construction began at the start of WWII at the British Columbia town of Beaver Creek. Building the road was in response to the bombing of Pearl Harbor, realizing the US was vulnerable to attack at the upper coastlines. At the time it was near impossible to get to Alaska by land until the 1,700-mile road was constructed to intersect the Richardson at Delta Junction. The road is said to be mostly paved, but I found a great deal of the highway, rough gravel. The original road has been shortened by three hundred and fifty miles with shortcuts not possible during the early construction. The ALCAN would have been my alternate route if I had not taken the ferry. How far I would ride it south when leaving Alaska was in question.

I came through the small town of Slana. An Alaskan Native village centered initially around mining. The federal government offered homestead options for people to settle here. It never took off, the highest point of employment generated a population of sixty people. Now the town was centered around the Slana Roadhouse, on the National Register of Historic Places. I found a trading post with picnic tables and got a cold drink, a bag of nuts and watched Indian children play in a grassy yard while noticing the smoke had dissipated to improve the visibility of the Alaskan Range.

Just up the road was an overlook to the vast openness where two trucks pulling campers were parked. Black spruce lined the edge of muddy waters in natural patterns of perfection, the brush thick with willow saplings and compliments of fireweed, aka, *Epilobium*, great willowherb or wickup; a purplish, mauve-colored perennial as ubiquitous as the black spruce. The plant grew in thick patches up to five feet high, spotting the landscape with an unusual hue. I was told it got its name because it grew abundantly in burned areas.

A series of historical plaques at the overlook detailed "Allen's Incredible Journey." A West Point graduate and Army lieutenant, Henry T. Allen was commissioned in 1885 to explore the Copper River area of Alaska. His exploration took five months and covered 1,500 miles and was compared to the Lewis and Clark Expedition. Looking out at the vast and open land I could not imagine where you would start with the brush so thick, offering neither path or trail.

Colored renderings of Allen and his men inspired me to do more research. Allen abandoned his exploration because one of his men had scurvy. I was impressed that he chose the welfare of one of his men over the accolades of continuing. He and his men suffered from malnutrition, frostbite, and exhaustion. They were true heroes.

Turning to Brother, the doors on both campers opened simultaneously as two elderly couples stepped out as if the act was choreographed. They appeared stressed, one of the ladies asking in a quivering voice, "are there a lot of bumps from where you came?" I shook my head and said, "none that concerned me." I passed areas that seemed to undulate with the roll of the land and a few bumps from poor patches but was of little concern to me on the bike. I had to think they were experiencing the knuckling of their trailer hitch with the long span of the wheelbase. Both couples seemed reluctant to continue.

I entered the confusing town of Glennallen; a scrambled collection of stores, gas stations, and a visitor's center. As with most Alaskan towns, there was no town center. The center was where the Glenn Highway met the Richardson Highway. The Glenn Highway was named after Captain Edwin Glenn who led an expedition in 1898 for the US Army.

At the visitor's center, I gathered a few travel guides then questioned a volunteer to make sure I knew which road was the Richardson. I walked over to a gas station for a cold to drink. Sitting against the cinderblock building I recognized a face from the bike rally. It was an Army vet from New York who was knocking out some serious miles — six to eight hundred a day. He was using vacation time on his Suzuki V-Strom adventure bike. He lit up with a smile when he saw me, and I asked: "How was the Dalton?" "Piece a cake," he said with a grin. From New York, he made it to the Arctic Circle and now was heading back. His face was red in areas his helmet didn't cover, just like mine. We talked for a minute, and then he was up and gone. His report on the Dalton was good news—and inspiring.

Valdez was discovered by the Spanish in 1790 and named after a Spanish naval officer, not present at the discovery. In 1898 the town began to flourish as a port. Before that, many came following rumors of gold, said to be in surrounding glacier fields. Most ended up frozen, crazy, sick with scurvy, and no more prosperous than when they arrived. Many during the gold rush years tried to get rich, but few did. I admired the entrepreneurs who sold shovels, tents, boots, and durable clothing choosing to earn a living over foolish attempts to become wealthy.

The port town of Valdez supplied much of southern Alaska with goods. Following the completion of the Richardson Highway in the late eighteen hundreds, the town thrived due to the connection to Fairbanks. Valdez has had its troubles. In 1964, the Good Friday earthquake shook the town badly, much of the shoreline slipping into Prince Edward Sound. Thirty-two people were swept away while unloading cargo and never recovered. Then in1989 there was the Exxon Valdez oil spill, which the town is best known for. The tanker Valdez was loaded with oil piped from Prudhoe Bay by way of an eight hundred mile pipeline and was ready to head for Long Beach, California. In the early seventies, the pipeline was a thing of urgency, a United States answer to Saudi Arabia's oil embargo.

The oil spill took place twenty-five miles from the terminal, running aground at Bligh Reef. It spilled an estimated thirty-eight million gallons of crude oil into the pristine waters of the gorgeous sound. At the time, it was the largest man-made disaster in history. It dramatically devastated marine life, covering 1,300 miles of Alaskan shoreline.

Getting close to Valdez, I saw snow-capped mountains of Thompson's Pass and the closer I got, the more dramatic the scenery became. High mountainsides appearing to be covered with moss that I realized was thick growing carpet-like black spruce. I slowed the bike to savor the experience. At one point I counted eight waterfalls at high altitude spilling long, perfect walls. I stopped roadside to one waterfall named Bridal Veil Falls, appropriately named because of the misty, thin, lacy transparency. The sun refracted through mist created from water splashing to project prismatic rainbows along the towering drop. Nearing Valdez, I was sorry the ride was over. Alden, my inspirational friend from the ferry, was correct. Thompson's Pass would be nothing I would ever forget.

I was as awestruck riding into Valdez as I was riding through Thompson's Pass. It was a fishing village on the Prince Edward Sound, surrounded by snow-covered mountains. From Valdez, I would take the ferry to Whittier for access to the Kenai Peninsula. I rode through the town to check motel options intending to stay several days. Valdez was unlike any place I had seen since leaving Virginia.

I rode back to a campground I passed entering the town with the idea of pitching a tent but saw a row of towable log cabins on wheels. I inquired, then rented one for three nights. The units were so small, once unloaded I had to be strategic with the arrangement of my gear and luggage to have a path from the bed to the bathroom. Standing in the shower was a challenge.

The wharf area was filled with boats, both commercial and recreational and a waterfront with restaurants and pubs. I was looking for fresh halibut—the specialty fish of Alaska. I chose a restaurant with views of the sound. I ordered a draft and read the menu, shocked to see a halibut sandwich was twenty-two dollars. Sitting close to a couple, it was impossible not to converse. The woman was younger than me by twenty years with a husband twenty years older than me. She was obnoxiously boisterous, creating an alcohol high, inspired by a celebratory vacation mood. Her husband had a "Let her do what she wants" look, relaxed, like parents with screaming kids who no longer hear their noise. She asked me questions and like so many interrupted when I began to talk. Defensively, I chose to listen, sip beer, and nod. The bartender delivered my expensive sandwich a middle-aged man took the seat between the older man and me and his loud wife. Before his butt hit the chair, he began a conversation that made me aware that he and the woman were "two peas in a pod," equally as loud, equally as wound up and he referred to her as "sister." Their voices escalated as they discussed Donald Trump. At one point I foolishly muscled my way into their conversation only to regret it. They were not conversing, or debating—it was verbal mud wrestling. I paid for my expensive sandwich and got out the door.

I woke the next morning in my tiny cabin on wheels to people talking. I found my path to the door and stepped out on the porch in my underwear to see two guys checking out my bike. I threw on pants and boots and walked down to make introductions, then discussed why they were in Valdez once I saw their adventure bikes parked at the next cabin. One guy was pretty banged up saying he had three broken ribs having rolled his motorcycle on the Denali road. He explained how he accelerated on a gravel curve, hit a soft shoulder, the front wheel bit, and the bike rolled. I asked about the pain, and he jokingly said: "hurts when I breathe." They were from Illinois, and I felt for the guy with the busted ribs, knowing how painful riding those bumpy Alaskan would be.

HIs friend was looking my bike over like a surgeon. Standing from a kneeling position, he said: "You've got a leak in this front seal." I walked over to see oil was seeping down my right strut. I was mad at myself knowing I had shock covers to protect the seals stowed in a pannier and had never installed them. The leak was reaching my brake disc to cause a slow stop. I was frustrated, but knew things would occur and rising to the occasion was a part of the adventure.

I had little optimism that I would find a bike shop in Valdez. Plus, I was hesitant to turn Brother over to just anyone. I found one mechanic who worked on boat motors who said there was nowhere between Valdez and Anchorage to perform the work. Online, I found a shop in Anchorage, called and was told to bring the bike in and they would take care of me.

I spent my remaining time in Valdez enjoying the town and the fantastic scenery. Glaciers between mountains were spread out smooth, covering extensive acreage tucked in the bosoms of flanking peaks. The views inspired my imagination to consider what it would be like to stand on one of the lofty glacier fields and look down at where I stood.

I walked past a Mexican restaurant several times and finally surrendered. In the Lower Forty-Eight, Mexican restaurants were ubiquitous and seemed to exist on every corner. Not true in Alaska. Reading the menu, I saw the price of a taco was on the same scale as halibut sandwich.

The next morning there was a knock at my door. I opened to see the owner of the campground inviting me to a fish fry. That evening a crowd of people enjoyed a summer evening and fresh grilled halibut, for a great last night in Valdez.

Following the heavy meal, I walked along the wharf, ending up in a dive bar that looked to hold some Valdez history. Inside it was only the bartender, a forty-something blonde who seemed bored and ready for company. She asked why I was in Valdez, so I shared my story. She wondered how long I intended to live this way as if I had a termination date for my new lifestyle. I explained my plan to continue as long as it was good for me. She questioned if I regretted the divestment of all my belongings, so I explained how I enjoyed my life as a minimalist. What I shared seemed to make her uncomfortable, and she seemed to not like the idea of not having a home. Her final question was, "Are you sorry you did it?" A telltale question of how tight she held her life, possessions, and family. Getting rid of earthly belongings was the tipping point for many to prevent them from ever making a move towards freedom—knowing it was something they would regret. Stepping off the edge, as I did, is not for everyone, and I knew that. I could only say that it was right for me.

26

STAGE XXIII: Miles 12,322-12,770

Ferry to Whittier - Tunnel of Horrors
Brown Bear - Motorcycle Shop
Seward and Hope

You are enough, you have nothing to prove."

—*Maya Angelou*

I RODE AWAY from my tiny log cabin on wheels in Valdez and headed to the ferry terminal for Whittier. There, a guy parked next to me, riding a Suzuki V-Strom that I saw at the bike rally. Striking up a conversation, we hung out for the three-hour crossing of Prince Edward Sound. I was looking forward to what I heard would be great views of surrounding glaciers.

We ratcheted our bikes down then headed up to the cafeteria. The fellow on the V-Strom was touring Alaska while returning to his home in British Columbia. Like me, he was in his early sixties.

Getting coffee, we took a seat on a life jacket locker at the starboard deck. Somehow our conversation turned to his misfortunes with an ex-wife and his years of struggle through a painful divorce. His confessions lured participation making me feel like Dr. Phil. I absorbed the minutia of what had occurred between him, his ex, and his daughter and all I could say was "I'm Sorry." He was a "good Joe," possibly a giver that found a taker resulting in his state of anguish. But he was making me feel selfish. I just wanted to enjoy the glaciers, the snow-capped mountains, and the ride across Prince Edward Sound. It was a cold shot, but I finally told him that he needed to turn the page and move on; otherwise, he was allowing his ex to own him. Then I shared the words of the Wolfman—"Don't look back, it's a wilderness of horrors." After that, we stared silently at floating ice chunks from glacier calving along the sound.

From the Port of Valdez, the ferry left the dock heading southwest through the Valdez Arm; an inlet to Prince Edward Sound. The Columbia Glacier was in view after departure. The glacier twists its way through the Chugach Mountains until meeting the Prince Edward Sound and was the fastest moving in the world according to scientists who followed its movement using satellite photos.

The ferry ride was mesmerizing, with a unique littoral scenery of snow covered mountains, at heights up to 15,000 feet. While docking I asked my friend if he knew about the long tunnel we would go through to get out of Whittier. I read that riding through the tunnel was fun, but to me, it did not sound fun. In fact—it sounded stressful, dangerous, and life-risking. I recall reading about the tunnel and shaking my head. On a motorcycle, tunnels had always been an issue, giving me a sensation of disorientation and vertigo, requiring total concentration from the entrance to the exit. For that reason, I chose to shelve the idea of the Whittier tunnel until I had to deal with it. And now, here it was—directly in front of me.

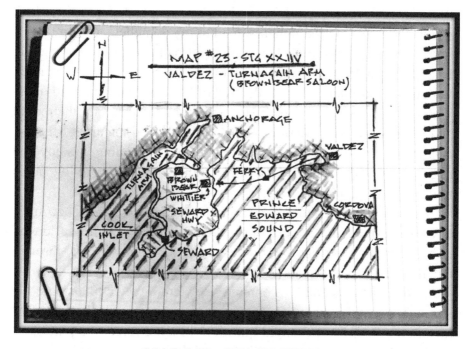

MAP # 23 - STAGE XXIIV
Valdez, AK - Turnagain Arm (Brown Bear Saloon)

The Whittier Tunnel was the second longest tunnel in North American. Its actual name, the Anton Anderson Memorial Tunnel passed through Maynard Mountain at 13,300 feet. It was carved out in three hundred and six days by an Army construction group at the beginning of WWII. The full length is over two and a half miles.

The town of Whittier was an odd place with a Cold War Russian look, due to unpainted cement complexes that covered hillsides. Now condominiums, they were built by the US government for civil servants with Whittier being the port of entry for US soldiers heading into Alaska.

We rode to the entrance of the tunnel with a sign that read "2 1/2 MILES." Tunnel personnel directed motorcycles in a group as we were informed we would go last. One biker asked why. The attendant said,

"Because motorcyclist go down and we can't depend on people in RVs to stop for them." The comment added to my apprehensive fear.

The tunnel was single lane with a railroad track down the middle, the track used for trains that transported cargo at night. The surface was crowned asphalt with a reflective oily sheen, that appeared questionable. The tracks were recessed with gaps to each side that could eat or trip a tire. The interior displayed the rugged manner of the excavation by explosives and jackhammers, and the ceiling was covered with fencing wire to catch rock chunks if they broke free. Yellow bulbs mounted overhead, in wire cages provided very little light.

The Whittier Tunnel was my most dangerous experience since leaving Virginia. I met serious motorcyclist that traveled the world who agreed with how terrible it was. We would talk about the ride through and awkwardly laughed about the horrific experience.

Once the cars and RVs entered, we were directed to a single file entrance, one biker shouting "Can we take pictures?" The attendant gave him a look for the stupid question. I maneuvered to a place so I would be last then stared at the dark, straight, long hole while centered between the tracks to enter the abyss. My only objective—the other side.

On gravel roads, I could follow tire tracks for miles to ride a flattened road surface. I was confused as to why I had such a fear of the single lane. Maybe it was the darkness, or the oily surface or the potential calamity if I crossed a track to twist the bike out of control and throw me against the rugged tunnel interior. Once I began, I thought that it would be easier than I imagined. It was not. I remained in first gear and stared far away waiting to see that light at the end of the tunnel.

At about ten miles an hour, I kept steady on the throttle and thought about shifting to second—but never did. I remained in a mummified position with a level of concentration similar to holding my breath. They said that at twenty-five miles an hour you would be through in six minutes. I choose a steady seventeen miles an hour, never shifting out of first gear. I thought of all the miles I had traveled using cruise control at sixty-five, my hands-free to stretch or rest across my tank bag, never having a problem. In the dark, hellish tunnel, with the narrow breadth between two rails, it was a different thing. The small spot of light was growing while I sweated every second to make it through, wondering who in the hell would think this was fun. When I saw the mouth of the tunnel, I shifted into second to put the short, "season in hell" behind me.

I was now on the Portage Glacier Highway, named for the town of Portage which no longer existed. It was located at the tip of what is called the Turnagain Arm, south of Cook Inlet. Portage was destroyed in the 1964 Good Friday Earthquake, the entire town sinking six feet and flooding. The highway delivered me to the Seward Highway, extending north to south between Anchorage and the Kenai Peninsula—the only road.

Population growth in the two locations caused the road to be thick with traffic. The Kenai Peninsula was a highlighted destination and would be a base to get to Anchorage and repair my front seal. The Seward Highway connected Anchorage to the town of Seward at Resurrection Bay, all the way south. Along the Turnagain, I could see why so many raved about the area. Another place of extreme beauty—vast, and surrounded with high mountains. The first town I passed heading north was Girdwood, where the brown bear got up to 1,800 pounds.

On the Seward Highway, along the Turnagain Arm, I turned in at a two-story log cabin called the Brown Bear Saloon. On the roof, big red letters read "MOTEL." Out front was an earthy young girl smoking a cigarette. She gave me a gracious smile when I asked if a room was available while still sitting on Brother. "Sure is," she said then walked inside. I followed her asking for a beer and how far it was to Anchorage. "About forty minutes," she said while placing a cold bottle of Coors on the wooden bar. The saloon was dark, moody, and cozy with a character that said Alaska. Room prices were cheap and exactly what I wanted; a bed, a toilet, a sink, and a shower. I paid for two nights, getting a room over the saloon with live music that would dictate my bedtime.

The Turnagain Arm is a vast inlet and one of two "Arms" as they are called. The second, the Knik Arm. Both were supplied by Cook Inlet, located above Anchorage. The Knik Arm was named after the

Knik Glacier at the Port of Anchorage. The Turnagain Arm was named by William Bligh, aka Captain Bligh of the HMS Bounty. Bligh was Captain Cook's sailing master and instructed to go up the Knik Arm to look for a continuous passage with no luck. He was then instructed to investigate the second arm. He did, to find it also terminated, so they turned around, thus the name Turnagain.

The body of water possesses one of the most extreme tidal changes in North America, similar to the Bay of Fundy in Nova Scotia. Tidal changes so extreme they produce a tidal bore; a wave up to six feet high.

I unload Brother, then was back in the saloon for a bratwurst sandwich while a band from Anchorage set up for the nightly gig. I felt like I had hit the Motherlode—cheap room, near Anchorage, across from the Turnagain Arm, and live music. Finishing what I called dinner and walked across the Seward. It was late in the evening and still daylight. I had to remind myself how late it got dark.

I found a deck to view the Turnagain with views to mountains on the opposite side. The tide was out with murky grayish water returning in slivering channels across mud flats. The shoreline was littered with huge rocks colored with earth tones of lichen. I was transfixed by the magnificent view while being grateful I survived the tunnel.

Back at the Brown Bear, the band had started. The saloon was a frontier classic with dollar bills tacked to the ceiling with the dank feel of an old roadhouse. It was nestled in a wooded area, private and cozy like a retreat. Deeper in the woods were rentable cabins, and the grounds were littered with discarded vehicles creating the atmosphere of a TV horror movie. The saloon was a hub for talent coming south from Anchorage and touring musicians looping through the state. The Bear, as I began to call it, was also a night spot between Anchorage and Seward.

In the morning I arrived at the motorcycle shop in Anchorage before it opened, so I found a cafe for breakfast. A robust motherly waitress with a "large and in-charge" attitude poured me coffee and questioned what I was doing, once seeing my open map. Giving her a quick synopsis of my new life she responded with a judgmental, "Hmmpt" then swaggered off. I believe she thought I was a vagrant, a bum, or a hobo and in her mind I was irresponsible. For a second I considered engaging her to try and turn her opinion and let her know that I had paid my dues to get where I was. Then I woke to the fact that her opinion about me just did not matter.

At the motorcycle shop, I parked among several motorcycles, while seeing a line to the maintenance desk. It gave me concern. I found the guy I spoke with while in Valdez, once noticing his name tag. He was a salesman, and I soon found out the facility was new, and there were territorial issues, specifically between the sales department and the maintenance department and I would be caught in the middle. The sales staff overcommitted the shop which created a grudge. Once getting my turn at the desk, a disgruntled young man told me I should have called the maintenance desk before bringing my bike in. I had stepped into a house divided.

I asked if they could do the work. The young man, who was in charge of the maintenance department, look down to avoid eye contact and said: "We'll see if we can fit you in today." I explained that I was living off the bike and got a cold blank stare. I was just another biker in the Last Frontier—one of many. In the Lower Forty-Eight, they would push bikes out of the way to repair your bike if you were on the road. It was an unspoken rule in shops. Not the case in Alaska, with so many bikers from the US, Canada, and Europe. Tour groups had arrangements with bike shops to get in and out fast with the promise of continued business.

I sat at a table in their waiting area on the sales floor. Being careful not to get abrupt with the shop manager I knew my best approach to get Brother repaired was to maintain face and checked progress in a passive-aggressive manner. It was a long, frustrating day and four o'clock before Brother was moved into the shop. I asked the manager if it would be ready before the shop closed to get a nebulous shrug,. I moped back to the waiting area as their hostage and changed my approach from a diplomat to a beggar.

Just before seven Brother was ready—the last bike out. Ready to roll, the manager put a hand on my shoulder and said: "Make sure you call me first, next time." I guess I was made an example of or a fulcrum for the shop to gain the advantage over the sales staff. Whatever! I was just ready for more Alaska.

On the Seward Highway, I was feeling free, following my day of confinement in the sterile, cold, synthetic atmosphere of the new shop. I preferred small, dank shops with history, the smell of oil, with a front counter in disarray of unorganized paperwork and parts. A shop where you could walk the floor among bikes and parts, fenders, and frames, and posters of girls in bikinis.

Back at the Bear, I felt like I was home. The girl with the friendly smile slid me a beer and asked about my day. I said it was good instead of boring her with the frustrating details. Tell someone about a bad time and you to live it again. I chose to think about my plan for touring the Kenai Peninsula having spent my day in the shop creating my own map. I had my room for two more nights and planned to explore the east side of the peninsula on a day trip.

Morning came, and I loaded Brother light for my ride directly south to the town of Seward at the end of the Seward Highway. The sky was heavy gray, and the air was moist. Not the weather I wanted, but I was antsy for the road and wanted to see more of the peninsula.

In Girdwood, I stopped for gas and coffee while watching a steady drizzle wet the parking lot. The locals were used to rain, so I adopted their mentality, choosing not to let it stop me. Standing at the gas pump, I looked at the miserable weather, wet road, thick mist, fog, and clouds as they drifted before the surrounding mountains. It was inviting and set a mysterious and surreal mood. I had Gore-Tex liners in both my pants and my coat which was the best I could do. It wasn't cold. In fact, it was a little balmy but knew that on the speeding bike I would be comfortable. Keeping my visor clear to see moose was my greater concern.

Having never seriously considered a trip to Alaska I was now glad that I saved the incredible state for my kick-off to retirement. There was no way I would have seen it the way I saw it on Brother. My thoughts about Alaska had always been in vague terms; Anchorage, Fairbanks, Nome, Skagway, and Homer and nothing specific about those places. Now the state was a newfound interest, and I was anxious to see as much as possible. Looking at maps of paved and unpaved roads I was making my plan to ride them, now thinking much harder about crossing the Arctic Circle.

The Chugach National Forest and the Kenai National Forest run through the Kenai Peninsula with icefields and glaciers. The name Kenai is said to come from the name Kenayskaya, Russian for Cook Inlet, a name that sounded Hawaiian to me. The country continued to be vast, open, with rich forest—a naturalist dream. The weather was messy, but I knew to come to Alaska in the summer it would be. For two hours down the straight road, I viewed big lakes from steep mountain climbs, through wet, foggy air. Black spruce continued to grow thick down sloping mountainsides, like a landscape painting by Bob Ross on his TV show *The Joy of Painting*. It was almost too perfect.

The town of Seward dates back to the late 1700s, settled first by Russian fur traders from the success of a fur trading post along Resurrection Bay. For thousands of years prior, the area had been the home of the Athabaskan and Alutiiq native groups. The town was named after William Seward in 1867, the Secretary of State under Abraham Lincoln and Andrew Johnson. Seward fought for the purchase of Alaska, bought in 1867 from the Russian Empire for $7.2 million; roughly two cents per acre. It was not until 1959 that it became the forty-ninth state—the largest state in America. The town is mile zero for the famed Iditarod, which mimicked the haul from the port city to the Anchorage, one hundred and fifty miles away. The initial purpose was to deliver cargo as quickly as possible.

In 1939, the Slattery Report was officially titled "The Problem of Alaskan Development;" a proposal produced by the Department of the Interior addressing the slow growth of the frontier. The US Government was offering options to entice movement and homesteading. Following WWII the government saw an opportunity with Jewish refugees escaping Nazi Germany, as a way to populate the state. Towns that endorsed the proposal to welcome the refugees were Skagway, Petersburg, and Seward. Non-supporting towns feared that Jewish settlements would institute socialism and Jewish immigrants did not favor the plan either, afraid the message would deliver the wrong impression with Jews taking over parts of the US. I had to wonder if the excuse was an elegant turndown to the Interior Department's offer, not wanting to be pushed so far away and into the uncivilized wilderness.

My entire ride to Seward was through heavy mist while passing the Harding Icefields in the Kenai Fjords National Park, where the Exit Glacier was located. In Seward, Resurrection Bay was socked in with fog. I parked Brother when I spotted a frontier saloon from the 1800s. Inside I got a seat at the old bar and coffee from the bartender. Jack White was playing loudly on the stereo, so we struck up a conversation about the incredible guitar licks from the mutually respected artist. The place was cozy and dry with the door open to a drizzling gray. Inside, the long wood bar had an equally long wood framed mounted mirror. Memorabilia plastered the walls, and dollar bills were pinned to the ceiling. After two cups of coffee and a brief conversation with locals I made my way back to the road. Cruising the streets of Seward my imagination went to a time when wooden ships were lining the docks and cargo loaded in sleds with deep snow and tracks for men mushing dogs to interior Alaska. It was a dangerous time filled with frontier people who chose to embrace a rugged life of survival.

Heading back, I took the turn for the Exit Glacier at the Harding Icefield, named after President William Harding. The drizzle had subsided, so I parked and walked through the visitor's center, then down a walking path beside the empty river bed of the receding glacier. Exit Glacier was named so because it was the route used to exit the Hardy Icefield. Walking the trail, there were stops with decks for viewing, each with a mounted sign of the year the glacier extended to that particular location of the empty river bed with the glacier in distant view. It was clever how the signs forced you to consider the recession of the glacier along with the controversial subject of climate change. Standing at one deck, I viewed the muddy river at a sign that read "1924." At the next overlook, 1939, then 1953—the year I was born. The year gave me a personal association—a reference point. It made me wonder if there was a concern for the receding glacier then having no idea how long the concept of global warming went back.

President Obama made a visit to the Exit Glacier out of concern for the continual recession of glaciers in Alaska, his tour, just a few weeks before mine. He considered global warming one of the major concerns in the country, and I confess, I questioned the depth of the matter. Rocks erode, beaches recede, and glaciers melt—how much can we control. Is it our extended lifetime? Or our excessive population? I understood the need to reduce the carbon footprint but questioned how much it would change the impact of global warming that was in motion. I wondered how much was the result of evolutionary and periodic trends. Trends to cause glaciers to melt.

My ride back was viewing the sun lighting layers of gray clouds with the air warming. I was relaxed as the ride, once again, passed back through the rugged forest along clean glassy lakes. The change in the weather was giving me a feeling of euphoria. It was Saturday, and back at the Bear, they were hosting a music festival, which I was in no mood for. I had read about the mining town of Hope, seventeen miles off the Seward Highway, on Resurrection Creek. The town was small with a population of fewer than two hundred people. The ride there was charming and picturesque—a sweet rolling gift of a ride. Someone told me the seafood chowder in the cafe was worth the trip so with a heavy appetite I was hoping for an early dinner.

Pulling into town, I could see the poorly brush painted letters, "CAFE," big and bold on a steep brown rusted roof of what looked to be an old shack. The place was jumping, and I thought it ironic that while I was trying to avoid the ruckus of the Brown Bear, here I was—at a party with live music. A band was playing with an overflow from the front door with a side deck where people stood, and young country girls danced with each in summer dresses and cowboy hats. I paid a small cover charge and stood in a long line at the bar for a beer. An undermanned staff worked hard, appearing overwhelmed. With a draft, I went back out to the porch to enjoy the music and stare at the old mining town where people lived a simple life.

Back at the Bear, I had dodged the big party but heard there would be a live band that night. I had my fill of entertainment in Hope, plus a good day on the bike to Seward and back. I canceled my stay for the next night with plans to leave in the morning to explore the west side of the Kenai Peninsula. That night I spent time reading internet comments from those who had taken on the Dalton Highway while listening to a band play below me in the saloon. I was weighing my decision.

27

STAGE XXIV: Miles 12,770 - 12,968

Aging and Ageless - Portal Glacier
Close Call to Calamity - Backing Out of Kenai
Cruciform - Homer

"Live before you die."

—*Chris McCandless*

I WOKE UP around eight in my simple room at the Bear. Opening the shades, I saw the Turnagain Arm under low-hanging black clouds, wispy fog, while raindrops hit the second story deck. It was disappointing with my strong intentions to leave. I washed my face, got in my gear, gathered and packed my luggage, and tossed it down near Brother.

Climbing on the loaded bike and putting on clear glasses, I reviewed the expectations of my day. Because of the rain, I wondered where I would be that night with my vague plan to cross the peninsula. First, I wanted to see Portal Glacier, following a breakfast stop in Girdwood.

Sipping coffee in the bakery, an elderly couple came in and sat close by. Soon after, another couple of similar age walked in and began talking to the sitting couple with an unspoken camaraderie because both had RVs parked outside. My observation of the couples was in contrast and how different they were in manner and conduct. I relaxed to enjoy their interaction like a movie.

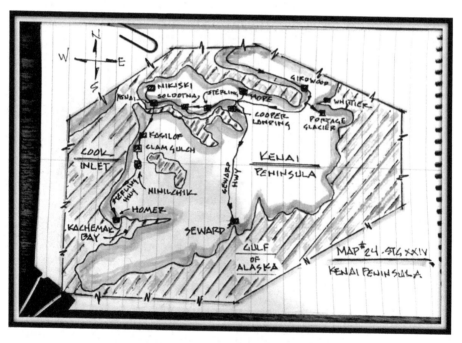

MAP # 24 - STAGE XXIV
Kenai Peninsula, AK

The seated couple was elegant and poised, well dressed, and of quiet demeanor. My impression was they retired and were making good on a long time promise to travel. At the same time, I perceived a discomfort in their makeshift life on the road while missing their domestic life. Were the "Golden Years" what they were cracked up to be? From what I saw the two were ready to head back to the routine of a life they trusted.

The couple who walked in was the polar opposite; gregarious, casual, carefree, and extroverted. The man entered and was on fire. He was ready to talk and ready for his day and showed little consideration to the seated couple easing into their day. The standing man began a conversation while standing over the seated gentleman, questioning his route to Girdwood. The man started a response as the standing man blurted the direction he traveled, holding a pointed finger in the air to draw an invisible map. I was being voyeuristic and omniscient with my face to the fishbowl and trying not be nosey.

The seated gentleman nodded while his wife appeared uncomfortable with the boisterous man standing above them. He tipped over their routine to awaken at their own pace. The standing man's wife held a constant smile and begin a statement only to have her husband take her subject and speak on her behalf. She was used to it, you could tell. The seated couple had the wheels turning with plans to escape.

For no apparent reason, the man standing began to tell the sitting couple about a dance contest they entered in Anchorage. He pulled his lady up to demonstrate dance moves. Her cheeks flushed as she straightened her leisure outfit while going into position like a trained terrier. Then they went into a waltz while sharing proud smiles to the seated couple. Then, in a snap, they two energetically displayed a jitterbug, beaming with brighter smiles to the two watching uncomfortably. I felt awkward for the seated couple with their insincere "paper cutout" smiles. Out of desperation the couple sitting stood, placed their coffee cups in the trash, gave a pleasant nod, and with quick steps in unison reached the security of their RV. I followed out the door too, sure the man would be seeking a new audience.

Climbing onto Brother I knew what I just witnessed in the bakery was a social statement. I had observed how two men were living their life that was probably a good indicator of how each man may die. One man may fade away in a reading chair wearing a cardigan while the other may explode with a massive heart attack while dancing in a Mexican resort. And, I saw no right or wrong in either.

The rain stopped, but not for long, with skies overcast and the air getting wet. Portal Glacier was ten miles away, and soon after taking off, I was struggling in wind-driven rain. At the visitor's center, I was soaked, a park ranger greeted me with "Little wet out there?" I smiled and asked if she knew the forecast being told that further west would be better, then suggested I watch the half-hour film on the glacier. So I took her advice for warmth and comfort. Coming out I could view Portal Glacier through a large glass window through hard rain and draping fog. I reminded myself that it was what I signed up for while buttoning my coat to take out.

On Brother, the hard rain was sideways in a steady wind. I was looking for the Sterling Highway to cross the peninsula west along Cooper's Landing. The highway began at Tern Lake, in the direction of the town of Soldotna where the road climbed a steep hill seeming endless with a surface of ground pavement chunks and the road prepared for paving. Jagged lines from a milling wheel left rough asphalt scattered and loose, coarse, and bumpy and the four-lane highway no longer marked with painted lines, resulting in an "every man for himself" mentality. The wind whistled through my half opened visor, too wet to see through. Being peppered by big raindrops made a noisy distraction while I stared through a narrow gap between the top of my glasses and the bottom of the plexiglass helmet shield—hanging onto what little view I had. I was looking for a place in the far right lane—the slow lane near the shoulder. Lanes were unmarked and nebulous in the worst possible scenario: hard rain, rough road, no visibility, while searching for my place among heavy, fast-moving traffic. I slowed down and knew that doing so was dangerous. The speed limit was, and I sensed an impatience from surrounding vehicles who wanted to go seventy while I struggled to maintain fifty with a feeling of urgency to get out of their way. I began to drift to the furthest place in the outside lane and possibly appeared to be pulling off on the shoulder. Struggling to battle the confusion I heard a truck accelerate behind me as it dropped into a lower gear to gain torque for the steep climb. From my side mirror, I saw the approaching vehicle and found the narrow shoulder to get out of the way, trying my best to stay out of the rough. Seeing the truck's tailgate in my peripheral glance I had a moment of relaxation, but then was immediately shocked to feel the passing of a large olive drab military boat in tow. The craft, wider than the truck, passed closer, causing me to prepare to be hit and pushed off the road. I held Brother firm with a simple objective—to remain upright. While these thoughts reeled through my head, the boat passed as I saw the transom gaining distance up the hill.

I was angry. A part of me that wanted to twist the throttle and flag the guy over. My wiser self chose to calm, gather, and appreciate my fortune of having had no misfortune.

The road construction ended, as did the rain. I was exhausted from the conditions and the close call, shaky, and aggravated at someone who could be so careless and aggressive to a motorcyclist in such weather.

The road knuckled south before Kenai Lake, then due west following the beautiful Kenai River. The sun felt good with the air drying my jacket and pants. Crossing a bridge, I saw a long row of fly fishermen aligned in emerald green, fast flowing water. They were throwing outlines in a disorganized rhythm—an eye-catching sight. Across the bridge, the river was to my left with black spruce covering steep mountains to my right. The small town of Cooper's Landing was sparsely populated, mostly cabins, fishing guides, canoe rentals, a grocery store, and a few motels, one had a restaurant, and a gas pump tucked in seclusion. I stopped for coffee to ponder the incident where I thought I was going to lose my life.

Following an hour of relaxation, I topped off my tank and continued west to the town of Kenai. The sky continued to clear, the ride a beautiful display of nature. I saw what you think of when you think of

Alaska—rough, wild, with a dreamlike perfection. How far I had come since Virginia and my plans for the Arctic Circle continued to gel.

It was after five when I arrived in Kenai, a town like many others in Alaska; spread out and no center. I found a high priced motel. In asking why so high, the owner just said, offshore drilling. In no mood to shop for a better rate, I surrendered to get a bed. Given the key, I rode to the back of the motel, shocked to see the parked truck and boat from my near calamity. My chest tightened in apprehension that I would encounter the driver, wondering how I would react. Parking Brother, I gave myself counsel to ease off any idea of confrontation.

Even if there had been no incident, I would have looked the craft over. I knew the boat from my previous life—my career. It was an Army Pusher Tug, used to arrange floating causeways to erect temporary bridges to support the mobility of troops. At the bow and the transom were stenciled black serial numbers with the military name; BOAT BRIDGE ERECT. It was all too odd, knowing the boat that almost killed me was a boat I knew. A spirit from my past, tapping on my shoulder.

Into my expensive, yet simple room, I took a shower, grabbed something to read and went to the restaurant. While reading a menu, a man walked in to begin a loud conversation with the bartender causing everyone to pay attention. He announced how he had been to Anchorage, bought a boat at a government auction and was towing it home. It was the driver, and I looked up to take note of who he was, immediately seeing he displayed a personality of someone who would drive uncaring and aggressive. The thought was judgmental but my honest assessment of the man. I was relaxed now with no desire for confrontation and open to the possibility that I may have wandered off the road to give the impression I was choosing to ride the narrow shoulder. With the fear behind me, I was granted the benefit of the doubt. Knowing for sure he was as confused and disoriented as I was in the bad weather.

I finished my meal and went for a brisk walk. Returning to my room, I passed the boat owner smoking a cigarette in the parking lot. He nodded with an expression of wanting to talk, so I decided to take the day full circle. "Your boat?" I asked. "Yea," he said, "just bought it at an auction in Anchorage." Then I shared my acquaintance with the craft. He was shocked, then told me he bought it for the trailer with plans to sell the boat for scrap. Then I told him "You know, you scared the hell out of me today passing me on the Sterling." He glanced at my bike and said "My God, was that you? I didn't know what you were doing and thought you were pulling off the road to stop. Passing, I noticed how close you were in my side view." Then he told me how he felt relief once seeing the transom had passed. That was when I relaxed too, I told him. "It was no one's fault," I said, then he concluded "sorry man, glad we got through it." We shook hands and said goodnight, and I felt it a rare case where I actually found closure—closure such a rare thing. Much of life is just moving on with no resolve.

It was one of those rare nights where sleep was elusive, with no known correlation to a reason why. Time passed, and I struggled, trying to sleep, but sleep was impossible. Night passed, and finally, I fell asleep, from around seven—until nine. I was exhausted, but my mind was set on leaving.

I made it to breakfast feeling buzzed and sleep deprived. In my numbed daze I began to change into my gear. Putting on a boot, I twisted to feel a sharp pain above my right hip—a pain I knew did not bode well for my next few days. I stood in hopes to stretch in a reversed direction, barely making it to a standing position with my lower back in spasm. I walked to the front desk in a bent posture and paid for another expensive night.

The next morning, no matter how bad my back was, I was leaving the town of Kenai. My intent was to camp on Homer Spit located along Kachemak Bay. On the way, there was a Russian Orthodox church I planned to visit. I did not find Kenai interesting, and it reminded me of Tok. Kenai was a Tanian word and meant flat area for trees. Once occupied by the Kachemak people dating back to 1,000 BCE, the town was settled in 1786 by Europeans in the fur trade.

It was a hundred miles to Homer, through numerous small towns. The first, Kasilof, a Russian fishing village from the late 1700s. I stopped at a grocery store for a cold drink and to stretch my aching back. The store was an "all in one" trading post with everything from eggs to shotguns. The next little town was Clam Gulch, no more than a stop for clam digging in summer months. The west side of the Kenai Peninsula was not as magnificent as the east, flat to rolling, plentiful with black spruce and moose grazing near the road.

Ninilchik was settled by Russians migrating from Kodiak Island in 1847. They spoke the language of Ninilchik; a mix of Russian and the language of the Athabaskan tribes. Down a dirt road, I found the old Russian Orthodox church located hillside overlooking the small town cliffside to Cook Inlet. Directly across was Lake Clark National Park, accessible only by airplane or foot.

The Church of the Transfiguration of Our Lord was built in 1901, a cruciform building; shaped to form a cross. It was painted bright white, trimmed in forest green, the front facing the inlet. It was closed, so I did not see the interior. Outside white crosses were mounted on gold painted egg shapes characteristic of Russian architecture. A white picket fence surrounded the church and a picturesque cemetery, thick with rich grass and spotted with wildflowers. The six crosses mounted on the church and those in the cemetery were unusual and not like I had ever seen. Each had three transverse members of different lengths. I researched the cross to learn the top, the smallest cross member, represented the plaque for the letters above the head of Jesus; INRI. The second cross down, the longest of the three, was for the outstretched arms of Christ, typical to Christian crosses. The lower cross, the shortest slanted to an angle and was where the feet were mounted; the right foot of Christ higher than the left foot. It served as a message, pointing in opposing directions. The message—choose between heaven or hell.

I wandered the churchyard on the flattened mound near a cliffside that offered an aerial view to the small town of Ninilchik. Houses and barns appeared to have had no planned arrangement in a quaint unorganized manner, fifty yards to the cliff at the inlet. Muddy roads flowed in spiral patterns making the town look like a fold-out picture in a child's book. Looking down at the town and back at the church, I felt a sense of calm for those that lived the simple life. The people remained back in time and denied the modern world. I imagined that there were no

TVs, computers, cell phones or internet, the thought making me aware of how I complicated the simplicity of living.

Continuing to Homer, I passed through the nondescript towns of Harbor Valley and Anchor Point, where Captain Cook lost an anchor. I got to Homer, the largest town since Kenai, and rode to the end; The Spit, a four and a half mile gravel bar between Cook Inlet and Kachemak Bay. Homer had a population of around five thousand and known as the halibut capital of the world. Its nickname was "The End of the Road," and more recently "The Cosmic Hamlet by the Sea." The Spit, was a collection of motels, restaurants, fishing docks, trawlers, coffee shops with funky names, and the Salty Dawg Saloon—famous in the state.

I checked into a campground that was an open, treeless field. My campsite was segregated by logs with a fire pit and a picnic table. I unloaded Brother and was trying to set up my tent in a steady wind that blew from open waters. My struggle with the flapping tent was frustrating, yet comic. A few campsites away was a parked hatchback with two young guys, one playing the harmonica. Both were grudgers in their twenties that I learned were from Seattle. One had dreadlocks and wore narrow blue-tinted hippie glasses and walked over to offer help to erect my tent while sharing travel tales. He and his friend had been camping north of Denali, having hiked the Stampede Trail. "The Stampede Trail?" I asked. One replied, "Yea, the trail Chris McCandless hiked to find the bus he died in." I read the book about McCandless, *Into the Wild* by John Krakauer. McCandless, the young man who hiked into the Alaskan wilderness in 1992 to live a life unencumbered by the pangs of society and the demands of established goals. He was educated and smart, an idealist, original in thought, but unwise with his preparation to enter the wilderness. I found his story sad. Chris was a mix of a troubled soul and a foolish idealist. At the same time, a hero of sorts. He followed his passion at the ultimate cost. I admired his ironclad determination to satisfy his ideal, but I did not respect the thoughtless manner of his preparation. Where his act was extreme, I'm sure mine was also extreme. Both took forethought and effort to step away to pursue a personal ideal. I wondered if Chris considered his attempt an experiment, as I did.

The two from Seattle told me about spending two nights in Bus 142, the bus Chris lived and died in. "His Bible was inside, brought by his mother" one said. And a journal for visiting hikers to sign and the bus interior covered with magic marker comments and quotes, several by McCandless. I asked how it felt, thinking about being inside the bus where such a person died from starvation.

There was little substance in what they shared. I felt it was more of a novelty to brag about with no meaningful spiritual experience. I questioned their lack of emotion and compassion for having spent time inside the bus. I would have considered it a cathedral, and if I had slept there, I am sure it would have been with a sullen mood to give me a cathartic chill about my own mortality. Chris was a unique pioneer and deserved a pause for soul-searching. I considered his short life emblematic of a troubled youth, one who chose to be proactive instead of being bitter and complacent. And for that, he won my favor.

I took a walk around The Spit. Homer was a fishing village and a tourist destination for halibut fishing. Oddly enough, Homer had a long history of coal mining, dating back to the late 1800s and the primary source of income until WWII. It was named after Homer Pennock, who established the town in 1896, beginning a gold mining endeavor and building living quarters for fifty men in preparation. Legend has it he advertised for gold mining, but when none was found he used the available labor for coal mining. Was he a charlatan or a smart businessman who knew how to turn horses mid-stream.

I found a deli restaurant where I ordered sautéed halibut with vegetables and roasted red potatoes. I was planning an evening at the Salty Dawg Saloon. Following dinner I walked to the bay to visit an elaborate memorial for fishermen lost at sea; a bronze statue of a fisherman holding a looped rope surrounded by plaques honoring the dead. Then I succumbed to the famous drinking hole unable to remember where or how I heard about the Salty Dawg, but each time I said something about Homer the response was "The Salty Dawg?"

The Salty Dawg Saloon was a single story, wood shingle structure with white trim and a lighthouse tower with a rotating Fresnel lens. The original structure was built in 1887 when Homer began. The structure was moved to the end of The Spit, following the 1964 Good Friday earthquake. The building has been a post office, a railroad station, a grocery store, and a coal mining office, then in the forties, it became offices for the Standard Oil Company. In 1957, just prior to Alaska becoming the forty-ninth state the building was purchased and opened as the Salty Dawg Saloon. In 1960 state representative, Earl Hillstrand bought the saloon and now stands as a historical landmark.

It was nine o'clock at night when I walked into the saloon while it was still daylight. In a corner, a guy played guitar while singing a Jimmy Buffet song. I saw an enclosed area in the back, isolated with a privacy fence so got a beer and stepped out to a sky slowly closing into some degree of darkness. I sat to think about how far I had come to now be in Homer, Alaska. Nearing fifteen thousand miles since leaving made me wonder when I would choose to stop. After two beers and seeing a bit more darkness I headed back to my tent, zipped everything up and read myself to sleep.

I woke to cloudy skies that would eventually bring light rain. Getting coffee, I sat on my picnic table while going through maps in the quiet morning. Relaxing to the idea of a leisurely day in the comfortable atmosphere of Homer I showered in their rustic facility and changed clothes for a sense of renewal.

For lunch, I walked up The Spit to a Chinese restaurant. My meal arrived as a man, and a woman came in and sat near me, both clad in Harley Davidson leather. I let them settle in before asking where they rode from. The man said New York, by way of the ALCAN, entering Alaska at Beaver Creek. He shook his head in frustration and said, "If I knew it was going to be that way, I would have not come." I asked why. "Rutted, potholed, deep gravel. "It was really bad," he said. I made little response. He looked tired and frustrated, and I could tell that his return trip on the ALCAN would be an irritating dread during his visit to Alaska. I considered the difference between his Harley and my Triumph then thought about the Dalton Highway.

Out of the restaurant I was in light rain so chose to go back to my tent to read. The hypnotic tapping of raindrops lulled me into a relaxing nap—rare that I let myself surrender to rest. I woke to an early evening not knowing the time disoriented while looking around to see myself enclosed by my belongings and not knowing where I was. Then I awoke to a moment of clarity, feeling content with my small place in the world and thankful for where I was, grateful for my choices.

Back to the campground office, I got more coffee. The rain had stopped, and the sky was a bluish gray with a yellow glow across the bay. I was in a trance-like state from my afternoon nap. I walked to the Salty Dog Saloon, got a beer and stepped out to the private area in the back to stare at the rotating beacon against the cloud layers. An orange life buoy on the weathered back door had a sign in the center that read "FUCK EXXON," a sentiment about the Valdez oil spill. A young couple came out in pursuit of privacy and engaged in some light petting, totally ignoring my presence. They lit cigarettes, occasionally staring in my direction with no acknowledgment. I ignored them to continue my slow process to wake from my nap.

Draining the can, I stepped back into the saloon and headed for the bar. I passed a table of rowdy guys ready to party. Talking with one, he shared how they had been fishing for salmon on the Kenai around Cooper's Landing and drove down to finish off their trip at the Salty Dawg. I asked how about the fishing and one gregarious fellow already pumped by a few Alaskan ambers jumped up to say it would have been great if it wasn't for the bears. "Bears?" I asked. "Yea," he said. "Big browns would run out of the woods and grab the fish off your line almost every time you hooked one" he added. Another at the table spoke up to tell me how they fished all week with pistols on their hips——.357 magnums. Knowing what the response would have been, I didn't ask if any were wearing holstered bear spray.

At the bar, I grabbed a stool next to two women who were in Homer for halibut fishing. We spent most of the evening chatting about life, work, and travel. I explained my divestment and my new life on the motorcycle. They were envious, and their enthusiasm caused me to give advice to make me feel awkward and pretentious, like a sage, a philosopher, even worse, a parent. My advice was on preparing a life for full-time travel, explaining how the goal should be to accumulate less as you age; possessions and property make freedom difficult. It takes a strong commitment to break free of what you have been conditioned to have and to unground yourself. For most, it's a dream they talk about but eventually discard. Ultimately, they're too weighted down with belongings for freedom to be possible, with all they own, ironically, owning them. Earlier in the day, I woke to see all I owned surrounding me in a tent to make me content with no regrets.

28

STAGE XXV: Miles 12,968 - 13,521

Don't do the Dalton - Back at the Bear
Wasilla - Talkeetna

"Knowing yourself is the beginning of wisdom."

—*Aristotle*

HAVING EXHAUSTED HOMER, I planned to retrace my route back across the peninsula. I tore down the tent, packed Brother, and on the way out stopped at a funky coffee shop that looked like a bait shack. I got a cup of designer joe and a muffin that I would call breakfast. Homer had been restful. Time there helped me in my effort to mold, shape, and transform my psyche—my experiment to see if I could change and adjust how I would spend my time on earth.

A Saint Bernard dog came up and sat to stare me down for some of my muffin. Pinching off a bite I tossed it up, and he caught it in his mouth. I could tell it was not his first rodeo. Looking at Brother, I saw a young couple circling, the guy pointing, making remarks to his nodding significant who could give a damn. I was enjoying my coffee, my morning, and the attention from the stunning dog. I was hoping the couple would not approach, in no mood to talk about my bike or myself. They connected my outfit to the motorcycle and walked over, we chatted, I finished the muffin, and the dog walked off with no more interest.

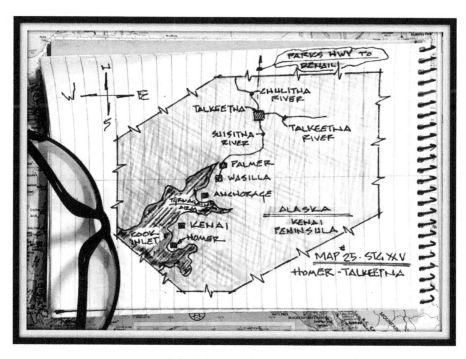

MAP # 25 - STAGE XV
Homer, AK - Talkeetna, AK

In Kenai, I stopped for lunch where a quiet time was disrupted with misbehaving children—a mother too busy on her cell phone to adjust their conduct. In a short time, I was back on the Sterling, once again passing the ultra-green water of the Kenai River. Through the narrow town of Cooper's Landing, located between the river and where the mountains climbed from the road I was lucky to find an inexpensive efficiency. An Asian lady behind the desk showed a lot of interest in my bike and my travels. She told me about her friend Craig, who owned a nearby roadhouse, saying he took adventure motorcyclists on world tours. It piqued my curiosity, so I made plans for dinner and to meet the man.

I showered, then rode the mile to the roadhouse. Built on a knuckle in the road, the structure was a creative use of space that gave it the mysterious and cozy atmosphere of a hideout. Walking in I passed through the bar to see the back of the restaurant was glass providing spectacular views to the fast flowing green river. A tall man with blonde curly hair, in his early forties, welcomed me. I asked if he was Craig. He concurred. So I told him about my travels to get to Alaska causing me to engage in an energetic conversation about motorcycles, travel and new adventure bikes on the market. So occupied with my choice to cross the Arctic Circle, right off the bat I fished for information about the Dalton Highway. When I did, he shook his head in the NO direction. "Don't do it, Man," he said. "It's hard on you and hard on your bike," he added. He talked about people, and their "bucket list" and how riding the Dalton Highway on a motorcycle was a big box they wanted to check. He repeated everything I had already heard— rough road, high speed eighteen wheelers, flying rocks off their wheels, and dangerous animals. Then he talked about the calcium chloride telling me how you can't get that shit off off your bike. "Dalton Pottery they call it," he said. Go ride the Steese out to Circle or the Elliot to Manley Hot Springs. "Both good roads—not so dangerous" he concluded.

He continued to say "I take people down to Tierra del Fuego, all so they can come back and tell everyone they rode from Fairbanks to the tip of South America. I think the whole bucket list thing is bullshit." I agreed with him knowing how much the term annoyed me. It was trendy and a modern day system to establish bragging rights which had never been my motivation. "Go ahead and ride the Dalton," he added. Then reiterated, "But my advice would be not to."

I got a beer and fresh salmon tacos hypnotized by the mesmerizing flow of the Kenai River while thinking about fist size rocks coming at my head—still inconclusive with my dilemma. I was being fickle and knew it. My struggle was metaphysical, knowing I had come too far not to pass the Arctic Circle while questioning whether or not it mattered. What pushed me more than anything was that I did not want to be sitting in a recliner at eighty-five, rubbing my forehead, reviewing my life, and regretting I did not cross the Arctic Circle on Brother when I was so close. There was such a range of opinions from, "piece of cake" to nightmare stories. Because of the danger, the idea continued to lure me, a decision similar to buying my first motorcycle.

Walking to my room, a young girl caught me before I entered. She and her boyfriend were headed to Anchorage for a flight and had a cooler of beer they couldn't finish. I grabbed a few and thanked them. She responded, "Hope you have a good Fourth." I crinkled my forehead, and she said, "Yea, this weekend is the Fourth of July." I had no idea. I called the Brown Bear and was lucky to reserve a room for two nights wanting to hold up and avoid heavy holiday traffic.

I spent the morning in a cafe, before reaching the Brown Bear Saloon, just a few hours away. I was preparing for my next move, with a map of Anchorage over breakfast. Back on the Sterling, I reached the Seward Highway, amazed at the congested holiday traffic near Girdwood. I made it to the Bear, against a straight non-stop stream of traffic coming south from Anchorage.

The following day I was in the near-empty saloon with the doors open to misty rain and a constant flow of traffic. Everyone was either going to Girdwood or all the way down to Seward. I set up my laptop at a wooden booth by a window that faced the Turnagain. The owner was behind the bar catering to a few patrons. I got hot coffee in a thick white mug and ordered another bratwurst sandwich for my late breakfast. Looking through a filter of misting rain I could barely make out the mountains across the muddy flow of the Turnagain. I spent my day at the window, comfortably avoiding traffic and rain, productive in organizing photos, narratives and scrubbing through my Alaska map for someplace I may have missed.

The owner was full of energy and occasionally would stand and stare out the open door, with his hands on his hips while sharing local anecdotes. He was a talker and not a listener, which was good since I was not in a talkative mood. The man possessed the local history and knew where the bones were buried. A flat-screen behind the bar was tuned to an annual Fourth of July event called Mount Marathon taking place in the town of Seward. It was a race to the top, then down Marathon Mountain at 3,200 feet. Entries were from all over the world. Locally, the event was a big deal and I got involved along with everyone at the bar. Most entries were marathoners and skilled competitors, trained to maneuver through areas of jagged rock and crevices going up and coming down the big mountain. It was dangerous and required not only a full body effort but the ability to let yourself go and glide down rock faces at your own risk. The owner of the Bear was excited with the race while sharing knowledge of how they trained, some coming a week ahead to run the mountain numerous times. Everyone was bummed when a guy from Spain was the winner.

I spent the rest of my day in the Bear with my office arrangement at a wooden booth. I was a curiosity to people who made their way in for a beer to get out of the thick traffic. The bar would fill up, then empty out with the gloom of fog and drizzle continuing. In the late afternoon, the traffic stopped, then someone ran in to report on a man being killed on a motorcycle near Girdwood while being chased by a police officer. The news ignited a torrent of scuttlebutt about the officer who pursued the biker, all the locals knowing him and having nothing good to say. The traffic went from a steady flow to a bumper to bumper stall that lasted over two hours. The energy from the race shifted to the Girdwood tragedy. I was glad to be where I was.

That evening a Bluegrass band arrived from Colorado and the saloon filled with a drunken holiday crowd that had been partying hard all day. In no mood for the rowdiness, I went up to my room to hear the music without the obnoxious drunks.

I got through the following day much like the day before, minus the Mount Marathon race and the motorcycle accident. I made a plan to visit Ted, my new friend in Wasilla, who had been emphatic with his invitation. I was going to take him up on his offer, knowing I would see more of Alaska.

Taking out on the fifth, I sat on Brother at the gravel parking lot of the Brown Bear for a for a long wait to find an opening in the thick, steady traffic returning north. Finding my place in the traffic, I made it to Anchorage and then further to the town of Wasilla. I left a message with Ted that I was in town and would get a room if I did not hear back from him. Then spent the afternoon in Wasilla, a place seeming to have little identity or personality—basically, a single highway filled with businesses, no town center, and considered a bedroom community for Anchorage. It was the hometown of Sarah Palin, who ran for vice president on the Republican ticket in 2008 with John McCain. I met several people in Wasilla who knew Sarah, most knowing her more for playing basketball than being Governor of the state or a vice presidential candidate. All considered her a small-town girl who did good.

Not hearing back from Ted, I got a room. It was a hot day, so it felt good to lay on the bed after a shower and watch mindless TV with the AC running full blast. After dinner, I got the call from Ted, and he apologized saying he had cell phone issues, so we arranged a meet up for the next day.

I slept late the following morning, then found a spot to kill time reading before making my way to a nearby watering hole. Once there, we walked in with for my friend to be greeted by everyone he passed—a person of notoriety in the small town. Taking a seat at the bar, a man walked up to discuss his panning operation He pulled out a glass tube about five inches long, an inch in diameter, with a removable cap and passed it over. I saw it partially filled with a fine crush of gold, the consistency of large pepper flakes. I asked how much that quantity of gold was worth. "Around two thousand dollars," he said. Asking how long it took to get that, he said about a week. He would not be the first I would encounter in Alaska that still pursued gold—doing what people originally went to Alaska to do.

After socializing at the bar, I followed my friend to his property about five miles out of town. Civilization quickly turned to wilderness once we turned into a gravel road carved through big spruce. The road to his home past an abandoned school bus, abandoned cars, and kitchen appliances strewed in the middle of high growth. In Alaska, the disposal of junk was a common joke and a real problem. Along the roadside, there were mounds of discarded junk, rubbish, and clutter as if randomly unloaded. I would pass areas piled high with refrigerators, couches, lawnmowers, baby strollers, on and on. It was a disgrace to spoil the natural beauty.

Pulling into Ted's property, I parked near a wooden staircase down to his two-story, wood-sided cabin homestead at Bruce Lake. Inside, it was a real "man cave," overflowing with sports equipment of every variety; bows, arrows, fishing rods, reels, guns, ammo, motorcycle helmets, jackets, skis, and ski clothes. In the central area of his small cabin was the kitchen, connected to a living space with a door to a deck. Big windows gave an open view of wilderness and the calm, pristine lake that reflected clouds and trees at the opposite shoreline.

His living space was a clutter of guitars, bongo drums, amplifiers, and songbooks that covered the kitchen table. We grabbed two beers and went out to the deck. He held his beer up for a toast and said in his perfect diction, "Glad you made it, brother." I gave him a "Thanks, man." Then he pointed at the Bruce Lake and said, "See what I was talking about?" I shook my head saying "It's incredible"—and it was. He shared how therapeutic and meditative it was to stare out at the lake, each and every day of his life. We heard the song of a loon and Ted went in for binoculars, focused them so I could see a mother loon with a baby on her back, swimming mid-lake. It was a precious sight, and I was impressed by how Tim had immersed himself in his environment to observe nature down to such small details. Handing the binoculars back we heard the cries of Arctic terns at one end of the lake. He told me that when the mother loon came too far to their area, the terns would get active, fussy, and fly in circles to convince the loon to return to her end of the lake. There were territorial issues with the wildlife that live on the lake.

We finished our beer, and I took my bike to Tim's fifth wheeler. I was pleased to see a view of the lake through a perfect row of black spruce saplings and dense growth of fireweed. The fifth wheeler was fifty foot long with a bedroom, a living area, a couch, and a table where I set up my computer. There was no power or running water, but—luxury camping.

We grabbed more beer and headed back to the deck. Having talked about playing guitars, Tim brought out one of his acoustics. I gave a demonstration of my blues, ragtime fingerpicking; mostly Robert Johnson and Reverend Gary Davis. I am not a singer but enjoyed the guitar. Learning finger patterns was relaxing, like solving a puzzle. It was also meditative. I was not a performer, but Ted was. At the rally, he explained how he was getting back into playing guitar and singing after a long hiatus. Now Ted was jamming with groups and performing at open mics. He took command of the instrument and was a solid chord player that knew how to accentuate bass notes to highlight a strong and direct strum. His singing, like his speech, was clear, deliberate, pure in diction, with honest clarity. He had a sheepish grin following his first song. It was not egotistical but more—"Well, this is me."

I enjoyed my four nights at Ted's homestead, tagging along while he played at local pubs. He was an example of my *Positive Attraction* and the type of people I was drawing into my life—divergent, self-reliant, visionary. He was doing a good deed for a fellow biker, but I knew he enjoyed the camaraderie, as much as I did.

I spent four days in Wasilla making travel plans while Ted worked to manage his business from the cabin. In the mornings he showed up with coffee, and we shared a conversation about where I should go while continuing north. Like many I had encountered in Alaska, he had not ridden the Dalton Highway to cross the Arctic Circle. He was confident that I had the off-road skills to handle the road by how I rode at the rally and the Top of the World Highway. Many bikers in Alaska did not ride the notorious highway for fear of bodily harm and concern for their bike. Most had not just taken the time to ride that far north—a long ride to get there, even in Alaska.

Ted made sure that I visit the town of Talkeetna, telling me about the views of Denali and how it was the most quintessential Alaskan town in Alaska. After four days off the road, I was chomping at the bit to leave. I liked the road and the changing scenery, and the mystery of where I would sleep. I needed to go. I was an introvert and needed time alone. I needed to recharge.

Packing to leave there were sprinkles with a threatening sky. It was Alaska, so it could be pouring, then ten miles up the road, sunny. The best I could ever do was take my shot. I was heading to Talkeetna, less than a hundred miles north by way of the Parks Highway to the Talkeetna Spur. The town was located at the confluence of the Susitna, Chulitna, and Talkeetna Rivers. Talkeetna was known as the jumping off place for those climbing Denali and, supposedly, the best view of the tallest mountain in the United States. If you wanted a real taste of Alaska, the town of Talkeetna was the perfect example and used as the filming location for the TV series, *Northern Exposure.*

I said goodbye to Ted and rode back through the ramshackle collection of makeshift homes, abandoned and rusted relics, and trash overgrown with wild grass. Skies continued to spit rain until getting close to Talkeetna, then it got hot and sunny. The road through town was a dead end at the confluence of the three rivers. I read that only about thirty percent of people coming to see Denali ever saw it. During the summer months, it was difficult, with high temperatures and snow mixing at the timberline forming a long thick cloud layer to obscure the view of the big mountain. At 20,320 feet above sea level, Denali was the highest mountain in North America. Alaska possessed two other high peaks in the Wrangel-Saint Ellis Mountain Range; Mount Blackburn at 16,390 feet and Mount Sanford at 16,227 feet. All three taller than Mount Whitney in California, the highest in the Lower Forty-Eight.

Denali was the name given to the massive peak by the Koyukon tribe of the Athabaskan people, indigenous to the area and the mountain's name for centuries. That was until 1896, when a gold prospector from Ohio decided to rename the peak, McKinley, after the twenty-fifth US president. Mount McKinley became the registered name by the Department of the Interior, although Alaskans continued to call the mountain Denali. It would be obvious you were not a local Alaskan if you referred to the mountain as McKinley. In 2015, the name was changed back to Denali, to satisfy popular favor.

Once in the small town of Talkeetna, I understood why it was recommended. It had all the essentials; grocery store, restaurants, bars, bookstore-coffee shop, and two historic motels. At the dead end or the gravel road entrance, there was a bazaar with a woman of native heritage at a picnic table and a sign—"Camping $10." Nearby was an asbestos shingled house in a grassy lot, enclosed in the rough growth of saplings on a sandy beach at the river. I noticed a shelter for firewood next to a shade tree and thought it would be a perfect spot to camp. I gave the lady a twenty for two nights and pointed at the area for permission. She nodded yes and told me I could get a shower at the Talkeetna Roadhouse for five dollars. I pitched my tent, rolled my jacket to make a pillow, and laid back fading into a lazy nap.

The Talkeetna Roadhouse got its start in the early 1900s, supporting gold prospectors that descended on the confluence of the three rivers. The establishment rented rooms served breakfast, dinner, and had an upright piano for nightly entertainment. From what I noticed they had a good business selling showers to campers.

Walking back from my shower, I began my survey of the town, first walking the river's edge with hopes to see Denali. The sky above the horizon remained covered with a thick white cloud line. I had to ask which direction to look if the mountain were to appear.

I walked to the town for an early dinner, finding a burger restaurant that appeared to be run by guys who looked like adrenaline, adventure junkies; wiry, covered in tats, body piercings, exuding alive in the moment credo about time on earth. I liked the vibe and settled in to vicariously suck it up. I didn't think these guys were on their parent's nickel. No! I saw them more like they were working it out on their own—sparse communal life, financially broke, true to a chosen path, and no intentions to cave and embrace a career. They reminded me of myself at that age. I recall having my W-2 tax forms sent to my father during my rambling years, and he would point out that I was living five thousand dollars below the poverty level. I never felt poor and recall being very content to just be free.

With so little darkness I split my day into two parts, heading back to my camp to read midday until early evening. Then I pursued live music and social interaction. Seeing there was music at the Fairview Inn, I stepped inside. You could feel the age of the frontier establishment with the open dance floor, an old stage, and a U-shaped bar below an antique carved oak framed mirror. Pictures of early settlers, maps, and mounted animal heads decorated the walls. A local group stood drinking PBR in cans while a Jamaican guy with dreadlocks set up for his performance with an electric bass guitar. People flowed in to make it evident that I was at the place to be. I met some who lived in Talkeetna for the summer then off to somewhere exotic and warm for the winter. Most, too young to afford such a lifestyle, caused me to question how they funded their globe-trotting lifestyle—so different than the adrenaline junkies at the burger joint. It made me aware of my middle-class mentality and how I evaluated the life of others while recalling the words from an old friend—"You can't count another man's money."

The Jamaican played his bass guitar against the sound of a box that played a melody. He thumped those heavy strings and sang with a loud, clear voice to keep everyone's attention. At a booth near the stage, a pretty young girl sat reading Tarot Cards for hire; the girlfriend of the musician. More entered to fill the periphery of the open room. I made my spot at the far end of the bar to enjoy the music and watched the antics of the crowd as they got drunk and animated.

A few hours made the music sound like noise, and the drunken crowd produced a droning buzz of mixed conversation. I walked out then down the gravel road to my campsite with the sun in some direction near sunset with the sky having gone from partially clear to stacked gray clouds. Before heading to my tent I chose to walk the sand trail to the flowing Susitna River, then north to the convergence of the Talkeetna and the Chulitna, which caused an unusual flow of eddies with muted reflections of the colored sky. There was a multi-colored glow of the sun's circular impression behind a layer of thick clouds. To the east, a separate and mysterious glow, a distinct sphere shape of the same brightness. The two were tied together with an elongated yellow glow of light, causing me to wonder if I was witnessing what I really wanted to see—the Northern Lights, the Aurora Borealis. No matter, it was a magnificent and quite a moment at the intermingling of three rivers and the illusive Denali peak somewhere in the distance.

I slept great in my tent and woke to people coming from river campsites to have breakfast in town. The day was bright, and I crawled out with hopes to view Denali. No luck, with a cloud layer blocking the big mountain. At a state provided restroom, I brushed my teeth, washed my face, then settled at a coffeehouse with a porch table for a breakfast sandwich. Then spent my morning organizing pictures and writing in my journal.

Talkeetna was active, but not uncomfortably so. I spent the remaining day reading, taking photos, and napping under the tree. I gave thought to how I had not had a job for over four months—my most extended period without employment since my twenties. I kept feeling like I was cheating the system and feared being caught and forced back. I took walks to the rivers with continued hopes to see Denali. The overhead sky was blue but in front of the big mountain, puffy clouds formed as the summer heat mixed with ice and snow.

Talking to the man who owned the property where I camped, he confirmed that few actually saw Denali. He said it was due to tourist coming in the summer months. The man was from North Carolina, telling me about coming to Alaska as a young man, falling in love with Talkeetna, a native Indian lady then never left. Like most I met living in the state, they held a deep connection with the natural beauty and the freedom. I told him about the lights I saw in the sky over the river and thought they were Northern Lights. Hearing my description, he said what I saw was Sun Dogs—too early in the year for Northern Lights. Doing the research, I read about the atmospheric phenomenon called Sun Dogs or Mock Sun or Phantom Sun or the meteorological name, Parhelion—I was sure it was what I witnessed. Sun Dogs occur when the sun is near the horizon and will appear as two suns either to the right or the left. The effect is due to the refraction of light through ice crystals and about twenty-two degrees from the location of the sun.

The remainder of my last day in Talkeetna slipped away in a relaxed manner while I enjoyed the peace of the little town, the views of the rivers, and optimistic hope of seeing Denali. For my last night, I chose the hypnotic and mesmerizing confluent flow of the three rivers over the raucous barroom.

The next morning I woke to the sound of a young couple forcing air from an inflatable boat. It made an unidentifiable screeching sound while I laid in my tent trying to figure out what the hell I was hearing. And all the while their dog barked at the annoying sound. I gave up, unzipped the tent and crawled out. A guy walked over to apologize for the noise while his girlfriend continued to deflate the boat. Asking what they were doing, he told me how they planned a two-day camping trip down the river from up north, then explained how the river flowed so fast their destination was finished in four hours, arriving last night.

He was admiring my bike and told me how he rode his dirt bike through Mexico and Central America two years ago. I shared how that was my initial intention, but had trepidation about traveling South America alone. He ensured me that there would be no problem and there was nothing to worry about. Then, in a casual manner, shared a tale of one guy he encountered who was later discovered off the main road, dismembered near his dismantled motorcycle. Then, once again, in the same casual manner, he told me I would have no issue traveling South America alone. I nodded and walked over to brush my teeth before heading north, far away from Mexico.

29

STAGE XXVI: Miles
13,521 - 14,129

**Denali Behind the Clouds - No Skinny Dick
Fairbanks - Steese to Circle – Fox
The Howling Wolf**

*"Life isn't about finding yourself, life
is about creating yourself."*

—*George Bernard Shaw*

AGAIN, ANOTHER HOT day in Alaska. On the Spur Road out
of Talkeetna, I rode back to the Parks Highway, then north towards
Fairbanks having no idea where I would end my day. A plan to have
no plan had become my choice—my luxury. There was summertime

traffic to deal with on the only highway going to Denali National Park. The Parks Highway was named after George Alexander Parks, governor of the Alaskan Territory from 1925 to 1933 and not after the park, as I thought.

I continued to nurse hopes to see Denali. I considered camping in the National Park, but also considered the crowds. Turning on the Parks, I saw a constant slow flow then a mile up the highway, I saw a viewing point for Denali at the edge of miles of rich summer growth, natural and lush. There was a full-length picture of the big mountain, identifying all the associated peaks. The picture was beautiful and such a tease for the big mountain I so wanted to see. Looking out over the layered greens I saw fireweed, black spruce, and willow saplings. Beyond that, the most massive mountain in America continued to be obstructed by thick clouds. I began to accept the fact that I would not see Denali.

Back on the Parks, I hit gravel—an asphalt surface ground in preparation for repaving. In Talkeetna, I was warned of excessive road construction near the park. I saw another overlook for Denali and pulled in with my eternal optimism—once again, no luck.

The gravel continued in heavy traffic as I approached the entrance to the park. Most vehicles were RVs the size of tour buses. I came to a collection of stores, shops, and restaurants where the park entrance intersected the highway. Getting mixed up in a thicket of humanity that did not appeal to me, I passed it all to continue north. I was stopped by a young girl wearing a neon vest, holding a stop sign which made me stop for almost thirty minutes. I got off Brother, removed my helmet and gloves and cooled off. Disappointed in not seeing Denali, the surrounding mountains were magnificent.

Finally, the park madness was behind me, so I drove away from any possible chance to see the massive mountain. Barely on the tarmac, I was stopped in another line of traffic—another young girl in neon holding a stop sign. Another frustrating, long, hot roadside stop.

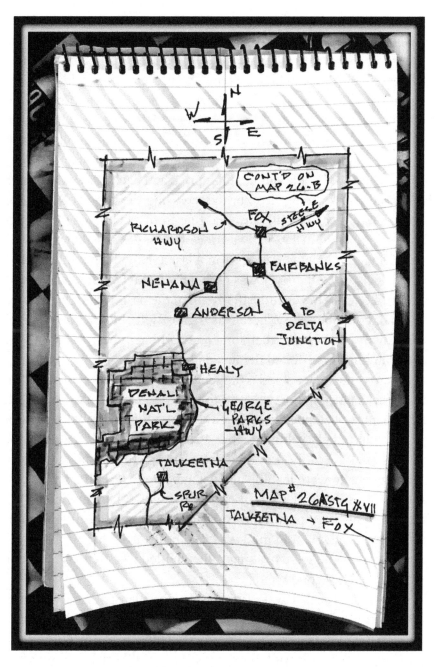

MAP # 26A - STAGE XXVII
Talkeetna, AK - Fox, AK

I passed through the town of Healy, that offered a few lodging options. It was too early to stop, and with the construction behind me, it felt good to have Brother in motion. I turned into Nenana, one of the larger small towns which had a main street, though odd makeshift construction, Alaskan style. I considered a motel of wood plank connected boxes, no doubt just a room, a bed, with an overhead lightbulb. I knocked on a door, and no one came, so I rode down to an old train station where I saw a message taped to the door with a number for rented rooms. I called to hear about the high price and backed away. From the old station, I saw a long truss bridge crossing the Tanana River, later learning the railway was the original line from Anchorage to Northern Alaska. Completed in 1923 it was once the longest single truss bridge in the US and remains the longest in Alaska. Now the town was dead, and the dock along the river was a clutter of heavy equipment, cranes, container boxes— the chaotic aftermath of the past. No activity, human or animal, could be seen. There was a ghostly feel to the mostly abandoned town with a sense that someone had been there once, but left, leaving an imprint of failed dreams and misfortune.

Across the street stood a rugged corner bar with beer boxes from twelve packs taped to the windows to make the place dark. I was up for refreshment, so I stepped in the seedy, smoke-filled, dimly lit cave. Besides an elderly lady behind the bar, there were three old men slumped on stools drinking sadly. A pool table at the far end entertained a couple of teenagers who were leaning against a cigarette machine making out. I ordered an amber and a bag of chips. A very old man mumbled in my direction in an attempt to talk to someone, making me feel sorry for feeling antisocial. He told me I was fifty miles from Fairbanks as if he knew where people were heading if they pulled into Nenana. Finishing my beer, I felt a second wind.

After my break I was surprised by the pleasant ride with areas enclosed in a thick forest—deep, dark, and perfectly vertical comfier growth. Along the way were numerous businesses that had gone belly up. I stopped at one to walk the property at an old brick building filled with cluttered remnants of some activity as I could see through wavy glass windows. Now it was just another Alaskan eyesore.

About thirty miles before Fairbanks I passed Skinny Dick's Halfway Inn, which I had read about. Skinny Dick was of some local fame, and his Halfway Inn was a bikers destination. I was not sure what the Inn was halfway between, too far north to be between Anchorage and Fairbanks. It was a bar and a novelty store where he sold a variety of items geared to a maturity stuck in adolescence. His big road sign displayed his logo—two bears fornicating. There was a line of small cabins with porches that appeared partially complete, unpainted, fabricated from untreated plywood, now weathered and warped. And like much of what I saw in Alaska it looked as if someone just walked away from the construction saying, "That's good enough." There were no cars in the lot and no light in the window of what appeared to be the bar.

I walked up a weathered and rickety staircase that looked to be fabricated from scrap wood. Stopping at a stoop, there was a toilet bowl filled with rocks and sand for cigarette butts. A neon Skinny Dick's bumper sticker was on the raised lid with the same logo as his sign—bears fornicating. I knocked on the door with little hope the place was open. Skinny Dick was portrayed as a cantankerous old fellow and said to give people a lot of grief if they did not show satisfaction for his only menu choice: a cheese sandwich, chips, and beer. I had steeled myself in the apprehension of him swinging the door open in anger for waking him but grinned at the possible encounter with a man named Skinny Dick. My impression was the place was shut down for good, and Skinny Dick was gone, possibly to the afterlife.

Into Fairbanks, I was surprised at how small the city was. I entered near the airport and made a run-up and down the main drag looking for motels. I found most overpriced, so I returned to a motel separated from the airport runway by a chainlink fence, in need of repair with a neon sign, similar to The Bates Motel in *Psycho*. The lobby was homey with three docile golden retrievers, one coiled in a wingback chair. The man behind the desk was near eighty, thin, hunched over with a drooping mustache covering both lips making him look like a cartoon character and causing me to wonder how he ate. For a moment

I thought it might be Skinny Dick, with a new career, but would feel odd asking "Would you happen to be Skinny Dick?"

While unloading, a Fairbanks police car pulled up with officers heading to the front desk. From there they approached a room to address a domestic dispute with a Native American lady having issues with a man. They told the man to get his belongings and leave the premises. By the time I had unloaded, the police were gone and see the man from my second storeroom walking down the gravel road holding a brown paper bag with his belongings.

I learned the motel was featured on the TV show *Alaska State Police* and the vibe I got was that it was a retreat for vagrants and misfits. I chose to give it a one night test. As it happened, I liked the motel and stayed three nights, using it as a base for getting mail and items I had ordered. A Denny's Restaurant near downtown was where I spent my mornings, later being told it was the most northern Denny's in the US. Those were down days in Fairbanks, and I surrendered to them, washing clothes, rearranging luggage, and researching maps.

I was close to the Dalton Highway and continued to think about crossing the Arctic Circle. While deciding, I planned to take Craig's advice and ride the Steese Highway out to Circle, north of Fairbanks. After three days in Fairbanks, I was ready to go.

I loaded Brother and took out to enjoy Denny's knowing there would be no lack of daylight.

The small town of Circle was located on the south side of the Yukon River and named Circle because it was initially thought to be the location of the Arctic Circle. Later it was discovered that it was fifty miles south of where the Arctic Circle exist.

The Arctic Circle is an arbitrary line and, due to the axial rotation of the earth, continually shifts its location where there is no darkness for one twenty-four-hour period, during a one year period. Above the line the Arctic, below the Northern Temperate Zone. The actual line is not fixed and dependent on the axial tilt of the earth, which can fluctuate at a rate of two percent over a forty-thousand-year period.

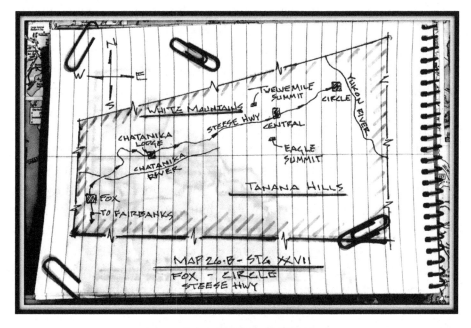

MAP # 26B - STAGE XXVI
Fox, AK - Circle, AK (Steese Highway)

Ten miles north of Fairbanks was the town of Fox. From there I could continue north on the Richardson Highway that terminates at the start of the Dalton Highway. Just before Fox I saw the Steese Highway and made the turn, not sure how much was paved and how much gravel, but ready and confident to take on what it offered. Now, no longer apprehensive of difficult road surfaces, I looked forward to where a rough road would take me.

Making the turn, I knew it would be a ride worth doing and deeper into the northern Alaskan frontier to pass small towns where people still panned for gold. The Steese was paved for seventy-five miles until the tiny town of Central. Past Central the road was gravel for another seventy miles to the historic town of Circle. The road rolled through majestic scenery with willows decorating both sides of the road.

About thirty miles up the desolate road, I came to Chatanika, the largest mining town during the Fairbanks Gold Rush. The Fairbanks

Gold Rush began in the early 1900s by the prospector Felix Pedro, during the period that Fairbanks was being established. The word got to Dawson City where most prospectors and stampeders had already left for the Nome Gold Rush. Gold mining was a fickle pursuit and once one place caught on another popped up with a scramble in that direction. Small towns on the Steese were there because of gold mining and people making money off a steady flow of prospectors.

I pulled in the Chatanika Lodge for coffee. It was a bar and restaurant, with rooms attached to each side of a log-constructed building. I inquired about a vacancy, not knowing what I would find down the road. The woman behind the bar was chatty, and it was too early in the day for her vivaciousness. I gulped my coffee and got back on the road.

I passed the three-story Long Creek Trading Post that was fabricated with overlapped wooden plank board and adorned with antlers from moose, caribou, and elk. Before Central, I rode up steady climbs from flat land. First was Twelvemile Summit, near three thousand feet. The second was Eagle Summit, near the same height. At the top of each were tall poles, bent at ninety degrees at the top. Their purpose was to identify the edge of the road in deep snow. Views from the precipice were open to the beauty of multiple mountain ranges, mixed with grayish blue clouds. The foreground was scattered with granite outcroppings and rich mossy grass. I admitted to myself that it was one of my better rides in Alaska, mostly due to the extreme peace and the silence of the emptiness. It was like I was the only man on earth.

The town of Central surprised me with how livable and quaint it was. The road passed by a few small homes from the fifties where there appeared to have been a neighborhood. The houses were asbestos shingled cape cods with screened porches, and porch swings, some abandoned and dilapidated, the tiny town appearing to have seen a better day. I spotted a store, restaurant, bar, and gas station all combined in one. They offered rooms, laundry, groceries, and meals. I wanted to carry on to Circle, but was hungry and wanted a meal. I had the tendency to eat sporadically, at a whim, often having to convince myself that I was hungry. I now lived by the lyrics of the ballad *Moonshiner*: "I'll eat when I'm hungry and drink when I'm dry."

I walked inside and through their grocery store, consisting of two rows of racks holding various staples. To the back was a standing freezer. Stepping into the restaurant, the decor was sparse with a few small tables and chairs made of stainless steel and Formica—a *Leave it to Beaver* look. There was a long bar with a few bottles of liquor sitting in front of a mirror next to a row of beer cans. A grandmotherly type walked up as I read their special of the day scribbled on a board by a pink grease pen in jittery cursive. She asked how I was doing and I asked how the meatloaf was—the special. Of course, she said it was good, so I ordered it along with black coffee. The meal was delivered quickly and the closest thing I had to home cooked food for some time; a large portion of meatloaf, mash potatoes, broccoli, yeast rolls, and a scalloped moat for dark gravy. I took my time and patiently enjoyed the act of dining in the honesty and unpretentious atmosphere of the frontier haven.

In walks a lady to sit two seats down. She begins an inquiry about my bike. My mouth was full, and I was too absorbed in my delicious meal to give much response. She started to tell me about living down the road and working on a house she bought a few years back. Then she stepped out on a fragile limb, offering a front porch to camp on if I wanted. All was happening too fast, and I was more intent on loading my fork than to consider her offer—the best meal I had eaten in weeks. She was not drunk or seedy and appeared, in my assessment, to be from a professional background. She probably chose the wilderness for some poorly considered concept of seclusion, not knowing that seclusion was synonymous to loneliness. I thanked her for the offer and told her I was not sure where I would be that night. She reiterated her offer, giving me directions to find her place if I changed my mind. I thanked her again while buttering a roll. She said goodbye, and I watched her return to her car from a window.

I could not help but question the casualness of the lady, who seemed to have been of clear mind, to approach a total stranger and invite him to her home. Where I was sure, she was lonely the woman appeared to be someone who would have exercised more discretion. I felt a bit sad for her, but not so sad as to spend the night on her porch and enter some odd predicament. As Einstein said, "A clever person solves a problem. A wise person avoids it." I mopped the gravy from my plate with my roll and thought how unwise it was to invite strangers to your home if you were lonely. Start doing that, and it's time to move back into town.

Back on Brother, I felt fresh and ready to finish the Steese at Circle. Just up the road, the pavement fell off to gravel at a yellow highway sign that just read "PAVEMENT ENDS." Thick river rock worked the front wheel, causing a to and fro wiggle. I was in no rush and enjoyed the wilderness in what was called Tanana Hills, a part of the Tanana Valley, seeing landscape leading back to Fairbanks. Fireweed lined the road like it had been placed by a landscaper. I made a turn and see a creek that leads to a small lake, so still, it offered a picturesque mirror of the clouds and a nearby mountain. Across the road was a hillside ascending that was littered with burnt trees and charred trunks. Fireweed grew thick along the blackened ridge. The burnt trunks looked like upright men who stood to protect the perfection of the crystal clear lake. I got off Brother to stand in the extreme isolation, wanting to gather the moment into me, to be aware, and not wanting to just pass through. I was looking for a deeper connection to my experiences than the constant passing through, using my eyes and mind as a filter to wash one magnificent view away with another. I stood and turned full circle to take in the entirety of the magical location, conscious of placing a panoramic picture in my memory.

Arriving in Circle, the road ended at the Yukon River, an area that was once was the city center in the early 1900s gold boom of Fairbanks. A large sign at a gravel lot read "Welcome to Circle City" stating it was established in 1893. At the bottom, the comment "Hub of Supplying Interior Alaska's Oldest Major Gold Camps." And at the very bottom, in large print, "THE END OF THE ROAD." In 1920 this was the furthermost road north in Alaska. Circle was once a boom town with saloons, gambling houses, dance halls, and an Opera House. Now, all that remained was a big sign. Unlike Dawson City, nothing had been preserved.

Circle was just too far off the beaten path to sustain growth without gold mining. For over thirty years it was only accessible by the Yukon River. Goods were brought by sled dogs during winter months and pack mules in the short warm season. The town grew fast and died fast and just another fickle notion as being the next location to pursue gold.

Across from the Yukon was a grocery store with an old gas pump that I pulled up to. I had to get gas or use what was in my jerrycan to get back to Central. The pump was off, and a sign on the door said closed. A lady came around the corner, telling me she would turn on the pump. The town was vacant and calm with people who chose to live removed entirely from society and civilization—so far away.

Leaving the gas station, I began the seventy-mile gravel road back for a room in Central. I passed abandoned; trucks, cars, earth moving equipment, and an old ice cream truck, all piled like children's toys. It was squalor and a shame in respect to what Circle had been. It was an ugly contrast to a town that once had an Opera House.

I got a room with a shared shower and sink. There was a party at the bar, so I took a seat for a cold beer before unpacking. A woman in her early forties said she passed me on the road coming from Circle. She spoke while lighting one cigarette to another—end to end. She said she lived in Circle telling me she ran the post office and was recently widowed. Then told me she owned a house on the river. She was talking with the grandmotherly lady about an abandoned mining operation and how she wanted to go through their sluice boxes. Other than what I learned in Dawson City and Wasilla, I had little knowledge of panning, dredging or mining, so I asked questions. She told me sluice boxes were of interest because of the remaining gold. "My husband was a prospector," she said and made his living panning for gold in the Yukon. He made enough to build a house on the Yukon. It was odd to hear someone speak about prospecting in this day and age, but found it more common than I would have imagined. It was a different way of life in the frontier wilderness and so much was based on simple survival.

I slept hard in another small, dank room and continued to be impressed with how I could find comfort in almost any location. It was a necessary characteristic if you chose to travel in the manner I was traveling. You had to be adaptable, pliable, and pleased to have just enough. My lifestyle was remapping my brain in regards to creature comfort.

I took a shower in one of their rusted sheet metal stalls then loaded Brother that was parked in a collection of squalor; auto parts, construction scraps, empty oil cans, and an unidentifiable carcass in overgrown grass, no more than skeleton and pelt.

I had a big breakfast before backtracking the paved portion of the Steese with no plan other than to enjoy the day and see what the town of Fox had to offer. I stopped at the Long Creek Trading Post to browse the store and walk the grounds, looking over their collection of antlers. It was another trading post with everything you would need to endure a full winter. Making it through a winter this far north must be a challenging, depressing, soul-searching endeavor. I spoke with one young man who made it through a Yukon winter, emphatically telling me he would never do it again. A full winter in Alaska could be from mid-September to early May. I wondered if I had the temperament to handle such isolation without going mad with cabin fever. As beautiful as the country was, I thought of looking out on a landscape of deep snow, with no way to escape. I considered the Athabaskan people and wondered if they had a specific and unique gene, allowing them to withstand so much isolation.

The ride from Central to Fox was leisurely and stopped back in the Chatanika Lodge for lunch. I enjoyed conversation with locals at the bar who were drinking too early. I was interested in what it was like to live on the Steese year round. The woman behind the bar said she was a local with family strewn all over northern Alaska saying she knew no other way of life. There was a lot of snow, it was cold, and they were used to it.

Into Fox, I wanted to check out a saloon I noticed at the crossroads of the Richardson and Elliot Highways. It was a big brick one-story building with THE HOWLING WOLF SALOON painted on the front. Walking in, I liked it. There was energy and a flow of gregarious, fun loving people at three in the afternoon. I saw cabins in the back, so I inquired. The owner was an avid biker and gave me a discount, so I paid for the night, ordered a beer, and took a seat at the bar with other bikers. I sat next to one from Vancouver, B.C. who explained how he was on a trip of a lifetime. He was a high school teacher who had that "Hall Pass" married guys get. I asked if he rode the Dalton and he said he did not, explaining how he did not trust his MotoGuzzi to take him that far. I explained that I had just about talked myself into taking it on. Having just completed the long ride through deep gravel between Central to Circle and back I felt confident. I had cut my teeth on plenty of rough roads in the Yukon and the Top of the World Highway. I lived through the Whittier Tunnel, the most dangerous thing I had ever done on a motorcycle, for that matter—in my life. The mentality that caused me to fear the infamous road was now considered through a mindset of experience, now thinking more about what an adventure it would be. With that mind-frame, I planned to get up in the morning, check the weather and put an end to an over-nursed quandary and ride the Dalton Highway to the Arctic Circle.

I took Brother around the back of the Howling Dog to a line of cheaply built one-room cabins in a thinly wooded area. Across a dirt path were several tents with parked motorcycles. The cabin had no bathroom or sink, just a table, a few chairs, and a bed. Toilets and showers were at the back of the saloon. I unloaded, got a shower and went back to the Howling Wolf to hear live music. The owner waved me in without the cover charge to a packed house and everyone excited to hear a band from Austin, Texas. Like the Brown Bear, I felt at home in the Howling Wolf Saloon. Let my love for saloons say about me what it will. I spent most of my evening talking with the owner, with a band on fire and a full dance floor. I stayed until midnight, then read myself asleep in my cabin.

I woke in the morning feeling energetic, positive, and ready to go. I walked to the saloon for coffee, then packed Brother. It was not a beautiful sunny day. It was overcast, misty, too common in Alaska to consider waiting for sunshine. At eighty-five I would not furrow my brow for passing up this adventure—Damnit!

30

STAGE XXVII: Miles 14,129 - 14,331

The Dalton Highway - The Arctic Circle

"What we do in life echoes in eternity."

—*The Gladiator*

I PACKED BROTHER and rode around the row of cabins to a filling station in the adjoining lot. I got coffee to wake up and a banana to take the gnaw out of my stomach, then paced the surroundings, browsing artifacts and rusted remnants from some bygone era. Finishing what I would call breakfast, I rode to the pump to stuff as much gas in the tank as possible. I had my gallon jerrycan filled and attached to the back of my luggage, knowing I would not see gas until the Yukon River, miles up the Dalton. Knocking my kickstand down a guy pulled up on a KTM adventure bike loaded like me. "You headed up the Dalton?" I shouted over. "Yea," he said. "Want some company?" I asked. "Another person would be good," he replied. Both of us had Texas plates, we made a quick introduction, and now I was riding with Nate.

Up the Richardson, we were heading for the no longer existing town of Livengood where the Dalton began. The Dalton Highway was built for the construction of the Trans Atlantic Pipeline; eight hundred miles of forty-eight-inch pipe that transported oil from offshore drilling in Prudhoe Bay to tankers docked in Valdez. Between 1974 and 1977 it was a massive undertaking, originating from the 1973 oil crisis, the result of an OPEC oil embargo. The embargo was in response to support provided to Israel in the 1973 Yom Kippur War. The pipeline was a way for the US to say they could be self-sufficient without oil supplied by middle eastern countries.

I remembered the oil crisis lasting from October of 1973 to March of 1974. At the time I worked at a filling station while going to college. I recall long lines at the pumps and anxious people and each day gas ran out, and frustrated people were turned away.

It was seventy-one miles to Livengood, and the road weaved through a thick mountainous forest, cut at ridge lines. Views were to treetops as far as could be seen. Livengood had a two-year boom when gold was discovered in Livengood Creek in 1914. A flood of prospectors infiltrated the distant area with prospecting short lived. Now all that remains is a small green sign—LIVENGOOD.

From Fox the Richardson was in rough condition, rolling and undulating with asphalt patches from areas damaged by frost heave. Like the road to Valdez, the damaged areas of the road were repaired quickly by dumping a pile of hot asphalt them rolling them flat with little attention to blending smoothly to the road surface. Dark black patches were a warning and allowed time to brace and stand on the pegs for the impact. My Texas friend followed close behind me. I could see him standing while chomping at the bit for the heavy gravel we were speeding towards. I wasn't used to riding with anyone, so I didn't know if I was riding too slow or too fast, so I rode my own ride.

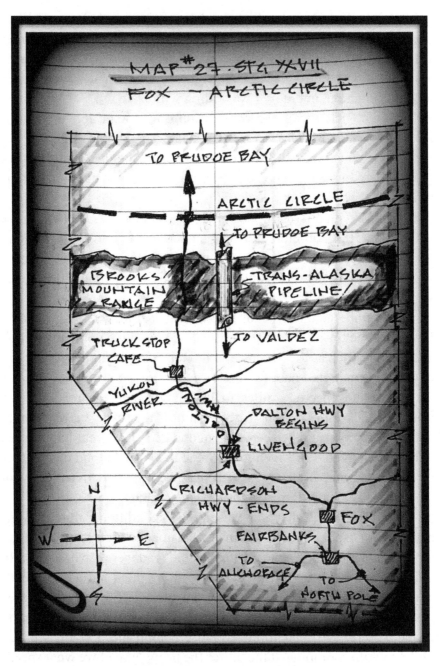

MAP # 27 - STAGE XXVI
Fox, AK - Arctic Circle

We were in deep wilderness, sweeping around turns that flowed against vast mountainsides while viewing miles of untouched forest. The sky was gray and moody with temperatures in the fifties, the atmosphere setting some tension for the pending highway. At a slight turn stood the same sign I saw heading to Circle—PAVEMENT ENDS. Gravel overflowed onto the Richardson, where one road began, and another ended. Turning, we passed a massive carved wooden sign, "Welcome to the Dalton Highway," below that, "Gateway to the Arctic - The Road to Prudhoe Bay." I saw people getting their picture taken with the sign. I was too involved in my first impression of the road to consider stopping. The gravel was deep, up to nine inches in places and wet from recent rainfall which made it heavy on the wheels. The beginning of the iconic road was a busy place with eighteen-wheelers, RVs and trucks, some turning around, apparently thinking the road a bad idea. A few vehicles passed me because of my cautious speed. Nate was well ahead, displaying the experience of a seasoned dirt biker. I passed another sign on the road that warned, Heavy Industrial Traffic. And then a sign for distances: Yukon River 56, Coldfoot 175, Deadhorse 414.

My first hill was the steepest hill I had even tackled on gravel. I read that some inclines were a twelve percent grade once crossing the Brooks Mountain Range. I held steady on the throttle to keep a positive grab of my rear tire—but not so much as to make it slip. I was unnecessarily cautious because of the reputation of the road. Going down steep hills was not as easy as going up, with the momentum of the bike gaining speed and braking causing the rear wheel to fishtail. You had to choose—either control the bike or let the bike go. Experience was needed, which I had and was getting more of. "Let the rear wheel follow the front wheel" would become my mantra. Over time I relaxed into that philosophy. It became a second sense.

Over a few big hills, I became conscious of how far away I had come since leaving Virginia. I remembered my Alaska motorcycle book sitting on my coffee table with a picture on the front of an adventure biker riding the Dalton. And now, here I was, and it was magnificent— much more than I thought it would be.

While I struggled through a thick section of gravel Nate pulled up. "I think we're riding at different speeds," he said, meaning he was faster or I was lagging. I understand," I told him, then said, "Ride your ride Man!" I gave him a wave to say go on, and he yelled out "Going to the Yukon for something to eat." I affirmed with the nod of my helmet. Then he spun around me, kicking up gravel down the hill. I continued at my novice to intermediate pace using my own discretion.

There was a truck stop at the Yukon River with gas and food. At the speed I was riding, I would be there in a few hours. In Anchorage, someone told me that heavy gravel was at the beginning of the Dalton to discourage people from taking the route if they were not serious about going so deeply in the bush. Once I hit hard packed gravel with calcium chloride, I increased my speed considerably.

Calcium chloride was a gray powder applied to rolled gravel roads, then hosed down with water turning it into a glue substance to connect the gravel for a hardened surface. After time and no rain, it became dry and returned to powder. Once caked on your bike it was difficult to remove, thus the moniker "Dalton Pottery." The change in the surface made it easier to ride, and I was up to fifty miles an hour in places.

Warnings of passing trucks were the most significant concern other than breaking down to be eaten by a bear. It wasn't until I encountered a passing trucker that I understood the danger. Injury and damage to the bike were common as was evident after the first eighteen-wheeler swept by with a blast of gravel, sand, and rocks in a tan-colored curtain. I would drop my helmet visor and duck low behind my windshield at the opposite side of the passing truck. Whether I would be hit by large rocks was between fate and luck. At the crest of high hills, you could look down to deep valleys to see fast approaching trucks creating a plume of whirling gravel and brown sand. It looked like a rooster tail at the transom of an offshore racing boat—the sight frightful, and all the while apprehensive of the outcome, each time relieved for an uneventful outcome.

Riding the Dalton made me wonder about the building of the road, a monumental task in a cold, rugged, and isolated environment.

The pipeline was a major boom for Alaska during a period when most of the US was suffering through a recession. Tens of thousands flocked to the state in pursuit of jobs in Anchorage, Fairbanks, and Valdez. In 1968 oil had been discovered in the Arctic Ocean off the coast of Prudhoe Bay. It was considered a reserve for just such a predicament as the oil embargo of 1973. The response to build a pipeline was immediate and a fairly direct route between Prudhoe Bay to Valdez. The eight hundred miles of pipe required a uniquely engineered mounting system to support the pipe over the rough mountainous terrain. John W. Dalton supervised the construction and was an expert in arctic engineering specializing in mounting large structure to the permafrost in a manner to prevent environmental destruction. He devised a method to float the footings above the frozen tundra. Having supervised the erection of towers for the Distant Early Warning Line that protected the Alaskan coastline. His knowledge of supporting towers transferred to the pipeline. The mounting feet were refrigerated to prevent melting the permafrost by heat created by the friction of flowing oil in the pipe.

My apprehension of the Dalton had turned to a pleasurable challenge, and I knew driving the road would forever be imprinted in my memory. I read that if you cared about your bike, you should not ride the Dalton. I cared much for Brother but bought the bike to ride such places. It was an adventure bike, and this was an adventure.

Before the Yukon River, there had been multiple opportunities to see the pipeline paralleling the Dalton Highway. The landscape was expansive with what had become typical Alaskan views—black spruce, willow saplings, with the massing of fuchsia fireweed. Most saplings were no more than knee-high indicating extreme winters and a short growing season. I kept a constant eye out for wildlife after spotting a handful of caribou mingling off the road.

I crossed the bridge over the Yukon, a longitudinal wooden-planked surface. It would have been like eel shit if wet and I was thankful it wasn't. Off the bridge and into the truck stop I saw Nate's KTM parked outside, the only other vehicle a big yellow earth mover. In the door for lunch, I saw him sipping coffee. "Had salmon tacos," he said with an approving nod, so I ordered the same. The place was a distant outpost with a burley-bearded man running the operation along with his kids who worked the counter, the kitchen, and a small alcove with souvenirs. I had to wonder where they lived and how they wound up there—possibly leftovers from the pipeline construction and never left. There was still plenty of traffic between Prudhoe Bay and Fairbanks, and I could only imagine what the place was like between 1974 and 1977—fast-paced, long hours, and heavy weather. Thirty-two people died during those years, and that did not include the truckers running back and forth at a steady pace through long hours in inclement weather.

Nate took off, and I stayed to finish my tacos. We made loose plans to meet up on the other side of the Arctic Circle. I relaxed with another cup of coffee and then topped off my tank for the next leg. The empty restaurant seemed to pronounce the isolation of my location. The Dalton has been on a number of reality shows, *Ice Road Truckers* being one. Also featured on *America's Toughest Jobs*, the job being driving trucks so far north in Alaska. And, a BBC series entitled *The Worlds Most Dangerous Roads.*

The scenery continued to be something out of an adventure tale with miles of open land heading for the distant Brooks Mountain Range—an abrupt stance of mountains, seven hundred miles long from east to west. They grew out of flat land like a large wrinkle in a tossed quilt with peaks ranging up to nine thousand feet. Views to the high mountains with a soft texture of moss that look ominous with partial snow at higher altitudes and a vibrant green landscape on inclined faces. Heavy gray clouds covered the highest peaks with floating fog. My approach felt like I was entering some mystical land—unknown and unexplored.

I thought the road had become less challenging, but I was not giving myself the well-deserved credit for my increased ability to handle Brother through rough gravel. I was feeling the ease of my experience of the challenging road surface, but would still not call it a "piece a cake" as the guy from New York said it was.

Twenty miles before the Arctic Circle, the scenery changed with an overlook at the Finger Mountains—an outcropping of granite rock